WORKER RESISTANCE AND MEDIA

Simon Cottle
General Editor

Vol. 18

The Global Crises and the Media series is part
of the Peter Lang Media and Communication list.
Every volume is peer reviewed and meets
the highest quality standards for content and production.

PETER LANG
New York • Bern • Frankfurt • Berlin
Brussels • Vienna • Oxford • Warsaw

Lina Dencik and Peter Wilkin

WORKER RESISTANCE AND MEDIA

Challenging Global Corporate Power in the 21st Century

PETER LANG
New York • Bern • Frankfurt • Berlin
Brussels • Vienna • Oxford • Warsaw

Library of Congress Cataloging-in-Publication Data

Dencik, Lina.
Worker resistance and media: challenging global corporate power in the 21st century /
Lina Dencik, Peter Wilkin.
pages cm. – (Global crises and the media; v. 18)
Includes bibliographical references and index.
1. International business enterprises. 2. Corporate governance. 3. Social movements.
4. Information technology—Political aspects. 5. Internet—Political aspects.
I. Wilkin, Peter. II. Title.
HD2755.5.D46 322'.2—dc23 2015008443
ISBN 978-1-4331-2499-0 (hardcover)
ISBN 978-1-4331-2498-3 (paperback)
ISBN 978-1-4539-1586-8 (e-book)
ISSN 1947-2587

Bibliographic information published by **Die Deutsche Nationalbibliothek**.
Die Deutsche Nationalbibliothek lists this publication in the "Deutsche Nationalbibliografie"; detailed bibliographic data are available on the Internet at http://dnb.d-nb.de/.

29 Broadway, 18th floor, New York, NY 10006
www.peterlang.com

CONTENTS

LIST OF ACRONYMS

AEEU	Amalgamated Engineering and Electrical Union
AFL-CIO	American Federation of Labour-Congress of Industrial Organisations
ADWU	Asian Domestic Workers Union
ACORN	Association of Community Organisations for Reform Now
BRIC	Brazil, Russia, India and China
CWU	Communications Workers Union
COSATU	Congress of South African Trade Unions
CSR	Corporate Social Responsibility
EU	European Union
GATT	General Agreement on Tariffs and Trade
GMB	General, Municipal, Boilermakers and Allied Trade Union
GIA	Girls Intelligence Agency
GFA	Globalisation from Above
GFB	Globalisation from Below
GUFs	Global Union Federations
HSBC	Hong Kong and Shanghai Banking Company Limited
HKCTU	Hong Kong Confederation of Trade Unions
FADWU	Hong Kong Federation of Asian Domestic Workers Unions

HOME	Humanitarian Organisation for Migrant Employees
HR	Human Resources
IAF	Industrial Area Foundation
IWGB	Industrial Workers of Great Britain
IWW	Industrial Workers of the World
ICFTU	International Confederation of Free Trade Unions
IDWF	International Domestic Workers Federation
ICEM (now IndustriALL)	International Federation of Chemical, Energy, Mine and General Workers' Unions
ILO	International Labour Organisation
IMF	International Monetary Fund
ITU	International Telecommunications Union
ISPs	Internet Service Providers
J4C	Justice for Cleaners
JFJ	Justice for Janitors
KCTU	Korean Confederation of Trade Unions
LAWA	Latin American Workers Association
LLW	London Living Wage
MAI	Multilateral Agreement on Investment
MNCs	Multinational Corporations
NUHW	National Union of Health Workers
RMT	National Union of Rail, Maritime and Transport Workers
NYCC	New York Communities for Change
NGO	Non-Governmental Organisation
NAFTA	North American Free Trade Agreement
PR	Public Relations
SEIU	Service Employees International Union
Telco	The East London Citizens Organisation
TQM	Total Quality Management
TUC	Trades Union Congress
TUPE'd	Transferred of Undertakings (Protection of Employment) Regulations 2006
TWC2	Transient Workers Count Too
USDAW	Union of Shop, Distributive and Allied Workers
WFTU	World Federation of Trade Unions
WSF	World Social Forum
WTO	World Trade Organisation

SERIES EDITOR'S PREFACE

We live in a global age. We inhabit a world that has become radically interconnected, interdependent, and communicated in the formations and flows of the media. This same world also spawns proliferating, often interpenetrating, "global crises."

From climate change to the war on terror, financial meltdowns to forced migrations, pandemics to world poverty, and humanitarian disasters to the denial of human rights, these and other crises represent the dark side of our globalized planet. Their origins and outcomes are not confined behind national borders and they are not best conceived through national prisms of understanding. The impacts of global crises often register across "sovereign" national territories, surrounding regions and beyond, and they can also become subject to systems of governance and forms of civil society response that are no less encompassing or transnational in scope. In today's interdependent world, global crises cannot be regarded as exceptional or aberrant events only, erupting without rhyme or reason or dislocated from the contemporary world (dis)order. They are endemic to the contemporary global world, deeply enmeshed within it. And so too are they highly dependent on the world's media and communication networks.

The series *Global Crises and the Media* sets out to examine not only the media's role in the *communication* of global threats and crises but also how they can variously enter into their *constitution*, enacting them on the public stage and helping to shape their future trajectory around the world. More specifically, the volumes in this series seek to: (1) contextualize the study of global crisis reporting in relation to wider debates about the changing flows and formations of world media communication; (2) address how global crises become variously communicated and contested in both so-called "old" and "new" media around the world; (3) consider the possible impacts of global crisis reporting on public awareness, political action, and policy responses; (4) showcase the very latest research findings and discussion from leading authorities in their respective fields of inquiry; and (5) contribute to the development of positions of theory and debate that deliberately move beyond national parochialisms and/or geographically disaggregated research agendas. In these ways the specially commissioned books in the *Global Crises and the Media* series aim to provide a sophisticated and empirically engaged understanding of the media's changing roles in global crises and thereby contribute to academic and public debate about some of the most significant global threats, conflicts, and contentions in the world today.

Worker Resistance and Media: Challenging Global Corporate Power in the 21st Century by Lina Dencik and Peter Wilkin perfectly resonates with both the global and critical thrusts of the series. Written by two expert academics in the field, this book provides a much-needed intervention into a conspicuously under-researched and under-developed field of media and communications scholarship. Perhaps it is the lingering 'methodological nationalism' identified and challenged by the influential social theorist Ulrich Beck that helps account for the continuing academic focus that—anachronistically in a globalized world—continues to conceive of its object of study as confined within national borders? Perhaps, more generously, it is the understandable political impetus to resist and challenge in, through and/or against historically forged political organizations, including the state and national labour markets, that also helps account for the continuing national focus in studies of labor movements around the world? In a globalizing world of transnational corporations and international flows of capital as well as migrant workers and movements of low-wage workers all seeking to survive as best they can in a world of corporate power and precarity of life chances, the researcher's gaze as much as that of the activist and concerned citizen needs to extend beyond 'the national.' When it does so a new panoramic view opens up, one of changing global corporate structures and systems of control as well as new forms of worker exploitation and resistance around the world.

This book is the first attempt to engage seriously with these new formations of corporate global power and forms of worker resistance, and does so with a keen eye on the possible opportunities and leverage that could yet be harnessed from new media and communication technologies. As the authors observe at the outset: 'The media occupies a long-standing and complicated place in the history of labour movements—as a space for visibility and resistance—but to a larger extent as an instrument for repression and social control.' They are also cognisant, however, of how 'the media environment is said to be changing, becoming more complex and differentiated, and creating new opportunities and challenges.' It is in this context that they pose a simple but politically crucial question. They ask: 'How, then, has the labour movement been able to take advantage of these changes in media platforms as part of the struggle to mobilise, organise and respond to increasingly global corporate activity?'

Worker Resistance and Media: Challenging Global Corporate Power in the 21st Century provides the first sustained, empirically detailed discussion of the changing nature of global corporate power and communications opportunities for the labour movement in the twenty-first century. It provides a closely argued and more circumspect argument than usual about the role and possibilities of communications in workers' resistance. The authors are not persuaded by those sometimes celebratory but empirically wanting claims now often heard about the democratizing forms and platforms of new media. Their study helps illuminate some of the complexities and difficulties involved, and it does so in part based on three fascinating case studies of different campaigns—Justice for Cleaners in the UK, Fast Food Forward in the US, and the domestic workers movement in South East Asia. As Series Editor I am particularly pleased to see a title on this little-researched but globally crucial issue in the series. Labour movements around the world are fundamentally implicated in a wide array of globally intersecting global crises. As the authors rightly observe: 'rational and humane solutions to the global crises facing humanity in the twenty-first century depend in fact upon a labour movement that can democratize the world-system.' This book in researching and reflecting seriously on the role of the media within processes of corporate control and worker resistance offers grounded discussion and a much-needed intervention into this little-researched but humanly and politically consequential field. I recommend it to you.

Simon Cottle, Series Editor

ACKNOWLEDGEMENTS

We would like to thank everyone we interviewed for this book for their time and kind generosity. Particular thanks to the New York IWW branch for hosting us during our fieldwork in New York City and to Cardiff University for awarding a grant that allowed us to carry out fieldwork in South east Asia. We would also like to thank Simon Cottle for his encouragement of the project and Mary Savigar at Peter Lang Publishing for her support in getting it published.

Lina and Peter

INTRODUCTION: LABOUR, MEDIA AND GLOBALISATION

This book situates the relationship between global crises and the media in the context of what we see as two central and interrelated developments in the twenty-first century: the rise of global corporate power and the decline of the labour movement. The media occupies a long-standing and complicated place in the history of labour movements—as a space for visibility and resistance—but to a larger extent as an instrument for repression and social control (Waterman, 2004, p. xxiii). However, the media environment is said to be changing, becoming more complex and differentiated, and creating new opportunities and challenges (Flew, 2007; Keane, 2013). How, then, has the labour movement been able to take advantage of these changes in media platforms as part of the struggle to mobilise, organise and respond to increasingly global corporate activity?

In order to understand and make sense of the current crisis in the labour movement globally it is necessary to take a long-term, structural and historical view of the development of the modern world-system. It is within this context that the labour movement has emerged and evolved, adapting to the changing nature of capitalism and the nation-state. What remains a constant is the continuing assault upon the labour movement by capital and the state, a reality depicted sharply in the recently established Global Rights Index created by the International Trade Union Confederation to rank countries in terms of how well they protect employment rights. Of 139 countries surveyed only Denmark was found to honour all 97 'fundamental aspects of employment rights as grounded in international human rights law' (Wearing, 2014). Historically gains made by the labour movement are always contingent and liable to be clawed back by capital and the state when the opportunity arises.

The development of a global capitalist economy driven by the need to accumulate capital and the transformation of economic relations to ones based on the private ownership of property has meant the need for labour to sell itself to an employer in order to live. Within this framework intensified and ruthless competition is enacted against much of the world's workforce (whether employed or not), forced into a contest with each other for survival in the workplace. At the same time many of the world's major markets tend towards oligopoly, not monopoly, and this has led to the transformation of the nature of trade, as we will discuss in this book. Thus the underlying principle is protection and subsidies where possible for economic elites, and competition for the world's workforce and unemployed.

At the same time we have seen the consolidation of an inter-state system driven by the political elites that govern states, at the basis of which lies military power. The dominant logic here, though not the only one, is to accumulate power, usually at the expense of other states and political and economic elites, and in so doing to promote and expand the interests of its own economic elites. This political logic can conflict with the logic of global capitalism as political elites have to manage various social, economic and political conflicts that are long-term rather than just the short-term imperative of making a profit that corporations face: in short, the state has its own logic (Dolgoff, 2013; Mann, 2011). This relationship between the state and capital remains central to understanding the structure of power in the world-system and how it manifests itself at different levels: locally, nationally, regionally and globally and in different zones: core, periphery and semi-periphery.

Within this emergence of capitalist social relations and nation-states all manner of social conflicts and resistance has engendered of which the labour movement is one of the most important historically. What is important is to avoid the idea that the modern world-system and its development have been inevitable or simply the outcome of large-scale structural factors. Agency and resistance to capitalism and the state have been constant features of the system and continue to be so (Mignolo, 2000; Tilly and Wood, 2013). Further, this resistance has long been global; as many writers have noted the labour movement has always been transnational in outlook since it began to develop and spread in the mid-nineteenth century (Schmidt, 2013; Berry and Bantman, 2010; Anderson, 2007).

Any attempt to describe and explain the way in which the labour movement has evolved since the mid-nineteenth century has to take into account the part played by a number of material and ideational factors: racism, sexism, the state, war and militarism, nationalism, political-ideological conflict, religion, science and technological innovation, the persistence of older forms of social life rooted in tradition and faith and finally the construction of large-scale bureaucratic organisations (Mann, 2012; Tilly, 1992; Moore; 1967). Within the context of these developments a number of major themes over the course of the nineteenth and twentieth centuries have helped to shape the direction of the labour movement including its relationship to the geopolitics of the Cold War, the spread and integration of capitalism as a global system, the relationship between the labour movement and political ideologies and parties, and the limitations and failures of the dominant approaches to trade union activity that emerged in the wake of the Russian Revolution and the end of the First World War.

Of particular concern has been the rise of the consciousness industries (Ewen, 2001). These are the forms of media that have helped to both construct and constrain social relations, from the print and broadcast media in all of their forms to the digital media and industries that have evolved in the twentieth century often with the specific ambition of trying to shape patterns of consumer taste and identity: public relations, marketing and advertising. The consciousness industries emerged at a time in the early twentieth century when both capitalism and the nation-state system faced tremendous challenges from socialists and the labour movement, amongst others, and as early proponents such as Bernays and Lippmann noted were explicit attempts to shape public opinion and encourage a particular kind of consumerism that emphasised status over class identities (Bernays, 2004; Lippmann, 2103; Ewen, 1996; Smith, 2003).

This book will examine the ways in which the labour movement is now trying to use evolving media forms, particularly new internet-based platforms, to promote and organise their activities in an age of unprecedented global corporate power and of governments that are largely retreating from welfare-state commitments, where they have existed at all. In short, how is the labour movement trying to counter the role of the consciousness industries and the changing nature of global capitalism and the nation-state? In particular our focus is upon two important strands of the current labour movement, low-wage workers who are proliferating throughout the world-system and migrant workers who are most likely to end up in low-wage jobs.

Historically, trade unions have often sought to develop their own media through newspapers, educational forums, and the creation of a vibrant working class culture through which they can tell their own stories in order to challenge the way in which they were represented in the capitalist media. This is understandable as a structural development over the course of the twentieth century has been the increased commercialisation of the mainstream or agenda-setting capitalist media. This process, in turn, has been accelerated by media mergers and takeovers from the 1980s onwards which have helped to consolidate patterns of media ownership and control not just nationally and regionally but globally (Keane, 2013; Herman and McChesney, 1997). This has been occurring in tandem with the relative decline of public service broadcasting, which, however limited and constrained, has historically been subject to some level of democratic and public control, unlike privately owned media (Keane, 1991; Tracey, 1998). The ability of unions to affect the mainstream media in a positive way or even to produce their own newspapers has declined due to two main factors: the increased costs of production and the need to secure profit from advertising revenue; and the spread of neoliberalism as the main ideological outlook of the world's political and economic elites, which is relentlessly hostile to the idea of an independent labour movement, which is seen as something to be contained, co-opted or crushed, when necessary.

None of this means that trade unions and the labour movement cannot receive sympathetic coverage in the mainstream media. They can and do. But as journalist Nicolas Jones observed of the media coverage of the UK miners' strike in 1984–85, a strike that was indeed a threat to the government and the state itself,

> While I would contend that broadcasters like myself tried valiantly to represent both sides of the dispute, we did have to work within what had become an all-powerful narrative: the country could not afford to continue subsidising uneconomic coal mines, devastating though that might be for their communities; the strike itself was a denial of democracy because there had been no pit head ballot, and the violence on the miners' picket lines, by challenging the rule of law, constituted a threat to the democratic government of the country. In the final months of the strike, once it became clear there was no longer any chance of a negotiated settlement, the balance of coverage tipped almost completely in the management's favour (Jones, 2009).

Jones' account of his experiences during the miners' strike is useful as it illustrates what is meant by the idea that structural and ideological factors can and do act to constrain journalistic autonomy, particularly when it concerns an issue of great importance, such as the legitimacy of the state and government (Thompson, 1991). These are issues that continue to mark the relationship between the labour movement and the media in discussions on its future.

Wide-ranging debates have been taking place in the labour movement throughout the twenty-first century as to its future direction, addressing issues such as the relationship between the labour movement and political parties, the need for global unions to tackle the impact of an increasingly global capital, new forms of unionism such as Community and Social Movement Unionism, and a revived emphasis on 'organising' as the means to rebuild the labour movement. The labour movement is at a crossroads in the twenty-first century as long-standing assumptions that have underpinned its development over the twentieth century have been found wanting, most obviously the commitment by trade unions to view the state and alliances with political parties as the means to *permanently* promote the interests of working people. As we will set out in this book, these assumptions have had profound implications for how the labour movement, in particular mainstream trade unions, have set out their strategies and tactics, whether in democratic or non-democratic nation-states. Since the 1970s global capitalism and the inter-state system have undergone profound transformations that the labour movement have had to reckon with in terms of strategies, tactics and visions for the twenty-first century. What seemed fixed and certain for much of the twentieth century has very quickly unravelled and been transformed into an environment that has caused a fundamental crisis for the labour movement.

What guides the research for this book, therefore, is a concern with the lessons that can be learnt from the history of the labour movement in order to address its future. In particular, we want to look at the ways in which the labour movement has sought to use media, especially new media forms, to organise and mobilise in the twenty-first century and analyse what role these technologies might have for challenging global corporate power in the current context. We have been particularly concerned with the growing number of low-wage service workers in this regard and have illustrated our research with three pertinent case studies within the labour movement today, looking at the campaigns Justice for Cleaners in the UK, Fast Food Forward in the US, and the domestic workers movement in South east Asia. The research for this book has been conducted over a two-year period and includes fieldwork and over 40 interviews with labour activists, trade union members, members of related social movements, members of Global Union Federations and academics and journalists specialising in the labour movement.

Our argument is that in order to go forward the labour movement will first have to rediscover the practices of independent unionism, pursuing a social vision of a good society, a point that Waterman makes when he talks about a revived labour internationalism (Waterman, 2002, p. 4). Without this social vision of a qualitatively different kind of world-system, the labour movement lacks the means by which to build wider social support and solidarity for its goals, regardless of the transformative potentials of media technologies. Given the dramatic challenges facing humanity in the twenty-first century (nuclear war, environmental disaster and global poverty and inequality) unions have a vital role to play in helping to overcome them and must situate uses of media forms within broader strategic shifts in how to win support in the struggle to transform the global system.

Situating the Labour Movement in the Modern World-System

Although the origins of the labour movement are sharply contested our argument is that to understand the way in which it has evolved globally over the past 150 years you have to situate it in the context of the emergence of the modern world-system. In using the idea of a *modern world-system* we are saying that it is a heuristically useful framework for describing and explaining the developments of the dominant political, economic and cultural tendencies that have emerged since the nineteenth century (Wallerstein, 2004; Palumbo-Liu, Robbins and Tanoukhi, 2011). As mentioned above, the modern world-system has seen the spread of *two* major material *and* ideational structures, both of which are undergoing profound transformation: the emergence of the modern nation-state system *and* the spread of capitalism as a global system of capital accumulation (Mignolo, 2000). These two structural and ideational factors each have a logic that cannot be reduced to the other. They are also the primary target for resistance on the part of those that Arrighi, Hopkins and Wallerstein have called anti-systemic movements; those social movements that have sought to challenge class divisions, racism, sexism and destruction of the environment (Arrighi, Hopkins and Wallerstein, 1989; Zibechi, 2010) of which the labour movement is pivotal. Throughout its existence the labour movement has been an agent acting to defend the interests of working people against capital and the state. The very fact that massive coercion and violence have been directed at labour movements throughout their history shows just how important agency, in the form of resistance, has been in the evolution of the system.

The modern world-system is the outcome of European expansion, conquest and exploitation of the world-system since the sixteenth century, establishing structures of unequal world trade that systematically exploited much of the world's population in the periphery and semi-periphery (Wallerstein, 2006; McNeill, 1979, chapter 19). At the same time there is a need to caution against portraying the actors in the non-European parts of the system (the periphery and the semi-periphery) as passive recipients of European power, capital and ideas (Mignolo, 2000). Like Khuri-Makdisi (2010) we argue that whilst recognising the central part that Europe has played in constructing the modern world-system, it is also important to recognise that while the non-European world was transformed by European conquest, the process was not simply one way. Europe (the core nation-states) was also changed by the process, often in deeply reactionary ways that generated powerful ideological frameworks that were racist or aggressively nationalist. Khuri-Makdisi's work on the rise of the labour movement in the Eastern Mediterranean in the late nineteenth and early twentieth century is a good example of this point in that it was the expansion of European power in Egypt, Lebanon and Syria that spread radical European migrants to the region who brought with them ideas of anarchism, syndicalism and socialism (not Marxism at this stage it seems) that were taken up in cities like Cairo, Alexandria and Beirut by local workers and other migrants from the region (Khuri-Makdisi, 2010). In turn, these ideas were developed, transformed and adapted to suit the needs of the local population rather than simply being transmitted from the core to the periphery.

In order to describe and explain the development of the labour movement (and other social forces) we argue that it is useful to employ an axis that distinguishes the practices and beliefs of social movements, institutions and social relations: from authoritarian to libertarian. The tension between these two perspectives regarding the organisation of social life underpins fundamental social conflicts be they about class inequality, racism, sexism or other forms of oppression. The dominant institutions and ideas in the modern world-system have tended to produce forms of social life that are hierarchical and authoritarian, embedded in a variety of relations and institutions: the state, political parties, corporations, patriarchy, religion, racism, aggressive and exclusive forms of nationalism. All of these suppose a hierarchy of power and authority over individuals that has often been viewed as natural and eternal and that becomes embedded in the systems of knowledge that perpetuate such belief systems: texts, symbols, sacred practices and events, cultural products, media outputs and so on (Rocker, 1937; Billig, 1995). As Dan Hind has recently argued, such systems of hierarchical power and authority are built on forms of prejudice, bigotry, faith and superstition that are often, but not always, in opposition to the universal goals of the Enlightenment, which tended to place individual liberty and equality at the centre of its social vision (Hind, 2008).

Countering this tendency towards hierarchy and authoritarianism in the organisation of social life has been the other end of the axis, those social movements that have argued and fought for a more libertarian social order in which people organise their social life around a different set of principles: co-operation, mutual aid, direct action and self-help. In theory the labour movement are clearly part of this latter tradition with their emphasis upon equality, liberty and democracy, ideas that go against the interests of entrenched economic privilege, political power and social hierarchy. However, this axial distinction between more authoritarian and more libertarian forms of social life is complex and far from straightforward. Trade unions, for example, illustrate this complexity in that in practice within the labour movement there has been a major division over the structure and organisation of trade unions. Over the course of the twentieth century, as we will see in chapter one, it became increasingly common for unions to seek to align themselves with political parties, the state and even business, in effect to align themselves with the very institutions that would threaten and end their independence. At the same time and within the very same mainstream (by which we mean non-revolutionary) unions there were often persistent and wide-spread grassroots activities that opposed such developments and sought to keep the union and the labour movement independent and true to its ideals. As Bookchin and Gallin argue, even explicitly libertarian unions faced problems, in reality, of authoritarian and dogmatic practices, despite their professed ideals (Bookchin, 1994; Gallin; 2014).

To illustrate this complexity further, consider the relationship between religion and the labour movement (Young, 2008). Clearly many religious movements have and continue to actively suppress the liberation and enlightenment of working people, afraid, no doubt, that their authority would be lost along the way. The Catholic Church is the major European and global example of this tendency. Conversely, at the same time and within the Catholic Church there have been movements advocating liberation for the poor around the world, encapsulated in the goals of Liberation theology. Liberation theology has revealed very clearly the division in the Catholic Church between a deeply reactionary political leadership and hierarchy as opposed to more radical and progressive elements in specific areas and amongst the grassroots of the church. In El Salvador in 1980 Archbishop Romero, a conservative figure, the head of the Catholic Church who had spoken out in defence of the poor and the rights of working people, was murdered by a state-run death squad, funded and trained by the US and its special forces. The 'crime' of Romero was that under his leadership the local Catholic Church was trying to organise peasant communities into self-help groups and peasant associations, to become an active part of the labour movement. Interestingly Romero's actions were denounced by the then pope and hierarchy of the Catholic Church, an illustration of what Fox describes as the deeply reactionary hierarchy within the Church centred around communion liberation, which he likens to a neo-fascist ideology (Lynd, 1992; Fox, 2012; 2013). However much religious movements have oppressed working people it is also the case that these movements are themselves complex and often split into conservative and progressive wings with the latter often being very important to the success or failure of union campaigns, as we will see later in the book.

Nonetheless, and despite this complexity, we argue that this axis of authoritarian and libertarian approaches to the organisation of social life (social relations and institutional organisation) is the most useful way of framing the development of the labour movement. Unlike much contemporary social theory that addresses the concept of complexity primarily through the spread of social networks we insist upon retaining the idea of causal structures, systems, agents and institutions (Waterman, 2001a; Tilly and Wood, 2013, p. 10). Indeed the focus upon 'networks' in social theory often fetishizes the concept of the network in ways that overlook the persistence of structures, institutions and systems, most obviously with regard to the persistence of the nation-state itself (Castells, 2009a; Tilly, 1992; Giddens, 1987; Mann, 2005, 2011). Unsurprisingly this tendency manifests itself most fully in some of the network-determining narratives that emerged after the 1999 WTO protests in Seattle (Castells, 2004; 2012; McCaughey and Ayers, 2003; Notes from Nowhere, 2003; Waterman and Wills, 2001). Networks exist, of course, and are important for the anti-systemic movements we describe but they exist in relationship to structures, institutions and the world-system. Indeed, the very focus and meaning of an anti-systemic movement as a network of opposition is directed against structures, institutions and systems of oppression; without them anti-systemic movements would have no meaning.

Thus we argue that social life is complex in the sense that the institutions, ideas and social movements that construct it are not simply fixed and static, and relationships between agents and institutions are not linear (Byrne, 2002; Byrne and Callaghan, 2013). Social life is patterned and regular, but it is not invariant as some approaches to social science have argued. Causality in the social realm is complex in the sense that social outcomes are the interplay of necessary and contingent causal factors (Wilkin, 1999; Sayer, 1992). The labour movement itself is also an example of this very complexity when one considers the divisions in the movement that emerged during the Cold War. These divisions, for example, led to conservative sections of the movement in democratic states actively supporting the CIA in subverting political processes and working to undermine genuinely independent trade unions in the global South (Gallin, 2014).

So one must be careful in terms of describing the development of the labour movement, as with any social movement, recognising the breadth and often contradictory nature of its actions. In this sense a social movement, following Dani, is a network of informal relationships between many individuals and organisations that share a distinct collective identity and mobilise around conflictual issues (Dani, 2000, p. 393). And this is why the twenty-first century represents such an important juncture for the global labour movement as it faces a series of fundamental questions about its future that can best be understood in terms of this axis between more authoritarian or libertarian modes of organising. Historically the tendency has been for authoritarian ideas and practices within the labour movement to win out, leading to formal relations with the state, political parties and business in the hope of permanent improvement in the conditions of their members. A long-term view of this material and ideational struggle within the labour movement that traces its development over the course of the twentieth century can only conclude that it has been a contingent and uneven success, bringing important welfare systems to specific parts of the core (Europe, Australasia, Japan and the USA) but much less so to other places. As a form of social and class compromise between the state, capital and the labour movement it has rapidly collapsed over the past 40 years. The question for the labour movement therefore is: what now?

The Labour Movement and the Media

As we will outline in this book, part of the debate on the future of the labour movement incorporates an important question about its relationship to media. The history of the labour movement and its relation to the mainstream media has long been viewed as one of antagonism and misrepresentation, and for good reasons. Given the oppositional role to capital and the state that the labour movement has often played, disseminating socialist-inspired ideas about a society built on principles of mutual aid, cooperation, self-help and direct action, it is hardly surprising to find that it has been viewed by the main political and economic institutions of privilege and power as something to be either destroyed, curbed or co-opted. Whether discussing trade unions in democratic or undemocratic countries, the idea of an independent working class movement that might bring about forms of social life that threatened to end economic privilege and transform political power has long been viewed by dominant social forces as something to be contained. In authoritarian and undemocratic societies this task has been and continues to be relatively straightforward for the state and governing elites to achieve through a mixture of force, punishment, violence and co-optation. Despite this there are many powerful examples of the labour movement around the world challenging and leading the fight for democracy in undemocratic states from the Congress of South African Trade Unions (COSATU) in South Africa to Solidarity in Poland and the Korean Confederation of Trade Unions (KCTU) in the 1980s and 1990s (Schmidt, 2013).

Nonetheless the idea of containing the labour movement has extended to include the part often played by important sections of the mainstream capitalist media. Orwell famously made the point that attempts to control language and meaning are central forms of power in a modern age of mass democratic societies, mass social movements and mass communication (Orwell, 2001). On this point he was in agreement with elite theorists such as Lippmann and Bernays (Lippmann, 2013; Bernays, 2005; Smith, 2003). The control of language and the representations of events through the media was, Orwell noted, also an attempt to control the way in which people thought about the social world. As he went on to argue, it is much harder to dissent from conventional opinion that in the main serves to defend economic privilege and political power when the very language that is available to you is a reflection of these powerful interests, a language that tends to normalise these social relations. Picking up this point from Orwell the philosopher Harry Bracken notes that it is precisely because people are not simply programmable automata, that they possess free will and critical faculties of thought and reason, that powerful elites and institutions have had to work so hard to try to curb and control the development of popular movements that might oppose political power and economic privilege (Bracken, 1983; 1994).

That said the labour movement have also sought to build a counter-media through their own activities in imaginative ways and often in the most challenging of circumstances. Common practices for all kinds of unions, for example, have been to establish newspapers, book clubs, libraries, social centres, educational programs and cultural activities where working people could gain a richer understanding of the history of the labour movement and discuss the ideas of a good society and the strategies by which it could be brought about.

A famous example of this occurred in 1913 when the journalist John Reed helped to support the striking Silk Workers in Paterson, New Jersey by organising a theatrical event staged at Madison Square Garden in New York, 'The pageant of the Paterson Strike', which gave an account of the atrocious working conditions under which a largely immigrant workforce laboured. The pageant helped to build wider community support for the strikers at a time when the balance of power lay firmly in the hands of the mill owners. Ultimately the strike failed to achieve its goals but it was a significant part of the history of the labour movement because of the way in which it was organised and the innovative tactics that developed during the course of the strike (Thompson and Bekken, 2006; Renshaw, 1999; Salerno, 1989; Shea, 2001; Golin, 1992).

Thus, the cultural life of the labour movement has been central to its historical success, aiming to build up and enlighten its members by providing them with the education and access to knowledge that had hitherto been denied them within the existing social order. Unsurprisingly in country after country where the threat of an independent and powerful labour movement that might challenge political power and economic privilege came into being, the state and business interests sought to curb or destroy these activities (Schmidt and van der Walt, 2009). Again, echoing Orwell, human agency and enlightenment depends in part upon access to alternative ideas and debates, so it is not surprising that the state and business have consistently sought ways to curb or contain the spread of such ideas, whether by co-opting union leadership into partnerships of varying degrees or through the development of the consciousness industries who exist to serve the interests of privilege and power (Fones-Wolf, 1995; Ewen, 1996; Beder, 2002, 2006; Miller and Dinan, 2008; Moloney, 2000; Bracken, 1983).

By the end of the twentieth century the labour movement was seen globally as being in retreat and as Paul Mason observes, the traditional narratives about working class life that had been handed down through successive generations of workers were being rapidly lost as patterns of work and oppression changed, breaking many of the community links that had sustained working class cultures around the world (Mason, 2008; 2013). However, the emergence of new forms of digital communication have opened up new possibilities for the labour movement in terms of its campaigning strategies and the possibility of both renewing itself and trying to build new forms of international solidarity, part of a process that numerous writers have described as Globalisation From Below (GFB) (Kellner, 1999). In an interview with us, Eric Lee, founder of *LabourStart*, an online support network for trade unionists around the world that operates by disseminating petitions in support of persecuted workers, said that such is the impact of these new technologies that the labour movement can think in real terms of building a new and perhaps the first genuine International that sees labour organising globally to challenge capitalism and the state. This, at least, is the aspiration, if not yet the reality. The case studies in this book examine the ways in which a series of campaigns in the labour movement that have emerged in the late twentieth and twenty-first century have sought to use these new forms of communication to build a form of GFB in resistance to the dominant recent trends in Globalisation From Above (GFA).

The Media as Fourth Estate

The role of the media in the building of modern nation-states and mass democracies cannot be underestimated (Keane, 1991; 2013; Habermas, 1992). In democratic theory, the media have a fundamental role to play as the Fourth Estate, the body that exists to criticise and scrutinise the actions of the powerful institutions and individuals that govern a society. In so doing they can inform the public of the reality of events taking place so that they can make their own rational judgments about political, social and economic issues. In this respect the media have a role to play in helping enlighten and make possible an informed public and, by extension, helping to build public opinion. However, in practice this model of the media has been severely criticised both by journalists themselves and academic observers, with many agreeing with Petley that the media have never actually played the role of the Fourth Estate (Petley, 2004).

The recent and dramatic example of the information leaked by Edward Snowden, which has begun to reveal the incredible extent of state surveillance of citizens and public figures, makes this point most clearly. Despite the fact that what has been revealed by Snowden's leaks is a clear subversion of what, in theory, liberal democracy is meant to entail (the state as public servant under political control by an elected government) the political and media debate has been dominated by a concern with whether Snowden's actions have endangered the lives of Western spies rather than with the obvious and clear threat to democracy that the surveillance represents (Snowden, 2013; Greenwald, 2014). In the UK it was *The Guardian* newspaper that broke the Snowden story originally and that worked with Snowden to release the information to the public. The response of much of the UK print media (*The Daily Mail, The Sun, The Daily Telegraph*) was to attack *The Guardian* and its editor, arguing that the government should prosecute them both for publishing the information (Petley, 2013). This example could not illustrate more clearly the limits of the capacity of commercial media in practice to act as a Fourth estate, instead subordinating themselves to state power. Here also public service broadcasting falls short. Previous head of BBC News, Richard Sambrook, has argued that the BBC has become politicised to such an extent that had the Snowden leaks come to them, they would not have published them despite their public interest value (Higgins, 2014).

The most well-known account of the historical development of the modern media is that associated with Habermas whose work on the emergence of 'the public sphere' describes what he views as the rise and fall of an independent media, charting its transition from small local newspapers to large commercial entities driven by profit rather than the need to pursue the truth at all costs (Habermas, 1992; Keane, 2013; Hind, 2012). As Herman and Chomsky argue, it has been the US mainstream print and broadcast media who have been at the forefront of this tendency towards commercialisation, despite fierce political battles in the US over the ownership and direction of the media (Herman and Chomsky, 2002). With the emergence of elite-led neoliberal political and economic movements in the 1970s it is the US model of commercial profit-seeking media that has now become the global norm, displacing public service models (Tracey, 1998; Thussu, 2006). There are significant exceptions to this, of course, in countries governed by various forms of dictatorship, but even here commercial media, heavily censored, are gaining influence, as is seen with *Star TV* in China. Dan Hind notes that the commercial media have evolved in such a way that they are now one of the main threats to the Enlightenment goal of establishing a form of 'public' based on reasoned debate and understanding (Hind, 2008).

In short, ever since they gained significance as a commercial enterprise the mainstream media have been subject to the interests and control of both their owners and eventually shareholders, and subject to direct interference and attack by the state itself. These trends have only intensified in the past 30 years, globally (Keane, 2013; Herman and McChesney, 1997). At the same time, as Keane and Mason emphasise, there has been an explosion of new media forms as part of the digital transformation of communication which have opened up the possibilities for a newly informed and critical public to emerge (Mason, 2013; Keane; 2013).

The Structure of the Book

We approach the relationship between worker resistance and media by setting out the historical context of the global crisis of the labour movement today. Chapter one sets out a schematic overview of the development of trade unions and the broader labour movement, from its emergence and spread around the world-system in the mid-nineteenth century onwards, paying particular attention to the acceleration of this trend in the later nineteenth and early twentieth century, the first wave of globalisation. These two periods were interspersed by a period of de-globalisation in which states sought to impose controls and obstacles to the movement of people, trade, capital and communication.

Our account of this development focuses upon the conflict between libertarian and authoritarian trends and practices within the labour movement and trade unions, a conflict that has been most manifest in terms of unions' strategic relationships to: the nation-state and the geopolitics of the inter-state system; political parties; prevailing forms of social hierarchy and authoritarian cultural practices (patriarchy, racism, homophobia); and corporations and the advancement of the global capitalist system. Whilst the form of these conflicts is always particular to the place where they occur (type of state; zone of world-system; balance of social forces; cultural traditions), it is always a conflict shaped by and in response to the relationship between labour and the world-system. This chapter traces these developments up until the global revolutions of 1968, which ushered a variety of anti-systemic movements onto the global political stage and which at the same time saw the emergence of the second wave of globalisation, driven by the movement towards a digital economy.

Chapter two picks up this story of the evolution of the labour movement and trade unions by providing an overview of the main developments in the state and capital in this movement towards an increasingly digitised world-system. Thus the chapter assesses the impact of this process upon corporations and the state, particularly when allied to the ideas associated with neoliberal ideology, which has been the elite-led political and economic expression of this transformation, an ideology serving to legitimise an intensified suppression of the labour movement over the past 40 years. As part of this struggle the modern corporation has transformed its organisation, structure and practices to take advantage of digitisation and as a means of undermining the unevenly distributed gains that labour had accrued over the course of the twentieth century. The chapter concludes by briefly examining how unions have sought to respond to these changes and the emergence of new ideas about the nature of trade unions in the form of global unions, community unionism, social movement and syndicalist unionism.

Chapter three considers the way these new ideas about the nature of trade unions have emerged alongside key developments in forms of media. It outlines some of the tendencies in the use of digital technologies within the labour movement, predominantly for the purposes of increasing the efficiency of existing services, rather than transforming bureaucratic structure and hierarchies. It also examines the emergence of social media as platforms that have helped to shape an array of corporate and social movement activities over the past decade and considers the main claims that have been made about the importance of social media as a mechanism for organising social movements and the labour movement in particular. It examines what may be considered a technologically driven narrative of the emergence of a 'new' protest culture seen in recent uprisings such as the Arab Spring, Occupy and more recently Gezi Park in Turkey and the Brazilian Free Fare Movement that attribute a fundamental role for social media. The chapter goes on to outline how the labour movement has sought to engage with social media protest, predominantly as an extended communication strategy rather than an organising tool, and considers what lessons can be learnt within the labour movement from recent protests and uprisings and subsequent debates around the role of social media in mobilising movements.

Chapter four, as the first of our three case studies, addresses the emergence of the global Justice for Janitors/Cleaners movement, which had its origins in the revived US Union Service Employees International Union (SEIU) in the 1980s and 90s. Such has been the success of the SEIU and its campaign that the union itself has actively sought to globalise its activities, establishing an international section to form strategic links with unions around the world with a view to disseminating its ideas and vision. Central to the success of these campaigns has been the ability to generate a form of public protest and counter-narrative to corporate propaganda that has used the internet and social media as means to mobilise and organise workers and to generate public support through by-passing the mainstream media. Thus in London over the past decade and as this chapter addresses, the Justice for Cleaners movement has won significant victories across the city around the issue of the London Living Wage. At the same time events in London have also drawn out some of the problems of the SEIU strategy and tactics that go to the heart of current debates about the future of the labour movement, and we will draw out these problems and offer a critical evaluation of the SEIU strategy and tactics.

Chapter five continues this debate by looking at a more recent SEIU campaign around fast food workers. This campaign has gained momentum in the past couple of years by engaging in direct action and protest with non-unionised fast food workers adopting movement tactics that seem more akin to protest groups such as Occupy than traditional trade union organising. It looks at the development of Fast Food Forward through the use of community groups and a heavy social media presence in what may be considered a move to create a more grassroots-driven appearance that bypasses the institutional 'baggage' of mainstream trade unions such as the SEIU. This is an important case study as it illustrates the concrete shifts in strategy towards community and social movement unionism that pertain to dominant narratives of social media-driven protest, but simultaneously highlights the challenges and problems with these narratives in relation to existing structures and institutions that significantly limit the possibilities of genuinely worker-led grassroots driven forms of unionism.

Chapter six shifts the focus to a different strategy of global unionism by examining the emergence of a domestic workers union movement that has only very recently been recognised by Global Union Federations. The amount of, predominantly female, migrant domestic workers sustaining global corporations in the modern world-system has grown significantly in the last couple of decades. This work has remained largely informal, often not recognised by labour law or unions as actual labour. However, a domestic workers movement seeking recognition as a labour movement with an emphasis on labour rights is gaining foothold, particularly in Southeast Asia. This chapter outlines developments in Hong Kong and Singapore as two contrasting contexts for the conditions under which domestic workers have been able to mobilise. In both places digital and social media have been hugely significant in the development of migrant communities surrounding domestic workers. However, despite the solidarity networks that have been built within these communities, they remain largely disconnected from the formal union structures that have been implemented around them, illustrating the extent to which social media practices amongst migrant domestic workers are embedded in the threats and constraints of the nation-state that has sought to squash any real labour mobilisation.

Chapter seven reflects on these case studies and builds on the debate regarding the possibilities and challenges of changing media forms for the labour movement by outlining the development of digital media in the broader context of the modern world-system and examining the ways in which the state and corporations have, in conjunction, sought to control online communication and activity. This forms a crucial part of our understanding of worker resistance and media as it highlights the threats and risks that labour activists are exposed to when they incorporate digital media tools into forms of worker resistance. Moreover, this chapter discusses the ways in which state-corporate control of digital media is being challenged by different groups, such as hackers and digital rights activists, and makes the case for these activities to form part of a broader political movement challenging state and corporate power in which the labour movement should be a central part.

In conclusion we draw together the narrative of the book and consider the role of online activism in new forms of workers' struggle. In particular we consider the problems for the labour movement with placing too much emphasis on media practices at the expense of other types of practices and discuss the potential for building a global labour movement that embraces its libertarian heritage of independent working class unionism. As we have stressed in this chapter already, rational and humane solutions to the global crises facing humanity in the twenty-first century depend in fact upon a labour movement that can democratise the world-system, and this book, in reflecting upon the role of media, should be considered as part of such an effort.

· 1 ·

TRADE UNIONS, THE LABOUR MOVEMENT AND THE FIRST WAVE OF GLOBALISATION

This chapter provides an overview of the historical development of the trade union movement and its relationship to the wider labour movement. In so doing we will highlight the choices made regarding overall vision, strategies and tactics at crucial junctures in the history of the trade union movement and the consequences of these choices for its development over the course of the nineteenth and twentieth centuries. It is the consequence of these choices that have, in part, helped to shape the current crisis of the union movement and that provides the context for understanding the place of developments in technologies, and digital media in particular, in current forms of worker resistance. Indeed many accounts of the trajectory of the union movement in the twentieth century have tended to reify these choices as though they were inevitable or natural in the context of the development of capitalism and the nation-state system. On the contrary, we argue that there were always powerful alternatives open to the labour movement and trade unions, choices that were part of their libertarian heritage of independent working class action, choices that were, in fact, pursued in many places, often against authoritarian tendencies within the trade unions themselves. Ultimately the libertarian idea and practice of an *independent* labour movement was suppressed or marginalised because of a variety of political and economic factors in the twentieth century, although it was certainly never extinguished. To this end former ICEM officer (now Global Union Federation IndustriALL) Vic Thorpe has called for a return to independent unions, an encouraging acknowledgment of the importance of the libertarian tradition (Thorpe, 1999).

There are, of course, many histories of the labour movement and trade unions available. However, and by way of contrast, we present a narrative that is different from those that have tended to dominate academic debates on the labour movement, and trade unions in particular. As we stressed in the introduction there is a libertarian narrative that has largely been downplayed over the course of the twentieth century in academic studies, which have been dominated by functionalist influenced and Marxist accounts of unions and industrial relations. Historically the labour movement and trade unions have had the opportunity to organise and direct their activities in contrasting ways: towards more libertarian forms of social life and organisation, or towards more authoritarian ones. In reality the labour movement and unions have often been drawn in both directions reflecting internal conflicts between leaders and rank and file and the influence of external agents, most importantly political parties, on trade union visions, strategies and tactics.

The overview we set out here explains why trade unions, in general, came to embrace the idea that the best route for social progress for the working class would be through various kinds of alliances with the state, political parties and business. In so doing we will draw out the significance of the libertarian tradition within the labour movement and trade unions that has begun to be reasserted in twenty-first century debates and activities, often linked with the rise of social movement unionism and community unionism and syndicalist tendencies (Waterman, 2001a, 2001b; Ness, 2014). We do this also because this tradition has gained renewed relevance in the context of a 'new' social movement protest culture that has emerged in recent years. The historical overview here is by necessity limited and schematic but nonetheless important as it serves to frame our understanding of the evolution of unions and the labour movement and their current circumstances.

The Meaning and History of Trade Unions

As we stressed in the introduction our focus is on the labour movement, broadly construed. By the labour movement we mean not only the industrial working class and those organised in trade unions but the peasant communities that are still hugely important, making up around 3 billion of the world's population, workers in non-industrial labour and services, the unemployed, the underemployed, the retired and the disenfranchised, disparate groups and communities who have struggled for both immediate short-term gains and also for more fundamental structural changes in the way in which social life is organised (Clawson, 2003, p. 24; Lynd & Gross, 2011, p. 11; Arrighi, Hopkins & Wallerstein, 1989; Bieler, Lindberg & Pillay, 2008a, p. xv). The trade union has proven itself to be historically the most important expression of the collective interests of the labour movement and this chapter will provide an overview of how trade unions have developed in terms of visions, strategies and tactics.

The meaning of a trade union is not fixed and has been open to significant contestation. The well-known definition set out by Webb in 1894, for example, views a trade union as being 'a continuous association of wage earners for the purpose of maintaining or improving the conditions of their employment' (Hopkins, 1995, p. 73). Others have viewed trade unions in terms of their potential for building a society based on socialist principles rather than accepting the Webb's more functionalist perspective. Historically this disagreement over the meaning of trade unions has played itself out in important debates and practises over the course of the nineteenth and twentieth centuries with regard to the directions that unions should take. The central issue in these debates has been over whether trade unions can work successfully within the framework of capitalist nation-states to deliver progress for their members or whether they need to articulate and struggle for an alternative vision of a different kind of society: In short, are unions to transform existing capitalist society and build a socialist future (Pouget, 1905)?

The origins of trade unions are equally contested with some viewing them as being part of the long-term Christian tradition, or perhaps a continuation of the guild system that had its origins in the fourteenth century (Moses, 1990; Davis, 2009, p. 32; Reid, 2004, p. 6). We are expressly concerned with the rise of modern trade unions as a part of the labour movement that emerged in the nineteenth century (Pelling, 1988, p. 3); initially developing in the UK they began to spread as an idea and practice to other parts of Europe, and through the effects of migration and colonialism, to the rest of the world (Rocker, 2004). The integration of working class communities into a capitalist world-system was crucial to the spread of trade unions in their diverse forms, whether covering industrial labour, so-called unskilled workers or peasant workers. There is, though, no single definition as to the purpose of a trade union. Academic debates have tended to be shaped by two main contrasting groups of theories, a functionalist/pluralist approach and a Marxist approach (Poole, 1981, p. 4).

The functionalist and pluralist approaches to industrial relations reflect a diverse array of sociological theories from Durkheim to Parsons, and schools of thought such as the Oxford school of industrial relations. These related perspectives view trade unions as organisations that are part of the overall and pluralist structure of a functioning liberal democracy, allowing for the aggregation, articulation and resolution of the interests of workers in their relations with employers. Echoing this point Ewing notes that the balance of union activity is towards providing services for their members (Ewing, 2005).

Although functionalism and pluralism are distinct approaches in their own right they share in common, as Clark notes, important assumptions about the way in which capitalist nation-states and their societies operate (Poole, 1981; Clark, 2000, p. 89). Importantly such approaches embrace what Wallerstein calls 'methodological nationalism'; they view the nation-state as the constituent unit of social life (Wallerstein, 2001). Such societies are bound within nation-states and are composed of an array of actors and institutions that have different forms of power that they can mobilise in order to pursue their interests. The state has a crucial role to play in this model in ensuring that no single group can use its power to dominate social life and decision-making. Such a view lends itself towards varied forms of corporatist models of industrial relations that see trade unions as a partner with the state and business in the organising of nationally-based industrial societies (Dunleavy & O'Leary, 1987).

By contrast, Marxist approaches in the academic literature tend to view trade unions as the manifestation of working class interests in a class divided society where conflict is structural and intrinsic to the nature of capitalism. This is most fully realised in the workplace where employers seek to exploit the worker directly and use a variety of methods in order to control the workforce. *Labour Process Theory* is the most well-known and important approach here, a tradition started by the work of Harry Braverman. This approach says that there can be no lasting or permanent harmony of interests between the state, business and the working class because of the structural conflict of interests between them. An assumption here is that class identity is shaped by and becomes conscious in the workplace in these conflicts over control of the production process (Braverman, 1998; Thompson, 1983; Thompson & Ackroyd, 1995; Gorz, 1978; Poole, 1981). For critical accounts of industrial relations the Labour Process approach has been justifiably influential in setting out the ways in which class as a form of social identity is shaped and transformed by relations in the workplace and the conflicts that ensue between managers and workers over work practices.

Both theoretical frameworks tell us things of importance when constructing any meaningful narrative of the development of trade unions and the labour movement over the course of the nineteenth and twentieth centuries. The functionalist viewpoint, for example, describes the goal of many trade unions to form a permanent relationship with existing political and economic institutions in society rather than to fundamentally challenge them in pursuit of an alternate vision of a good society. In the core democratic states of Europe and North America this led unions to seek partnerships with political parties, the state and businesses as a way of trying to manage social conflict in order to defend the interests of their members, a goal that remains important for most mainstream unions (Gumbrell-McCormick & Hyman, 2010; Oxenbridge & Brown, 2004; Ewing, 2005). Such an approach to industrial relations aimed to ensure the continuity and gradual transformation of the existing social order. In undemocratic states unions were by necessity subordinated to the authority of the party-state, reflecting the powerful Leninist idea that they were to act as the 'transmission belts' of official ideology to the workers. In the states in the periphery (largely to be found in Africa, Asia and South America) this kind of functionalist perspective was realised in the postcolonial period when many trade unions became intimately linked with newly elected nationalist and populist governments, part of the governing system rather than an independent voice within it (Koonings, Kruijt & Wils, 1995, p. 106). So in many respects the functionalist approach to the role of the trade unions has merit as a description of how trade unions developed during the course of the twentieth century.

By contrast the Marxist perspective in academic literature on trade unions regards the functionalist view as essentially a conservative defence of the existing social order that fails to recognise the irreconcilable differences of interest at the heart of capitalism and the exploitation of the working class in the workplace itself. As Moses says, for the Marxist perspective the resolution of this class conflict can only come about through a revolutionary transformation of the existing social order. However, for Marx unions were not enough in themselves and needed to be led by political elites and a party if they were to become revolutionary, a point taken up most successfully by the later Marxist-Leninist tradition (Moses, 1990, p. 50; Glockstein, 2011; Darlington, 2013).

However, our view is that both Marxist and functionalist/pluralist approaches are missing something crucial as descriptions and explanations of the development of trade unions because they fail to give an adequate account of the libertarian history of trade unions and the labour movement, by which we mean the idea that there can be an effective labour movement that is *independent* and *autonomous* of the state, political parties and business (Christie & Meltzer, 2010, pp. 37–50). In contrasting ways both functionalist/pluralist views and Marxist narratives have written out of their accounts the idea that an independent labour movement is either likely to be successful or is indeed desirable as a means of generating social change (Darlington, 2013). We argue, therefore, that both the functionalist/pluralist and Marxist accounts provide us with only a partial understanding of the development of the labour movement and trade unions and in part our aim is to correct this but also to make the case that the libertarian tradition is becoming more relevant in the twenty-first century with the rise of new forms of union activity and worker resistance more broadly. Lambert, for example, claims that at the beginning of the twentieth century the global labour movement was largely Marxist and believed in the Marxist story of history; but this is clearly a very Eurocentric view of the labour movement as other Marxist writers, including Eric Hobsbawn, have conceded that the libertarian (anarchist and syndicalist) currents were far more important and popular at the time amongst the global labour movement and well into the 1930s (Schmidt, 2013; Damier, 2009; van der Linden, 1998). Marxism really began to develop in the union movement outside of Europe in later decades in the twentieth century (Hirsch & van der Walt, 2014; Koonings et al., 1995, p. 105; Lambert, 2002, p. 185). In similar fashion Mary Davis says in her account of the history of trade unions that socialists advocate central planning of the economy in the hands of the state (Davis, 2009, p. 164). In fact this only applies to the authoritarian (statist) wing of socialism, libertarians advocate a federal and decentralised system of worker-controlled and self-organised workplaces allied with community councils that would produce under the control of the local population. They would, in turn, form voluntary agreements and coordinate their activities across territory independently rather than under direction of the state (Shannon, Nocella & Asimakopoulos, 2012; Lee & Bekken, 2009; Bekken, 2009; Forstater, 2009).

The labour movement was originally shaped in what many now view as the first wave of globalisation (1870–1914) by the flows and fluidity of migration and the movement of capital, people and ideas (Baldwin & Martin,

1999; Solimano, 2001). It was as much an international social movement as it was also a nationalist one. What we see over the course of the late nineteenth and early twentieth century is the emergence of structural and systemic constraints (material and ideological) on the internationalism of trade unions and the labour movement, most importantly the increased control of nation-states over the movement of peoples allied with the deepening of aggressive forms of nationalist identity, which often conflicted with the internationalism inherent in the labour movement (Waterman, 2001a). Coupled with already existing and divisive discourses of racism and sexism, nationalism served to seriously undermine the idea of international solidarity, liberty and equality in trade unions. This type of outlook, still prevalent in unions, is reflected in the comment by General President of the International Brotherhood of Teamsters union in the USA, Jimmy Hoffa Jr, that 'there's always somebody that will work cheaper. There's always a guy in a loincloth' (Brecher, Costello & Smith, 2000, p. 54). As Silver and Arrighi note, there was little international support by workers in the core nation-states for Chinese workers in the 1920s (mainly organised by anarchists) trying to organise unions who were violently crushed by the state. There was, however, plenty of anti-Chinese racism expressed within sections of the labour movement, in accord with the spread of nationalist ideologies that were built on biological arguments about inferior/superior races (Silver & Arrighi, 2001, p. 68).

Thus, we will reframe the debate around the labour movement and trade unions in terms of the development of the modern world-system. Globalisation can be seen as occurring in two waves: 1870–1914; and 1968 onwards. These tendencies towards globalisation were encouraging the increased interconnection of the world-system in terms of the flow of capital, communication, goods and people, measured in terms of both volume and speed. The continual crises that these developments generated culminated in World War I and the retreat by states from globalisation. Political and economic elites had to face a reality that had been apparent to the labour movement and socialists for many years: free trade was socially destructive. Thus, this led to the period between the two waves of globalisation that is best understood as a period of de-globalisation that saw states in the core (primarily) imposing restrictions and boundaries upon the flows of people, capital and communication in order to preserve their political power and economic privilege (Solimano, 2001; Scholte, 2008).

Within this historical and structural framework we argue that there has been an axial division amongst all social movements (including unions) towards either more libertarian or authoritarian forms of social organisation and practice. Ultimately, as we will show, both the Marxist and functionalist/pluralist views have lent themselves towards an interpretation of the history of trade unions and the labour movement that reifies authoritarian modes of social organisation and practice: for the functionalist/pluralist perspective trade unions and the labour movement are part of a functioning society within a nation-state whose role it is to help produce and reproduce hierarchical social order in partnership with the state and business; for Marxists, they are the potential agents of revolutionary change but *only* when led by a Marxist political party as the latter possesses the necessary scientific credentials to objectively lead them to socialism (Forman, 1998; Moses, 1990, p. 58; Harrod & O'Brien, 2002a, p. 7; Callinicos, 2013). Thus both approaches share in common a denial of the idea that the interests of the labour movement and of unions can best be realised by their independence of state, party and business; rather, in one form or another, it must be subordinate to them.

We argue that the functionalist idea that trade unions can play the role of partner in some form of corporatist structure has proven to be increasingly outdated in the twenty-first century, abandoned by capital, political elites and the state but still clung to by many union leaders in the hope of a renewed social partnership (Kapstein, 1996, p. 16; Hodkinson, 2001, p. 2; Ackers & Payne, 1998; Terry, 2003; Bieler et al., 2008a, pp. 1–11); while the Marxist idea that the labour movement has to be led by an enlightened Marxist political party has, at best, had very mixed results, and at worst been disastrous both for the working class and for socialism, with a legacy that still opposes independent unionism (Christie & Meltzer, 2010; Buketov, 1999; SolFed, 2012). Both perspectives ultimately undermine the idea of trade unions as the expression of *independent* working class activity in favour of workers being *represented* by an external authority (union leadership, political party, the state) (Pouget, 1905; Burgmann, 1995). These perspectives, therefore, endorse an authoritarian view of trade unions and the labour movement, which tells us that they can only be effective (in terms of promoting socialist reforms or revolution) when represented by some external authority that is in a more enlightened position than the rank and file members: either the state in partnership with business and union elites (as C. Wright Mills noted); or a Marxist political party in possession of the scientific account of historical change that sets the direction that the labour movement and trade unions must follow (as Moses has shown) (Mills, 2001/1948, Moses, 1990). These accounts of trade unions and the labour movement defend and reify social hierarchy and their subordination to an external authority who will represent them. Even now Waterman notes that most trade unions and socialist political parties overvalue hierarchy and hierarchical forms of organisation (Waterman, 2001a, p. 215).

Trade Unions and the First Wave of Globalisation 1870–1914

The first wave of globalisation is now seen by many writers as taking place in the late nineteenth and early twentieth century, with the dates 1870 to 1914 commonly accepted (Silver, 2003). This period refers to a number of important trends that have been usefully described as globalisation from above (GFA) and globalisation from below (GFB) (Siebert, 1999; Wilkin, 2001; Brecher, Costello, & Smith, 2000; Tilly & Wood, 2013, pp. 100–104). GFA refers to developments driven by nation-states and governmental policies; corporations and changes in the nature of capitalism; the cumulative and complex interplay of interests and motives underpinning the goals and decisions of political and economic elites. The consequences of these complex processes are three-fold: they are destructive of the environment (social and natural); they undermine democracy by enhancing the power of capital over national governments and international organisations at the expense of the public; they attempt to subordinate working class communities to the demands of capital and the state (Brecher et al., 2000; Wilkin, 2001; Hind, 2008).

The second part of the globalisation narrative, GFB, by contrast, focuses upon the ways in which grassroots activities of groups and individuals have sought to challenge these changes driven by GFA in favour of very different ideals based around equality, liberty and solidarity in order to bring about a system based upon social justice rather than inequality and exploitation. GFB can be viewed as the actions of what Arrighi, Hopkins and Wallerstein called 'anti-systemic movements', those groups who can only achieve their desired goals (the end of racism, sexism, class divisions and privileges) by fundamentally transforming the current world-system (Arrighi et al., 1989; Brecher et al., 2000; Wilkin, 2001). GFB is not inherently a progressive force, however, and there are many nationalist, right-wing and neo-fascist movements gaining strength across the world-system (Swank & Betz, 2003). The crucial difference is that the fascist and far-right movements want to take over the state and use it as a mechanism to impose their beliefs upon society and to reorganise hierarchy and privilege along racist/nationalist lines, whilst the libertarians aim to find ways to dismantle the state and all oppressive institutions and relationships. Paradoxically unions have played roles in both GFA and GFB, both promoting progressive social change and at other times undermining it.

There are a number of major developments in the first wave of globalisation that have been particularly significant for the trade union movement that we want to highlight here. The first of these developments has been the consolidation of the nation-state, the construction of forms of 'bad nationalism' and the rise of democracy. In this period nation-states began to develop as coherent political entities, establishing relationships amongst their populations that were increasingly built upon discourses of nationalism, race and exclusivity (Mair, 2013; Wallerstein, 2011; Tilly, 1994; Tilly & Blockmans, 1994). It is in this period that nationalism becomes firmly associated with right-wing political movements whereas previously it had also been a part of the language of progressive social movements (El-Ojeili, 2012). Mestrovic, following Durkheim, usefully distinguishes between 'good' and 'bad nationalism'. By 'good nationalism' he means those forms that embrace a culture of compassion and peaceful coexistence. This connects with some of the ideas associated with the libertarian (anti-statist) wing of the Romantic Movement in the eighteenth and early nineteenth century who defended the diversity of cultures and forms of national identity against the homogenising tendencies of modern states. 'Nation' and 'state' are not to be seen as the same thing, hence the hyphen in nation-state (Humboldt, 1993). 'Bad nationalism', by way of contrast, refers to those forms that have tended to dominate the modern world-system and is based upon ideas of national (and often racial) superiority and aggressive disdain for other nations. It also valorises the state in defence of the nation and is a form of nationalism that states have sought to construct and control over the late nineteenth and early twentieth century. Thus good nationalism refers to the diverse forms of national identity and cultural practices that help to construct our ideas of community and social solidarity; bad nationalism refers to the rise of nationalism as a statist ideology that is aggressive, divisive, exclusive and often racist in its ideological framework. Mestrovic makes the point that given the endurance of national identity in the world-system it is important that good rather than bad forms are promoted. The issue for the labour movement here is finding ways by which to reconcile national identity with the desire for global solidarity. Realistically, simply dismissing national identity *in toto* as being in contradiction with the ambitions of a global labour movement is to run the risk of perpetual failure to achieve any goals at all (Mestrovic, 1994, p. 9). Where appropriate we will persist with these distinctions in the book.

In the core states of Europe and North America this sense of national identity became bound up by the states actions with wider discourses of racial superiority and militarism, in short, with the promulgation of Mestrovic's 'bad nationalism'. This process of cementing national identity with the state and the promotion of bad nationalism that accompanied it was pivotal for the development of nation-states and has had seriously malign consequences for the labour movement. As Rocker wrote, nationalism was to become the secular religion of the state, binding people together in opposition to the state's official enemies (Rocker, 1937). The tension between bad nationalism and internationalism in the trade union movement has proven to be a lasting one and remains pervasive. During this first wave of globalisation, however, the loyalty of working class communities to the nation-state was far from straightforward as it was apparent to many that the state as an institution had not been built to reflect their interests but rather to control them (Hopkins, 1995; Wilkin & Boudeau, 2015).

Thus, within the union movement there were conflicting political viewpoints on how unions should view the nation-state and these, as we will see, played out most famously in the First International. Nonetheless, the core states began to exert their power and spread their activities into wider areas of social life with the goal of building up a particular and exclusivist form of national identity and, by extension, developing nationalist ideologies (Wimmer & Schiller, 2002). In the core states this often meant forms of bad nationalism that espoused variants of national and racial superiority over those peoples living in the periphery and semi-periphery, the majority of the world's population, in turn helping to legitimise colonial domination (Wallerstein, 2006, Amin, 1989; Wallerstein, 2011a). Education and welfare were two important means by which the nation-state sought to increase its influence over the lives of its citizens, intensifying the idea that membership of the nation transcended other forms of identity, most importantly that of class (Rocker, 1937). At the international level geo-politics was largely the preserve of the dominant European and North American states and their political elites who constructed a system for international diplomacy and law, which, in theory, served to constrain aggression whilst at the same time preserve the power and interests of these states' political and economic elites as well as, ultimately, legitimise their annexation of colonies. For trade unions the development of the nation-state was a hugely important and divisive issue. The elusive promise of democracy within the nation-state was that unions could gain all that they wished through national parliaments if they were successful in broadening the franchise to the working classes. Out of this tradition emerges the various and important forms of social democratic and to a lesser extent business unionism in the twentieth century (Bieler, 2012). The meaning of the nation for working class communities proved to be more powerful as a form of identity than that of class and despite the theoretical objection of many socialists (from Marxists to Anarchists) the nation, unlike the state, could not be meaningfully understood by reducing it to being merely an expression of ruling class interests.

The second major theme to emerge in this period was the spread of the labour movement itself, the development of socialist ideas and of trade unions as the key institutional expression of working class interests. GFB was being driven by the spread of ideas through newly developing transnational networks of workers and political activists, mainly in the early period through the activities of anarchists, syndicalist and anti-state socialists (Anderson, 2007; Hobsbawn, 2007; Hirsch & van der Walt, 2014; Gorman, 2014; Mason, 2008; Levy, 2010; Mattick, 1978). The labour movement began to take root globally as workers sought to organise themselves in resistance to the coercion and exploitation they faced from the state and capital. In particular, socialist political thought, emerging from the labour movement itself, also began to spread in this period and separated into two distinct branches, like the trade union movement: libertarian and authoritarian (Rocker, 2004, p. 19; Damier, 2009). The libertarian wing of socialism adopted principles that opposed both the state *and* capital, emphasising that workers' emancipation depended upon their own actions in their conflict with the ruling classes. Such actions were directed by adherence to a number of important principles including: mutual aid, self-help, direct action and solidarity (Hopkins, 1995, p. ix; Shantz, 2013; Christie & Meltzer, 2010; Schmidt, 2013). This meant in practice that the libertarian wing of socialism rejected participation in parliamentary politics as a means to bring about lasting and permanent changes for the benefit of working people. This perspective connects a variety of socialists (anarchists, syndicalists, anti-state Marxists, independent socialists) who shared in common a rejection of the belief that the state could be used as the means for liberating the working classes. For some libertarian groups this rejection of the state was an absolute (no good could come of the state) whilst for others a more pragmatic approach was adopted that sought to force the state to institute reforms that would ease the burden on working class life, whilst always striving to attain the long-term goal of constructing a new society without the state or capitalism (Amdur, 1986; Chomsky, 1999; Nettlau, 2000; Schmidt & van der Walt, 2009). The authoritarian wing of socialism ultimately adopted the idea that the state could be used to bring about reforms or even revolution that would emancipate the working class. This view would lead to the development within socialism of two distinct trajectories: social democracy and communism (as set out by Marxist political parties). Globally, however, in this period, trade unions and ideas of working class communities organising and defending themselves independently spread rapidly through the migration of workers and militant independent unions. These movements were largely shaped by libertarian ideas, operating as a form of counter-power and counter-culture around the world, prioritising mass organisation and mass education as the means of building up working class self-defence (Suriano, 2010; Shantz, 2013, Schmidt, 2013).

The first wave of globalisation is seen by many writers as a period where industrial society and the move towards increasingly urban social environments took hold in the core states, ushering in a movement towards the massive expansion of cities and of the production of consumer goods and services. Industrialism also led to important political and cultural changes with workers being swept up into factories where radical ideas and ideologies were debated and became a part of everyday working class life. Industrial society also meant the development of social and economic organisation based on alleged 'scientific and rational principles', of which the most famous examples are the Taylorist and Fordist processes that emerged in the USA (Thompson, 1983; Bieler et al., 2008a, p. xiv). As Baldwin and Martin note, the first wave of globalisation led to the industrialisation of the core and the deindustrialisation of the rest of the world (Baldwin & Martin, 1999, pp. 4–5).

Of great importance to the organisation of capital, the inter-state system and social movements during this period were innovations in global communication and transport infrastructure. Peter J. Hugill has written extensively about the impact of the new communication technologies in the nineteenth century upon the development of capitalism and the inter-state system, in particular the advantages that it gave to the core states in terms of their ability to shape trade, investment and the spread of ideas, often in the form of propaganda. The UK, in particular, remained at the forefront of communication and telecommunication advances from the mid-nineteenth century until the mid-twentieth century, laying the first trans-Atlantic cables for telegraphy over the period 1858–1866 (Hugill, 1999; Wolf, 2001). This proved decisive in prolonging its position relative to other states. The spread of global telecommunications was also crucial in the development of trade unions in this period and of union internationalism, enabling unions to campaign and build solidarity with workers in many countries, most famously in the wave of dockworker protests that occurred in 1889, itself an example of GFB, as British dockworkers gained crucial financial support from Australian unions (McKay, 2015; Todd & Coates, 2008; Mason, 2008). The extension of railway networks and their integration with shipping and canals also enhanced the rapid distribution of goods in this period, helping to increase consumption and to build massive profits for some of the world's major capitalist firms.

The first wave of globalisation also highlights the fact that capital was highly mobile in this period as there were hardly any national capital controls at the time (Baldwin & Martin, 1999; Hirst, Thompson & Bromley, 2009). Capital controls developed after and as a result of World War I. In this period money was largely interchangeable on global markets, a process that had evolved in an *ad hoc* manner rather than as the deliberate outcome of an international summit and treaties. The UK, as the dominant global capitalist nation-state, was the hegemonic actor in this period, underwriting the financial system and helping to maintain the rules of the inter-state system, which were largely shaped by the interactions of the states in the core. Some accounts suggest that this was a period of almost untroubled growth in the global economy but this is far from the case with depressions affecting major states such as the UK and the USA and the long-depression lasting from 1873–1896 (Rosenberg, 1946). Nonetheless it was a period of unparalleled integration and liberalisation of global financial markets.

Underpinning the geo-political expansion of European nation-states and their economic power was an aggressive form of imperialism. The 1880s saw an intensification of imperialism and colonialism as the core nation-states in Europe began to fight for new territories in Africa, Asia and the Middle East. This process was driven by a number of geo-political and economic factors including the need at the time to export capital, the search for new markets to sell goods, the theft of wealth and resources from the colonised countries and the intensification of the geo-political conflicts that had shaped Europe since the sixteenth century. As Vltchek has persuasively argued, this European system has exported barbarism and conducted slaughter in much of the world-system, from wars of conquest, the extermination of indigenous populations through to the slave trade and world wars generated by conflict amongst states in the core. As part of this process it led to the creation of structures and relationships that persist and continue to shape contemporary patterns of exploitation (Cowie, 1986; Vltchek, 2014). The impact of these processes on trade union development are two-fold: first, it helped to spread ideas about trade unions around the world as workers migrated into and out of these newly controlled territories; second, it helped to fuel bad nationalism and racism in the core nation-states in ways that fed into popular culture and helped to legitimise the process of colonial rule. Racism has been one of the fundamental ideological factors underpinning the modern world-system and the justification and popularity of imperial rule in many countries helped to undermine the idea of solidarity that would cut across class and race (Cowie, 1986, Davis, 2009, p. 88). Unions have had at best very mixed histories of dealing with racism, sexism and indeed all forms of hierarchy and oppression. Wrench, for example, describes the union movements as follows: 'in reality, history shows the record of the trade union movement to be characterised at worst by appalling racism and often by an indefensible neglect of the issues of race and equal opportunity' (Wrench, 1986; Burgmann, 1995, chapter 6). But the resistance to imperialism and its ideological underpinnings also emerges in this period in many unions with perhaps the most celebrated example being that of the Industrial Workers of the World (IWW) who were the first union in a core nation-state to organise amongst all sections of the labour movement and to actively oppose racism, sexism and the militarism underpinning imperialism (Salerno, 1989). The global impact of the IWW and its approach to organising and building a counter-culture of working class resistance to capital and the state has been hugely influential (Kornbluth, 2011; Schmidt, 2013).

The mass migration of peoples into and out of Europe is the most dramatic illustration of GFB in this period. This is particularly important to the spread of radical ideas around the world as there was a widespread migration of radical activists, particularly from European nation-states to its colonial territories. As Anderson, van der Walt, Schmidt and others have shown in important recent research, this networked transnational workers movement was driven by syndicalists, anarchists and anti-state socialists, primarily articulating libertarian ideas about the need for workers to build their own movement in pursuit of a world beyond nation-states and capitalism. Importantly it is these libertarian currents that have the biggest impact around the world in this phase, spreading ideas through people and in writing that led to the establishment of mass workers' movements and trade unions for the first time in countries as far apart as China, Korea, Argentina, Mexico, Brazil and South Africa (Suriano, 2010; Rodriguez, Ramos & Samis, 2003; Laforcade, 2014;

Dirlik, 1993; Hobart, 1977; Yerrill & Rosser, 1987; Ruiz, 1976; Morris, 1994; Simon, 1946; Shaffer, 2013; Anderson, 2007; Schmidt, 2013; Mbah & Igariwey, 1997; Hwang, 2014). In this period Marxism was much more limited in its appeal to the union movement, largely rooted in Europe, and nowhere near as influential amongst workers. This tumult of migrant workers, driven by changing patterns of demand and investment in global capitalism and the increasing pressure of nation-states in Europe to deport unwanted radicals, established transnational networks that spread radical and socialist ideas and helped to build the first forms of global solidarity.

The First International: The Libertarian and Authoritarian Divide

The First International is important in clarifying the subsequent direction that trade unions have tended to take in terms of their relationship to political parties and the state. The main issues in the dispute that eventually led to the dissolution of the First International and the subsequent development of other internationals of libertarian and authoritarian outlooks are of most concern to us here rather than the feuds that developed amongst the various protagonists (Guerin, 1970, 2012). The ambition of the International was to develop the coordinated action of a global working class. Although Marx was the major figure in directing and administering the organisation of the International he was never in a position to really control its activities as he wished to. The British trade unions, for example, were lukewarm to the International, tending to pursue more pragmatic, conservative and national-based objectives but happy to let Marx run things, up to a point (Dolgoff, 1988; Cole, 1970). As Lowy and Braunthal argue, for long periods the International worked effectively and the subsequent divisions between the libertarian and authoritarian wings were kept in check as there was much agreement amongst the different unions as to the goal of creating a socialist world (Lowy, 2014; Braunthal, 1967).

From the perspective of the trade union movement the division between libertarian and authoritarian perspectives hinged upon a mixture of personalities and principles with regard to the state, politics and the organisation of the International itself. Schmidt has argued that both syndicalist and anarchist influenced unions far outweighed the members of the International who identified themselves as Marxists. For the former the organisation of the

International should be based on federalist principles, promoting the voluntary and coordinated activities of militant unions. For the latter group based around Marx's ideas it was important the International was under centralised control so that discipline and organisation could be controlled by the leadership (Braunthal, 1967; Thorpe, 1991; Schmidt, 2013, pp. 34–35). However, the division around organisation reflected more permanent fissures between the libertarian and authoritarian wings of the labour movement that can be seen as reflecting three significant points of disagreement.

The first of these points concerns the relationship between the means used and ends pursued in struggling to promote social change. More broadly this raises issues of prefigurative ethics and the idea of what constitutes a good society. The question of means and ends was to prove fundamental to the libertarian-authoritarian divide in the International and reflected in the dispute over whether the International should be organised along federalist or centralist lines. For the libertarians the means by which social change could be brought about were intrinsically linked to the ends desired, what is often termed a prefigurative ethic (Cole, 1970). In short, if the society you want to build is one based on solidarity, equality and liberty then the means by which you bring it into being will be crucial to achieving this goal. The use of authoritarian (centralised and hierarchical control) means will not produce a free society, only one governed by another form of authority. This led to Bakunin's by now well-known observation that 'We are convinced that liberty without socialism is privilege, injustice; and that socialism without liberty is slavery and brutality" (Bakunin, 1992, p. 12.) This point was later developed by Max Weber in his account of the rise of the bureaucratic state and his criticisms of the revolutionary left who he felt held to a naïve view of power and hierarchy that failed to recognise that a socialist state would obliterate the individual (Weber, 1977a, pp. 49–50).

Thus the libertarians were insistent that only through the actions of workers themselves could a free society be established, which meant adhering to principles of mutual aid, self-help, direct action, independence, voluntary activity and solidarity, ideas that were at the time reflected in the activities of unions often with very different ideas about socialism and its appeal, in fact (Holton, 1976; Reid, 2004, p. 109; Shantz, 2013; Schmidt, 2013). A new society could only be built by working people if they came to want it and desire it, which meant that they also had to be pivotal in the steps that led to such a society, transforming themselves along the way. The authoritarian section of the International had a number of criticisms of this position that led them to the view that some form of political party would be needed to lead the working class who lacked the necessary consciousness and scientific knowledge of the steps they needed to undertake in order to bring about a socialist revolution. Ironically it seemed that despite Marx's belief that the emancipation of the working class could only be the outcome of the working class itself, in practice Marxism meant a working class *led* by a political party that shared Marx's ideas (Darlington, 2013; Dolgoff, 1988).

The libertarians also held to a broader view of the agents of social change as including not only industrial workers but also peasants and other groups in society who possessed the revolutionary spirit. For the authoritarians it was the industrial proletariat who were in possession of the highest form of revolutionary consciousness and who would be instrumental in building any revolution (Marx & Engels, 2003/1848). The libertarians tended to recognise and accept diversity and difference as a fact of social life (peasant, industrial worker, unemployed, intellectual, artisan and so on) and that any revolutionary strategy had to allow for this; not everyone was or would become part of the industrial proletariat and a revolutionary movement had to recognise this (Bakunin, 1867, p. 106). The authoritarian position, shaped by Marx's analysis that the industrial proletariat would expand and come to share a class consciousness derived from its material conditions (though still needing to be led and educated by a revolutionary political party) viewed, and still does view, diversity as a problem to be overcome (Waterman, 2001b, p. 3). In this sense unity requires uniformity of consciousness and outlook, not just organisation, and as Hyman notes many unions sought to *impose* a sense of shared values and interests upon their members (Hyman, 1999, p. 3). Contemporary debates about the future of the labour movement often focus on diversity as a problem to be overcome as though it were inevitably in opposition to solidarity and this idea follows on from the Marxist view that unity is derived from having a shared working class identity and that without it solidarity is problematic (Hyman, 1999; Clawson, 2003, p. 194). As we will see in our case studies, this is a tension that continues in the labour movement today.

The second main dividing point to emerge from the International was with regard to the relationship between the labour movement and political parties. The fears that the libertarians held about the nature of political power leading to the co-optation and suppression of liberty and independent thought and action were subsequently captured in a speech that Trotsky delivered in 1924 at the 13th congress of the Bolshevik Party where he said,

> None of us desires or is able to dispute the will of the party. Clearly, the party is always right ... we can only be right with and by the party, for history has provided no other way of being in the right (Cliff, 1960).

The libertarians in the International were at best highly sceptical of the argument that the emancipation of workers would be the result of political activity of the kind advocated by Marx and his supporters. Rather they saw politics and political parties as leading to the co-optation and corruption of even the most sincere and principled individuals, the gradual surrender of political representatives to the forces of existing political power and economic privilege (Christie & Meltzer, 2010; Cole, 1970; SolFed, 2012; Graham, 2015). Bakunin described this process as follows: 'take the most radical of revolutionaries and place him on the throne of all the Russia's or give him dictatorial powers ... and before the year is out he will be worse than the Czar himself' (Guerin, 1970). As Proudhon had observed of his own experiences as a Deputy in the French Chamber after the 1848 revolutions, those in government lose all touch with the people they are there to represent, an experience he extended to himself (Hyams, 1979, p. 134). Thus, for the libertarians the political process could only neutralise the ambitions of the workers movement. Worse, it meant in practice a political party claiming power and authority over the working class on the basis of the superiority of the party, as Trotsky later advocated. By contrast those members of the International grouped around Marx saw the possibility of using the political process as a means to alter the balance of forces in society in favour of the workers.

It should be stressed here that Marx, like Proudhon before him, argued that only the working class could emancipate themselves, an argument that the libertarians entirely agreed with (Guerin, 1970). Indeed, most libertarians drew a great deal from Marx's writings, which were always a mixture of libertarian and authoritarian ideas but that were, as Bakunin observed, of crucial importance for the revolutionary movement (Schmidt & van der Walt, 2009). This duality in Marx's work can also be seen as being reflected in the future development of *Marxism* as a political project—an authoritarian and statist tendency that has tended to dominate Marxist political parties and movements, a more minor libertarian and anti-statist tendency that remained true to Marx's original observation about working class self-emancipation (Guerin, 1970, 2012).

The problem of party politics for the libertarians in the International was that they saw the political process itself as being one of *representation*, whereby the workers would surrender their right to direct and control their own affairs to an external authority and process (the political party and the state) that they neither controlled nor designed. Ultimately the libertarian view saw Marxism as advocating loyalty to the political party not the working class, and also as the promotion of uniformity through indoctrination, not unity. In comparison the libertarian wing of the workers movement were never bound by a commitment to a kind of political theology as many Marxists were. As Jun has written of the libertarian current, there was never a fixed theoretical framework but instead a set of principles that underpinned an evolving series of strategies and practices: how best to extend the realm of workers' freedom and control over their workplace and communities (Jun, 2009, p. 505). The libertarians were driven by the need to produce answers to practical questions and less inclined to become driven by theoretical debates (Turcato, 2009, p. 452). As the anarcho-syndicalist Sam Dolgoff described it anarchism is simply a 'guide to action based on a realistic conception of social reconstruction' (Dolgoff, 1970). This issue of the relationship between the labour movement and political parties is central today as many unions that have been historically wedded to political parties have begun to question the strategic wisdom of such relationships. At the same time influential unions like the SEIU have made it clear that they will work with any political party that supports their goals.

The third main division in the International was over the relationship of the union movement to the state. As Moses notes in work that is largely critical of libertarians and anarchism, anarchist and communist aims were directly opposed on the issue of the state and of the need for a political elite to lead the revolution (Moses, 1990, pp. 53–55). For the libertarians the state was a fundamental enemy, built by and in the interests of a ruling class that was composed not only of capitalists but also political elites. The libertarian theory of class was much broader than the Marxist emphasis upon economic relations, seeing hierarchal division and domination in general as the problem to be overcome rather than just economic relations (Cole, 1970). The state was viewed as the institution that underpinned hierarchy and oppression in society and not simply a neutral instrument that could be taken over and driven by the workers (Long, 1998; Schmidt & van der Walt, 2009). Thus, a good society could not be brought about by a workers' state or any other kind of state as the state was itself a relationship that had its own logic of hierarchy, power and privilege, a logic embedded in its institutional framework. This did not mean that the state could not be forced by unions to make concessions to improve the lives of workers and the rights of unions, merely to recognise that such gains were always contingent, never permanent, and did not in themselves alter the essential characteristics of a hierarchical society. Only the end of the state and its replacement by a decentralised and federal system of councils linked through free and voluntary agreements between communities would really transform the lives of all oppressed groups (Rocker, 2004, p. 62; Mattick, 1978; Kropotkin, 2010; Malatesta, 2014; Proudhon, 2011; Cleaver, 2000; Pannekoek, 2003; Bakunin, 1992; Mintz, 2013).

In many respects the authoritarians fully understood this position and Marx had written on the class-based nature of the state in various places and in ways that made it clear that he saw it as an instrument of class domination. However, even in the *Communist Manifesto* and its famous 10 points it is quite clear that Marx and Engels saw the idea of a workers' state as being fundamental to the construction of a socialist society. Despite Marx's trenchant criticism of the state in capitalist society there is also clearly an instrumental view of the state in his work that is later developed by Lenin, amongst others, which says that the state can be the mechanism to initiate workers' liberation when guided by a Marxist political party and elite (Tabor, 1987; Darlington, 2013; Lenin, 1987; Marx & Engels, 2003/1848). This point has profound importance for the subsequent direction of trade unions that came to embrace political parties, the state and ultimately corporatism as the means to promote workers' interests. The division amongst statist trade unions and socialist parties became a choice between social democracy, Marxist political party led revolution or a pro-capitalist form of business unionism that eschews union democracy in favour of hierarchy (Mills, 2001/1948, p. 3; Moody, 2007, p. 163).

The libertarian response was summed up by Bakunin, who said of the idea of a socialist state that, 'one can change the label of a State and its form … but the foundation will remain unchanged … Either the State must be destroyed or one must reconcile oneself to the vilest and most dangerous lie of our century …: Red Bureaucracy' (Guerin, 1970, 47). A good society, for the libertarians, would be made by the workers themselves and the task of the union movement was not to move towards the state but to encourage and help workers to build institutions *away* from the state, what van der Walt and Schmidt have called counter-power (Schmidt & van der Walt, 2009). By this they refer to the ways in which workers at numerous times and places sought to take over the running of their own workplaces in conjunction with their local communities, to place the production of goods and services at the benefit of all citizens. This meant, for example, an extension of factory committees and works councils in the direction of self-managed, democratically controlled sites of production that would be directed towards the needs of the community (Pannekoek, 2003; Montgomery, 1979; Alperowitz, 2011). The point here, to reiterate, is that a good society could only emerge from the appropriate means, which meant one built on new relationships, social experiments and institutions that were to be run and controlled by workers and communities, it could not be brought into being on behalf of them by an external authority such as the state. In the current era where workers' rights globally and the legality of actions taken by the labour movement have been undermined by the transformation of state policies under the direction of neoliberal ideas the labour movement faces a critical question regarding its relationship to the state and the extent to which it must be bound by punitive and restrictive labour laws.

Although there are other points of importance in these divisions in the International we take these to be fundamental in providing the ideological arena within which the developments of ideas about the union's relationship to the state, capitalism, socialism and revolution subsequently developed and remain pertinent today. The split in the International, largely driven by Marx's desire to control its policies and actions, sharpened this division in both socialism and the union movement itself (Dolgoff, 1988; Cole, 1970). The libertarian tendency was reflected in anarchist, syndicalist and anti-state socialist currents that evolved and were adapted by workers and their communities around the world well into the 1930s. The authoritarian tendencies tended to move towards forms of Marxism, social democracy and business unionism, all of which, despite their differences, saw the state as an instrument to be used by trade unions (Shantz, 2013). Until World War I the libertarian ideas tended to dominate the spread of the union movement around the world, establishing movements based in communities that built their own cultures of resistance to the state and capitalism, often in the most impoverished and vulnerable of circumstances. The spread of forms of revolutionary unionism in this period, exploring ideas of syndicalist and anarcho-syndicalist approaches, was truly global (SolFed, 2012; Schmidt & van der Walt, 2009; Jennings, 1990; Amdur, 1986; Guerin, 2006). The Russian Revolution and the First World War proved to be decisive in many countries in ultimately helping to rein in the libertarian wing of the union movement for reasons that we can now turn to (Cannon, 1955).

The Great Transformation: War, Nationalism and Revolution in the Period of De-Globalisation

The first wave of globalisation came to a crashing halt in 1914 as the inter-imperialist rivalries that had been played out in the geo-political actions of the core states in the late nineteenth century generated industrial warfare on a colossal scale (Tilly, 1989). This brought with it massive losses to the labour movement and a transformation in the outlook of states, political elites and those Mills called 'sophisticated capitalists' towards unions (Mills, 2001/1948, p. 26). By 1914 the union movement globally had taken different forms and saw different kinds of unions that could be categorized in terms of their organisation into industrial, craft and general unions (Harrod & O'Brien, 2002a). They could also be categorised by their strategic and ideological outlook into unions that sought to win change and influence through the political process at the national level, often in alliance with a socialist or social-democratic party; and those unions that adhered to the libertarian idea of independent working class action in opposition to the state and capital and indeed to wider forms of hierarchy and oppression (Silver & Arrighi, 2001). Those unions adopting a social democratic platform shared in common with the libertarians the ambition to democratise the organisation of social and economic life, to enable the working classes to take control of their lives. In practice the reforms brought about in many core states by the impact of these unions' efforts has been immense in transforming working class life, though as we will show, always subject to the ability of capital and the state to undo these advances.

The First World War sharply divided the trade union movement in Europe and effectively killed the progress of union internationalism (Rocker, 2004, p. 92; Forman, 1998). Despite important and principled opposition to the war by an array of union activists and leaders across the political divide, in the main, unions supported the line that they had to work with the state in order to defend the nation (Davis, 2009, pp. 144–145). The impact of this for many unions in the core was to lead to a number of important developments: first, this helped to legitimise the union movement as a responsible actor in the nation-state rather than a potential threat to the existing social order. Thus political elites and the state could look to union leaders for support and attempt to integrate them into the political process by offering places in government to support the war effort. Second, the war enhanced the status of trade unions amongst the working population and led in many core states to an increase in union membership. The third development is that the war itself led to important changes in the outlook of national governments in that after the war they moved to impose new kinds of controls and restrictions on the movement of people and capital, reinforcing the power of the state in terms of its ability to construct the story of 'one nation' bound by common culture and history, but also leading to a more integrated and corporatist outlook. At the same time the state had to find ways to work with the unions and manage the extension of democracy to the working classes at a time when revolutionary outbreaks were either taking place or were feared in many regions (Cronin, 1989). One important strategy was the consolidation of forms of state welfare provision that had been taking place in many core countries since the late nineteenth century, which served the purpose, in part, of building a new relationship between the state and unions around the provision of public services (Haimson, 1989a, p. 24). This proved to be a powerful development that encouraged many union leaders to believe that it was possible for the working class to gain all that they wanted through democratic control of the state and to avoid social conflict by the gradual introduction of social reforms (Haimson, 1989b). As noted, in many core states these reforms have been profound in terms of transforming the circumstances of working class life.

Elsewhere the First World War saw a number of governments take the opportunity to repress independent trade unions and other left-wing groups that had adhered to more radical libertarian ideas. In countries such as Argentina, Spain, Brazil, Germany, Italy, China, the USA, Korea and Uruguay nationalist governments used their military forces and police to arrest, imprison or kill those radical trade unionists who had sought to build independent labour movements and unions that would transform the existing social order (Simon, 1946; Schmidt, 2013).

The corporatist idea, rooted theoretically in fascism as well as Hegelian philosophy, nonetheless proved to be a plausible and attractive option for many trade union leaders as it seemed to offer the possibility of achieving the union movements' goals without the need for what was regarded as its only alternative, a violent revolution. Although it took time to take root this kind of corporatist outlook found favour amongst democratic and authoritarian governments alike as a way of handling the problems presented by the new era of mass democracy and citizenship allied with mass communication. The fear of independent working class opposition to capital and the state could be circumvented by processes of either co-optation or corruption of union leaders, as has been noted by many writers on the history of the labour movement (Davis, 2009, p. 142; Fitch, 2006). In many core countries national systems of industrial relations began to consolidate while in the colonial world unions enjoyed far more limited legitimacy. This institutionalisation of the union-state relationship was allied in many countries with the move towards more professional unions with paid and trained full-time officials, representing a move towards a union structure composed of members who looked to their professional national leadership for direction (Heery & Kelly, 1994). This transformation was not straightforward, of course, and at the same time grassroots and radical unionism persisted both within and outside of the mainstream unions. Indeed, syndicalist unions were still global amongst working class labour movements in the 1920s and into the 1930s, Communist Parties were not then in the ascendant world-wide (Rocker, 2004, p. 94; Davis, 2009, p. 129). The opposition between a union driven and controlled by its grassroots as opposed to being under the direction of centralised leadership that was invariably incorporated into national systems of governance has been a persistent theme of union history over the course of the twentieth century (Armbruster, 1998).

At the international level 1919 saw the establishment of both the League of Nations and in particular the International Labour Organisation (ILO), which were also attempts by the core capitalist states to find ways to stabilise and secure a world-system that was facing continuous economic and political crises. The ILO was set up with the view of promoting a kind of global corporatism, as Wilkinson notes, issuing conventions that were never binding and trying to provide a way to encourage compromise rather than class conflict (Munck, 2002, p. 29; Wilkinson, 2002; Clawson, 2003, p. 148; Croucher & Cotton, 2009, p. 14). The institutionalization of trade union activity also evolved in this period through the further development of the original global unions, the International Trade Secretariats (renamed as Global Union Federations in 2002), which attempted to coordinate and enhance communication amongst national unions around the world. For Gallin they helped to improve organisation, policy agreement and democratisation within the union movement (Harrod & O'Brien, 2002a, p. 5; Lee & Mustill, 2013; Croucher & Cotton, 2009, pp. 8, 39). Their limitations were similar to those faced by the ILO, too often too remote from actual trade unionists, lacking resources and unable to get unions to overcome what became more firmly entrenched national outlooks rather than international ones. Solidarity itself faced the powerful obstacle of exclusive and state-centred forms of bad nationalism amongst union officials and members. Just as the trade union movement has always been struggling to define itself between more libertarian and more authoritarian outlooks, so too it has had to deal with the complex conflict between nationalism and internationalism.

In the aftermath of World War I many union leaders and rank and file union members saw the need to work with the state, government and business to achieve their goals. The war itself had revealed the terrible consequences of mass industrial warfare and created a desire for peace that permeated the class divide. More importantly perhaps the nation-state had developed in a way that cemented many unions in the core and in the periphery more firmly in partnership with it: nationalism, the parliamentary process, an end to free trade and the need to protect the national interest seem to provide a guarantee and certainty to union leaders that this was to be the future for the international system and their members. Nonetheless the world-system remained very unstable and the functionalist picture of the inevitable and gradual transition of unions to becoming reform minded partners in a social order regulated by the nation-state was under threat in countries in the core and the periphery of the system, certainly until the end of World War II. It was the Russian Revolution that proved to be the decisive moment in this period with regard to the direction that the global trade union movement was to take, ushering in a Cold War that really begins in 1917 as a war against independent working class movements that had also emerged in the core states, notably Germany and Italy.

The Russian Revolution had a profound impact on the global labour movement and the development of socialism, effectively encouraging a split within the movement (Croucher & Cotton, 2009, p. 23; Munck, 2002, p. 138). In the long run over the course of the twentieth century it served to undermine the appeal of the libertarian tradition in socialism and gave great credibility to authoritarian ways of organising political parties and trade unions. One consequence of the revolution was to split socialism into two main statist camps: social democracy and communism. Whilst each differed profoundly on fundamental points they both embraced authoritarian ways of bringing about social change through the state and the leadership of political parties guiding and controlling the activities of the working class and trade unions. The attack on the idea of independent unions and self-organising working class communities stems not just from the antipathy of a ruling class of economic and political elites in capitalist nation-states. It is also reflected in the realities of the Marxist revolutions and political parties around the world that followed in the wake of the Russian Revolution. From China to Africa and South

America, as Marxist political parties gained power and strength throughout the 1930s onwards there was a familiar pattern that followed: the crushing of independent union activity and of working class communities.

Despite the new-found authority of the Bolshevik government in the Soviet Union, initially securing support from all manner of socialist and anarchist groups, it very quickly revealed its authoritarian instincts as has been ably documented, instituting a form of state capitalism that centralised power in the hands of the Bolshevik Party and away from the revolutionary instincts and practices of the independent Works Councils that sprang up after the February Revolution (Wallis, 2011; Avrich, 1973, 2006a; Brinton, 1970; Berkman, 2009; Goldman, 2003; and Voline, 1982). The long-held fear of Bakunin that the rise of a red bureaucracy and the tyrannical nature of socialism without liberty had proven to be entirely accurate. The Bolsheviks moved very swiftly to centralise power and crush independent groups in the Soviet Union, quickly embracing all of the facets of state tyranny that had been a feature of Czarism and surpassing them in terms of barbarism and cruelty (Moore Jr., 1987; Tabor, 1987; Avrich, 1973; Conquest, 1968). Lenin's oft-noted admiration for capitalist efficiency and organisation very swiftly saw the massive expansion of management and administrators across the major cities of the Soviet Union to control production and, allied with the Cheka police force, to eliminate any independent union or working class opposition (Avrich, 1973; Avrich, 2006a; Schmidt & van der Walt, 2009; Lee, 2005b). Lenin's contempt for those who criticised Bolshevik methods was revealed in his exchange of letters with the anarchist Kropotkin who had returned to Russia after the revolution to witness the swift descent from the promise of the revolution itself, the outcome of independent workers and communities across Russia, to the reality of what was in effect a counter-revolution by the Bolsheviks who showed that the seizure of the state could indeed be used to bring about a Marxist state, if not to actually liberate the working classes (Shub, 1953; Lovell, 1984).

In the democratic capitalist states union leaderships tended to move towards forms of social democracy, Christian democracy or in many cases, explicitly business unionism (Baccaro, Hamann, & Turner, 2003, p. 121; Fitch, 2006). All of these approaches sought to build on the developing national structures within nation-states. This nationalist-minded business unionism is a kind that has a long history and that has placed its hopes on the possibilities of the development of a nation-state that could be directed democratically through the parliamentary process and in alliance with the state and the ruling class (Fitch, 2006). This process of incorporation with the state and capital required unions to marginalize and crush the left in the union movement in many countries, including Communist Party members who operated in the union movement in democratic countries. The return for this was to be an increasing share of the nation's wealth for the working classes but only in the core, whose struggles had forced the state and capital to adopt a more conciliatory approach to the distribution of wealth. Indeed, this outlook is still dominant in many of the world's major unions and is encapsulated in the recent autobiography of Andy Stern (see chapter 4), the former president of the much revered US Service Employees International Union (SEIU) who said, 'business, labor and policy makers must form a new compact for the twenty-first century USA' (Stern, 2006, pp. 20–21).

The Consciousness Industries and Crises in the World-System

The interwar period also saw the emergence of the consciousness industries, those institutions that were explicitly concerned with trying to influence and control mass society through the tools of propaganda, initially in the form of advertising but later developing into sophisticated systems of public relations and mainstream mass media (Beck, 1999; Miller & Dinan, 2008). The goal was to win the hearts and minds of workers and to help instill the identity of individual consumers amongst the populace (Bernays, 2005/1928; Lippmann, 2013/1922; Keane, 2013; Tedlow, 1996; Olasky, 2011; Smith, 2003). For Bernays, PR was to be a function of management, in this case the management of workers and consumers alike (Solis & Breakenridge, 2009, pp. 22–23). This process has been an important aspect in the building of nation-states in the twentieth century. In totalitarian nation-states (fascist, communist or military-nationalist) propaganda was crude and backed by the persistent threat of force. In democracies the process was more complex as there citizens enjoyed hard-won formal rights and freedoms that meant more sophisticated strategies had to be used to win the ideological battle. In the core states the fear of working class radicalism was explicit amongst the ruling classes and there was a need to devise tactics that would undermine this (Ewen, 1996; Hind, 2012; Carson, 2002; Smith, 2003).

The interwar period was one of many crises of democracy in the core and also of the promotion of ideologies of nationalism that tended to be exclusivist and often aggressive in outlook, buttressed by 'red scares' that could be used to demonise all forms of left-wing activity, not just that of Communist Parties but also of independent libertarian trade unions (Fones-Wolf, 1994; Ewen, 1996; Schmidt & van der Walt, 2009). Political elites in the core states had to find ways to manage mass democracy and the workers movement and a variety of strategies were embraced including, as noted, co-optation and corporatist type arrangements. However, and as the union leader Pelloutier noted, capitalism needed to win a cultural battle amongst the population in order to succeed over time, and this was a conflict played out at a psychological level (Shantz, 2013, p. 39; Pelloutier, 1896). At its crudest, and as Fones-Wolf has documented, this meant attempts by employers to indoctrinate masses of workers through the production of educational films, programmes, speakers and political talks that workers were forced to attend as employees (Fones-Wolf, 1994). These strategies of mass propaganda, often allied to popular entertainment, were pivotal for nation-states in promoting both national consciousness and loyalty to the nation-state (Ewen, 1996).

The consciousness industries emerged in the USA in the 1920s as by then it was the most advanced liberal democratic nation-state (Ewen, 1996). Both advertising and public relations sought to use a variety of psychological techniques to influence public opinion, as had been famously demonstrated by the Committee on Public Information (also known as the Creel Commission) during World War I, which was set up by President Wilson with a view to making US public opinion pro-war rather than isolationist as it had tended to be (Zaharna, 2004). These developments confirm Rocker's and Pelloutier's point that the nation-state and capitalism were underpinned by a sustained ideological assault on the general populace in the practices of the consciousness industries, against which union resources were far more limited. As we will see later in the book, by the time of the second wave of globalisation and the end of the Cold War the consciousness industries had developed into institutions that were formally embedded in political, economic and cultural processes, from the sponsoring of cultural events (art, sport and leisure) through to the organising of political culture through public relations and the management of image. Power, as Castells noted, resided firmly in the means of communication as a means to manage what he called the 'public mind' (Beder, 2006; Moloney, 2000; Castells, 2009).

The Golden Age of Capitalism? The Cold War and the Geo-Politics of Trade Unionism

World War II served to reinforce the incorporation of trade unions into national state and political structures—as in World War I those independent and libertarian unions that resisted this were subject to brutal treatment, imprisonment or execution (Moody, 2007, p. 63). The transformation of the union movement in the first half of the twentieth century was driven by a complex interplay of political, economic and ideological factors, most of which served to undermine and render less attractive the libertarian idea of an independent union movement.

At the end of World War II, as Gallin says, trade unions around the core democratic nation-states looked to be in a good position. Having been incorporated into the fight against fascism and indeed leading it in many occupied countries they were in a position to advance their interests against a business class and corporations that had been exposed as fascist sympathisers and collaborators in many countries (Gallin, 2002, p. 235). However, the end of World War II also left the USA as the pre-eminent global nation-state and its own unions were cemented into a business union outlook, particularly after the New Deal economic recovery programs of President Roosevelt in 1933–36 (Bronfenbrenner, 2007, p. 22). In return for US financial and political support the largely destroyed European economies had to accept conditions that placed restrictions on political activity and involvement of the left in postwar politics and society. These restrictions on left-wing political parties, unions and general elections affected France, Greece, Italy, Japan and Germany, amongst other countries (Mair, 2013). At the same time fascist supporters in these countries were also returned to positions of power in politics and the economy as they were seen as a bulwark against the real threat to political power and economic privilege: the possibility of an independent working class movement. The postwar political, economic and social reconstruction of Europe and Japan was supported by a US-led Western alliance that helped to usher in the formal era of the Cold War, leading to the establishment of NATO and later the Warsaw Pact, itself largely a response to the incorporation of West Germany into NATO in 1955.

For trade unions around the world the Cold War meant a number of things. First and perhaps most fundamental it saw the separation of international trade union organisations into a communist and capitalist camp: the International Confederation of Free Trade Unions (ICFTU) and the

Communist-led World Federation of Trade Unions (WFTU). The geo-politics of the Cold War became embedded in the union movement with leadership in US unions and others in the Western bloc persuaded, inclined, co-opted or corrupted into support for anti-Communist Cold War policies. This led union federations like the American Federation of Labour-Congress of Industrial Organisations (AFL-CIO), for example, to actively support governments and dictatorships in South America and Africa that were trying to destroy independent union movements: the emergence of what became known as 'trade union imperialism'. British unions, too, were involved in similar activities in Africa (Waterman, 2001b, p. 123; Munck, 2002, pp. 141–143). Silver and Arrighi note that this Cold War division had a crucial North-South component that pitched unions in the North into a competition and opposition to unions in the South in terms of their perceived interests, a problem that persists today as the greatest obstacle to labour internationalism (Silver & Arrighi, 2001).

In the expanded Eastern bloc of the Cold War system unions were incorporated and subordinated into the direction of the national-level Communist Party, ultimately subordinate to Soviet leadership. Class conflict, however, remained part of the new Marxist political systems in Eastern and Central Europe. The Soviet Union had enormous ideological appeal to postcolonial states in the decades after World War II both for offering a successful state-led model of nation-state building, and also for having stood up to and opposed Western intervention in the global South. The Soviet Union was not tainted by the history of imperialism and colonialism in the global South that the West was, only in central and Eastern Europe. A number of important states entered this bloc, of which China remains the most significant, but all of them adapted and introduced their own forms of Marxist authoritarian government that exercised control and coercion over the working class.

Finally, in the periphery and semi-periphery (most areas of South-east Asia, Africa, the Middle East and South America) the Cold War was fought against independently minded social movements and trade unions that were resistant to being incorporated into either a Western or Eastern bloc system (Chomsky, 2002). Trade unionism in the postcolonial period was a complex affair, as Thomas stresses, and has to be understood locally and regionally (Thomas, 1995b; Ahmad, 2007). Geopolitically both the US and Soviet-led blocs wanted to expand their influence at each other's expense, using money and arms to support sympathetic postcolonial governments, though by 1980 the US influence in the global South far exceeded that of the Soviet Union

(Chomsky, 2002). These governments were invariably run by newly empowered political elites who were often willing to sacrifice the interests of their own citizens in return for privilege and power. As Frantz Fanon warned in 1960, national liberation that replaces one set of colonial elites with another set of national elites will do nothing to liberate the global South (Fanon, 2006). Fanon's warning remains pertinent and the example of the former leader of South Africa's National Union of Mineworkers, Cyril Ramaphosa, illustrates this point clearly. Where once Ramaphosa was at the heart of the global union opposition to apartheid, instrumental in the major 1987 strikes, now he is a billionaire shareholder in African mines who was instrumental in breaking the strike that led to the Marikana massacre in 2013. Ramaphosa denounced the 'dastardly criminal' striking platinum miners who were subsequently executed by the police, many shot in the back of the head. He is also deputy president of the ANC (Munusamy, 2012; Hattingh, 2013; Hattingh, 2014). As Bakunin once noted in response to Marxist ideas of using the state as a short-term mechanism to bring about socialism, 'politicians do not change the state, the state changes politicians' (Guerin, 1970).

As with unions in the core nation-states of Europe and North America, those in the periphery and semi-periphery have also been undermined by internal divisions around patriarchy, racism and sexism (Mies, 1998; Thomas, 1995b; Silver & Arrighi, 2001; Jakobsen, 2001). When unions in the global South did seek to assert their independence or promote the interests of their fellow citizens rather than that of ruling elites or foreign capital, as occurred in many South American countries in the interwar period, they were described as 'internal enemies' and subject to brutal military assault, almost invariably backed by Western governments (Koonings et al., 1995; Chomsky & Herman, 1979). This support was driven less by a fear of Soviet expansion as it was the fear of losing geopolitical and economic control over the periphery and semi-periphery. The enemy, as ever, was less the Communist Party and the Soviet Union than an independent working class movement, including trade unions and their communities. The Cold War was war on the global South far more than it was a war between East and West. In the main the US backed counter-revolutionary forces and governments of the most savage and brutal kind where it did not intervene directly itself, with the Soviet Union tending to support national liberation movements (Herman & Chomsky, 1979; Blum, 2014a; Silver & Arrighi, 2001). Those unions that thrived in the global South during the Cold War were often those that were co-opted into existing national structures and who were proponents of the nationalist ideology of the new ruling political, military and economic elites (Gallin, 2002, p. 237). This legacy remains a problem, as Waterman noted, that unions in the global South remain either Leninist or nationalist in outlook (Waterman, 2001a, p. 152).

This period is often viewed as being the 'golden age of capitalism' as for a period of around 20 years after World War II there was significant economic growth in most of the core nation-states and their working classes enjoyed unparalleled increases in their standard of living (Henwood, 2012; Brenner, 2005; Munck, 2002). The golden age of capitalism thesis is, of course, heavily Eurocentric, measuring progress in terms of the experience of the core nation-states of Europe, Japan and North America (Sklair, 2002). Much of the periphery and semi-periphery, however, remained subject to the hierarchical control of often highly corrupt political elites, intervention or subversion primarily by the global power of the US-led West to undermine independent movements, and to increasingly authoritarian forms of state and political systems governing their national territory. When nation-states attempted to break free of US or Soviet power they were subject to various forms of intervention from invasion, coup d'états, economic destabilisation and other subversive acts, for example: Hungary, Cuba, Iran, Iraq, Indonesian, Vietnam, Czechoslovakia, Nicaragua, Guatemala, Brazil and many others. William Blum presents an almost endless list of interventions in the global South during this period (Blum, 2014a, 2014 b). Many unions in South America and Africa, for example, willingly embraced authoritarian policies that excluded women from the workplace and helped to entrench chauvinism and the subordination of women (Burgmann, 1995; French & James, 1997). Mihyo and Schiphorst have noted the corruption of many African trade unions by political elites, which has only served to encourage authoritarian and patriarchal outlooks (Mihyo & Schiphorst, 1995). For the working classes in the global South the postcolonial period was a false dawn that promised liberation but in fact ushered in new and nationalist based forms of authoritarian government and political elites who were frequently openly corrupt and who depended on the USA, or to a far lesser extent the Soviet Union, for support. It is easy to understand how by the mid-1960s the Cold War system, violent and potentially globally destructive as it was, also looked to be a fixed and permanent structure shaping the geo-political landscape and the development of the union movement. But as Fairbrother, Williams, Barton, Gibellieri, & Tropeoli have noted, those old certainties about the relationships between states, unions and societies are over (Fairbrother et al., 2007).

· 2 ·

LABOUR AND THE SECOND WAVE OF GLOBALISATION—DIGITISING THE WORLD-SYSTEM

The global revolutions of 1968 mark an important turning point in the modern world-system. They signify a point of rebellion against many of the forms of social hierarchy and oppression that had underpinned the world-system both ideologically and materially: movements challenging racism, sexism, homophobia, imperialism and militarism all emerged around the world alongside a growing peace movement, human rights and environmental movements (Arrighi, Hopkins & Wallerstein, 1989). The consequences of this explosion of ideas and social movements were felt across the political divide as political parties and established organisations such as trade unions had to rapidly come to terms with them. Unions were subject to an array of criticisms for their bureaucratic, hierarchical, conservative and exclusive practices, including sexism, homophobia and racism (Wrench, 1986; Briskin & McDermott, 1993; Munro, 2001; Wallerstein, 1989). For radicals the unions were also accused of having, in reality, served merely the sectional interests of those they represented rather than working to improve the conditions of the working classes generally (Hyman, 1999). This was a revival of the criticism originally made by the IWW in its founding days, which said that the existing union movement divided rather than united the working classes and that what was needed was One Big Union for all workers (Thompson & Bekken, 2006; Renshaw, 1999; Dubofsky, 1987).

At the same time the 1968 revolutions presented major challenges to the state and capital and this chapter addresses their responses to these challenges. The turbulent 1960s and early 1970s were a high point for the working classes in the core states in terms of winning workers' rights and increased wages (Gumbrell-McCormick & Hyman, 2013; Clawson, 2003; Silver, 2003; Brenner, 2006). This period also saw a wave of revolutionary movements emerge across the periphery to challenge imperial power. However, in the middle of this turbulence, governing political and economic elites were rapidly reorganising themselves in terms of an ideological reassertion of the power and legitimacy of capital and a reorganisation of the state in ways that would undermine and end the social compact that had led to uneasy class compromises in industrial relations in the core states in the middle of the twentieth century. This ideological outlook became known as neoliberalism but has its roots in developments in the 1970s sponsored by corporate think-tanks and roundtables such as the Trilateral Commission, which brought together political and economic elites from the core states to discuss how to deal with what was viewed as a 'crisis of democracy' (Gill, 1992; Beder, 2006; Harvey, 2007).

The developments of new forms of information and communication technology, culminating in the ongoing transition to a digitised world-system, were fundamental technological developments that the state and capital were able to use initially to their advantage against the labour movement and wider forms of social and political protest. This second wave of globalisation was driven by forces from above and below, as was the first wave. Whilst it shares much in common with the first wave (increased and cheaper means of communication, liberalisation of the flow of capital and labour) it also differs qualitatively in terms of the volume and speed of global communication, the unprecedented levels of global inequality, unemployment and poverty that it has generated. Whilst the first wave of globalisation did much to industrialise the North whilst it deindustrialised much of the South; the second wave has tended to reverse this process (Baldwin & Martin, 1999). The 24/7 multimedia age ushered in by digitisation has created a global environment within which social movements (globalisation from below) have also been able to develop in historically unprecedented ways, establishing forms of global solidarity and networks that have been dramatic and often effective (Juris, 2005; McChesney, 2013; Khatib, Killijoy & McGuire, 2012; Graeber & Schmid, 2012; Waterman, 2001a).

For some critics trade unions have been made redundant by these developments, maturing as they did in an age of Fordism where work and social life appeared fixed and unchanging, providing a constant stream of new (largely male) recruits for the union whose officials often worked in tandem with management to oversee production and maintain their sectional interests (Munck, 2002, pp. 35–40; Moore, 2011, pp. 43–45). As the second wave of globalisation shattered this nation-state based framework of industrial relations so trade unions began to shed membership in the late 1970s in what has been a global trend (Fairbrother, 2000; Ebbinghaus, 2002). Multinational corporations, adopting complex new patterns of ownership and forms of organisation, have been instrumental in shaping the second wave of globalisation (Sklair, 2002). The question raised by many is whether trade unions have a future (Munck & Waterman, 1999, Waterman, 2005; Castells, 1997). Are they, in fact, already dead, zombie-institutions that have been killed by the forces of capital and the state, still staggering around in the same old way as though the world remained locked in the 1950s? The answer to this question is not straightforward, as this chapter will explain. Clearly trade unions have to change and our argument is that they have to change radically if they are to be effective in combatting capital and the state, but that they remain very significant and relevant.

This chapter will set out the ways in which both corporations and the state have tried to shape the second wave of globalisation to their own advantage as the dominant forces in GFA, before turning to the response by trade unions to these developments. Two main tendencies have been prevalent in contemporary corporate models: the tendency for corporations to change their identity very rapidly as they engage in takeovers, mergers and frequent reorganisations, and try to escape any bad reputations they have acquired in the past; and the growing casualization of the workforce (including such developments as temporary labour contracts, franchising and the imposition of self-employed status on people who are *de facto* employees) (Chen, 2014). The archetypical contemporary corporation is owned by a constantly changing constellation of asset holders who trade their shares in it electronically. It makes use of a diversity of labour-service contract forms in order to bring together fluctuating combinations of workers and dispense with the need to have any actual employees (Crouch, 2004). There has been a shift of focus from production to brand images (Klein, 2000) in which social media is transforming businesses in their aim to build and safeguard corporate reputations.

The world-system is going through a period of increased turbulence and social crises, plagued by endless wars, environmental disaster and ruinous poverty and unemployment. A rational and humane solution to these problems will, in part, be built by the activities of trade unions and the labour movement, or it is unlikely to emerge at all. On this point it is important to recognise the enduring legacy of trade unions and the labour movement. For all of their imperfections and major faults, which must be acknowledged in the current debates about their future, they have also been at the forefront of the trends that encapsulate the most civilised aspects of the modern world-system: human rights, democratisation, campaigns for equality, social solidarity, anti-militarism, education, health care and social welfare for working people, are all symptomatic of the activities of trade unions. They remain the largest and most democratic social movements (Clawson, 2003, p. 117; Croucher & Cotton, 2009, p. 4). The reality for the vast majority of people, whether employed, underemployed or unemployed, remains simply a basic struggle to survive. Over half of the world's population exist on $2 per day or less, so they are certainly not shopping online or at the mall or accessing social media. And the trend towards exploitation of working people and the destruction of the public services that they depend upon is now global, not just a problem for the periphery. This is the reality that trade unions and the labour movement have to live and deal with, what Beck called the 'Brazilianization of the West' (Beck, 2000).

Resurgent Capitalism and the Ideology of the Corporation

The second wave of globalisation has its roots in developments in political and corporate culture and technological innovations in the 1960s and 1970s and was driven from above, by the political and economic elites who govern state and corporations; from below, by social movements. This section will concentrate on the ways in which GFA has been imposed upon trade unions and the labour movement through political, economic, social and technological reorganisation. These have proven to be a highly effective series of strategies that have led to the crises of the labour movement that frame this book. The implications of these developments have been profound, leading to the erosion of democratic control over political and working life, the destruction of the environment and the normalisation of corporate propaganda as a part of everyday life in much of the core. The exception to this trend in the world-system, and an important one, has been the development in South America of a succession of post-dictatorship democracies that have taken some important steps towards freeing themselves of US intervention, developments which have been shaped by a plethora of grassroots-led social movements across the continent (Zibechi, 2012; Klein, 2000; Beck, 2000; Miller & Dinan, 2008).

The modern corporation has its roots in the core states in the interwar period before spreading dramatically after World War II as US corporations effectively disseminated their form globally (Brenner, 2006; Dicken, 2010); its ideological roots are in fascism and the idea of the corporate state, as the political economist Robert Brady has shown in *Business as a System of Power* (Brady, 2012/1942). Brady showed how the ideas underpinning the modern corporation directly paralleled those found in fascist political forms. This is an important point to consider as there are powerful arguments in contemporary political culture and academic literature that argue that democracy is, in fact, necessarily rather than contingently linked with capitalism, a reversal of Brady's claim (Friedman, 2009; Fukuyama, 1992b). Writing in 1942 Brady's analysis has proven to be insightful in terms of setting out the way in which corporations would subsequently develop if not checked by social and political movements. Brady makes the point that corporations are systems of private power, organised in a way that parallel fascist organisation of social and political life: they are intrinsically totalitarian, built upon systems of hierarchy and bureaucracy that place the corporation and profit-seeking activities at the centre of their activities. Milton Friedman reiterates this point, too, when he argues that making money for share-holders is the only thing that corporations are obliged to do (Friedman, 1970; Bakan, 2005; Guerin, 2005). As in fascist political systems, the individual is tolerated to the extent that they ultimately conform to systems of private economic power. Corporations are anti-democratic in that they seek to control all major decisions over economic policy and direct it to their private ends, not public good. Indeed, democracy is a problem for corporations as it raises the spectre of workers gaining control over the production process and directing it towards the satisfaction of human needs rather than private profit (Smith, 2003; Bakan, 2005). As a consequence the political system has to be subject to corporate control either directly through the funding of political parties or indirectly as when, for example, governments are elected who voice the idea of promoting policies that would benefit the public in general (Mitterrand in France in 1981, Clinton in the US in 1992), through threats of disinvestment, closure of plants and the relocation of jobs to the periphery. All of this is now a familiar part of 'normal' political culture: corporate politics.

Brady traces the evolution of the ideas of fascism and the corporation in the interwar period, setting out the relationship in their ideas about corporate control of social and political life. The model of corporate domination of social and political life has now become commonplace and despite the reorganisation of corporations in the second wave of globalisation, the underlying principles have been applied more intensively than ever. In the post–World War II period corporations in the core were integrated into nationally-based forms of state capitalism, receiving important subsidies and protection from their states without which much of the research and development that has shaped the global economy in electronics, agriculture, computing, pharmaceuticals, aeronautics and so on, would have taken place (Mazzucato, 2015; Bremmer, 2009; Dicken, 2010; Chomsky, 2011; Wang & Winters, 2000). In short, this period deepened and entrenched the idea of public subsidies for private profits, a theme that has become increasingly transparent in the current global financial crisis where banks and insurance companies have been bailed out by unprecedented amounts of public money whilst at the same time funding for public services have been cut (Ferguson & Johnson, 2010).

In the postwar period corporations themselves tended to be organised within nation-states with fixed chains of hierarchy and decision-making over the organisation of production. Corporations adhered to and perfected what are often described as Fordist forms of production that drew upon Taylorist social psychology to organise production, applying behaviourist methods to control the workforce and the rate of production (Brenner, 2006, Braverman, 1998). The social psychology of behaviourism that Taylor's work established in industrial relations has strong resonance with fascist ideas, it being about techniques of psychological manipulation and the hierarchical control of the workforce in undemocratic institutions (Chomsky, 1988, pp. 177–178; Mannheim, 1971, p. 215; Sobel, 1990). The need to control the masses, whether in the form of workers or citizens, is the issue here and fascism and the corporation both face the same problem and share the same fear: an independent and democratically organised working class that seeks to organise social life for the common good, not private interests. Hence the need to subvert, co-opt or destroy independent trade unions and the labour movement as they have been at the forefront of these trends towards democratisation and the common good.

For trade unions this period of Fordist production was important in that it seemed to establish a pattern of working life and production that was fixed around a specific community and workplace, making capital and the corporation somewhat vulnerable to the power of the union to act strategically, when necessary, to promote workers' interests. This period is often viewed as one of Keynesian demand management within which the state and political elites in the core supported their nationally-based corporations and sought to build up national forms of capital through intervention in the economy and agreements with unions (Dunn, 2004). In addition, the aim of the mass production of commodities for a domestic market was central in shaping this period, though what came to be called Multinational Corporations began to develop, too, across the core states. The utopian idea of free markets as set out by Adam Smith was long abandoned by political and economic elites due to their socially destructive consequences, producing inequality, poverty and social conflict in the core (Polanyi, 1944). Political and economic elites in the core realised that the future of their own political power and economic privilege depended upon accepting a compromise forced upon them by the working class, or alternately facing the possibility of social revolution. The state was to be the instrument for the transformation of capitalism. It is this social compact that rapidly unravels in the second wave of globalisation, transforming the state and corporations as part of this process. What, then, are the main changes that have taken place?

Neoliberalism and the Corporate Counter-Revolution

By the late 1960s and early 1970s corporations from the core faced a number of significant problems: they suffered declining profits, increased worker militancy that was often beyond the control of union officials, nationalist governments in the periphery and semi-periphery attempting to take control of their natural resources from corporations from the core through nationalisation, and the apparent spread of radical social and political movements who were opposed to capitalism (Brenner, Brenner & Winslow, 2010; Brenner, 2006; Wallerstein, 2003; Shaikh, 2013, 2014; Leimgruber, 2007). It was in this phase of the second wave of globalisation that corporations in the core began to reorganise themselves politically and economically in order to reassert their power and legitimacy, in part by transforming the organisation of the corporation itself.

On a political and ideological level the 1970s saw leading US corporations begin to develop already existing or build new links with think-tanks, the media and universities, establishing an elite network for discussion, analysis and coordination of responses to the problems generated by what came to be known as the 'crisis of democracy' (Peschek, 1989; Gill, 1992; Beder, 2006; Leimgruber, 2007; Hossein-Zadeh, 2014). This 'crisis' for many political and economic elites in the core states was a concern with the fact that the public had become increasingly active in social and political life, seeking greater say in and control over work and community life and seeking to control and curb the aggressive activities of US-led imperialism (Gill, 1992; Crozier, Huntington & Watanuki, 1975).

As a consequence major corporations saw a need to develop and promote a political ideology that would require the support of the state to enforce it, a form of capitalism that freed markets from social regulation and that would prioritise corporate profits over social concerns or the common good (Harvey, 2007; Peck & Tickell, 2002). Major principles established in this period were the need for political parties and governments to embrace the liberalisation of the economy, the privatisation of publically owned assets and the deregulation of the workplace from social control from the private sector. The consequences of these policies for workers have been dramatic: liberalisation has seen the destruction and relocation of major industries in much of the core to parts of the periphery and semi-periphery as firms sent their production off-shore in search of cheaper labour. Privatisation has led states to sell publically-owned assets (invariably tending to undersell them) to private corporations in areas that guarantee profits. As Hudson notes, unearned profits based on rent not the production of goods have driven the recent boom and bust cycles in the global economy as corporations, hedge funds and major shareholders take over utilities, property and land and exact profit through ownership (rent) rather than production (Hudson, 2012a). Privatisation has had the knock-on effect of driving down work conditions and pay in the public sector as jobs have been outsourced to private firms providing cheaper services such as cleaning and catering, ultimately helping to drive down wages in a race to the bottom with many workers in the private sector (Hudson, 2012b). Again, the cheapness of these services is invariably driven by paying workers the lowest wage possible, as we will see in our case studies, and frequently falls on the shoulders of female workers (Standing, 1989). Deregulation has meant the removal of restrictions on the ability of corporations to exploit their workforce in terms of hours to be worked, health and safety regulations and rendering unions more vulnerable to corporate attack in the courts for their 'illegal' activities (Colling, 2009; Hudson, 2012a, 2012b; Mason, 2008). None of this would have been possible if corporations had not been able to build political alliances to support these policies, as Gill notes (Gill, 1992). This kind of 'free market' that maximises the exploitation of workers requires a strong and often violent state. This has happened as unions have sought to rebuild forms of partnership with the state and business in a largely failed attempt to defend their members (Citigroup, 2006; Hyman, 2001; Stevis, 2002; Bieler, Lindberg & Pillay, 2008b).

The origins of these neoliberal policies can be traced back to developments in Brazil after the US-sponsored military coup led by Vargas in 1964 and Chile under Pinochet after 1973. Both were dependent upon military-political alliances using the state as a tool to destroy unions and working class resistance whilst conducting what was, retrospectively, a utopian socio-economic experiment in the periphery. In the latter case neoliberal ideology was directly imported from the Chicago school of economists whose ideas were eventually adopted by the military dictatorship. The impact was dramatic with the economy of both countries devastated by the implementation of neoliberal policies, producing massive inequality and poverty for the majority. The introduction of these policies was only made possible because of the overthrowing of democracy, supported by the core states (Klein, 2008).

By the late 1970s the twin crises of inflation and unemployment in the core states led to the implementation of neoliberal policies by the Thatcher government in the UK and more importantly the Reagan administration in the US. The impact of Treasury Secretary Paul Volcker's policy of increasing interest rates from 11.2% in 1979 to 20% in 1981 was crippling for US industry but far worse for much of the developing world who had borrowed heavily from the US and Europe in the 1970s when money was cheap and suddenly found themselves unable to repay the interest on their loans, triggering the first wave of the global debt crisis that has continued ever since (Branford & Kucinski, 1988; Bond, 2008). This provided a crucial lever for the core, led by the US, to use the debt crisis to force many major economies in the periphery and semi-periphery, such as Brazil, Mexico and Argentina, and later South Korea and Japan to submit to IMF restructuring packages that effectively imposed neoliberalism upon populations who were given no choice in the matter (Chossudovsky, 2003). This, in turn, produced a massive transfer of assets and resources to the financial industries in the core and at the same time opened up the possibility for corporations in the core to relocate either whole or parts of industries (ship-building, coal, steel, automobile, manufacturing) to the periphery and semi-periphery in search of cheap labour (Harvey, 2007; Wallerstein, 1998). The impact of these policies on the lives of people in the periphery and semi-periphery were devastating with a dramatic drop in incomes, massive unemployment, cuts in what public services existed, and rising prices in food and basic necessities (Branford & Kucinski, 1988; George, 1991; Bello, 1994). As Bello argues this was effectively a recolonisation of much of the periphery and semi-periphery through the world's major financial institutions and international financial agencies such as the World Bank and the IMF. It created a never-ending cycle of debt repayments that could only ever cover the interest accrued, not the capital. Worse still these were, in many instances debts accrued by authoritarian governments, not democratic ones. So the general population was being held to account for debts incurred without their consent, what is often termed *odious debt*. All of this worked much to the advantage of financial institutions in the core that reaped the debt repayments through the interventions of the IMF and to some extent the World Bank (Bello, 1994).

At the same time they also wreaked social disaster for citizens in many of the core states as traditional industries were relocated to the periphery and semi-periphery, devastating communities and leaving a trail of mass unemployment and underemployment that has never been resolved, building up Marx's 'reserve army of labour'. Again these developments were normally backed by military regimes in the periphery and semi-periphery that would act to crush any resistance to these policies in savage fashion. It is these policies that governments in the core are now trying to impose upon their own populations as a way of subsidising the cost of bailing out the banks and insurance companies in the core in the current financial crisis (McNally, 2011).

So corporations were central to the political and ideological spread of neoliberal policies and practices globally in this period and by the 1980s were able to use new forms of information and communication technology to transform the organisation of the corporation itself in ways that undermined the ability of unions to organise as they had done over the previous 50 years. Where once corporations were based within a single nation-state, with a community-based workforce that enjoyed a degree of fixity and continuity, with clear lines of command and control in the corporation, directed by a centre that could be targeted by unions, this was to change rapidly and dramatically for many major corporations (Croucher & Cotton, 2009; Beck, 2000). The impact of computer technology and subsequently the internet itself meant that corporations could abandon traditional structures of organisation for new, more flexible forms of production, in many instances eschewing direct need for a workforce and instead contracting out work to a plethora of smaller units to organise and control or by employing new techniques of worker participation and flattened hierarchies. The latter encourage worker participation but, of course, not control or self-management (Kahmann, 2003, p. 7).

To be clear, this does not mean that hierarchy, system and structure disappeared (Jessop, 2002, p. 229). On the contrary, the dramatic inequality of wealth and poverty that neoliberalism generates has led to increasing power and decision-making in many industries in the hands of fewer agents and institutions than ever. Many markets have become effectively state-subsidised and protected oligopolies, rarely monopolies, with relatively few mega corporations able to take part and compete. This is what the economic historian William Lazonick refers to as a system of guided or coordinated, not 'free', markets, subsidised and protected by the very visible hand of the state rather than the invisible hand of the market (Lazonick, 1993). Telecommunications, aerospace, pharmaceuticals, electronics, finance and insurance are all dominated by a relatively small group of corporations from the core states, corporations that have often grown through mergers rather than through increased profits or market success. They have also benefitted from a great deal of protection and subsidy from national governments in the core who have been happy to espouse the rhetoric of free trade whilst at the same time strategically pursuing mercantilist policies of protection of their own industries, another characteristic feature of contemporary imperialism that is now based on both territorial control and the control of markets (Mann, 2011; Harvey, 2007; OECD, 2010; Chang, 2002).

Thus, many companies have taken advantage of the digital economy to abandon traditional forms of production and control and to outsource many of their activities to smaller companies who carry the risk and burden of producing on time for their major corporate partner, effectively decentralising the production process and making it much harder for unions to take action against them (Monks, 1992). Nike, for example, now sees itself as being primarily involved in research, brand identity and marketing; it leaves production of its goods to others whom they contract work to and who have to impose the necessary discipline upon the workforce on Nike's behalf (Gallin, 2014).

These new networks of production exist within the framework of broader corporate structures of ownership and cross-ownership, backed by states in the core (Gumbrell-McCormick & Hyman, 2013; Dicken, 2010; Antcliff, Saundry & Stuart, 2007), making it much harder for unions to know where to apply pressure effectively across the supply chain.

Despite much popular and academic talk of the move to a risk society and a 'new economy' shaped by the internet and digital entrepreneurs there is clearly little risk involved here for corporations; it is the public that carries the risk for their losses as they are compelled to subsidise or bail out many major corporations deemed 'too big to fail' (Hudson, 2012a). Indeed the nature of the industries that are associated with the new economy are in fact a product of state investment and often military directed research, only in the later stages of development when profit is guaranteed becoming marketed by private companies (the internet, satellite TV, digital innovation, computing). Corporate risk has been socialised by the state in the core since the emergence of the post–World War II international economic order known as Bretton Woods, and the public have permanently underwritten the costs of research and development by the state through taxation (Mazzucato, 2015; Wilkinson, 2002; George, 1991; Cavanagh, Wysham & Arruda, 1994). This is what the economic historian David Felix describes as the strategic role of the state in 'cherry-picking' the industries they wish to develop and protect (Felix, 2003). There has been a good reason for this system emerging, largely to do with the chronic inefficiency of markets that are driven by the need for short-term profit and return. Significant research and development needs a long-term investment on projects that may ultimately lead to nothing. No private company has an interest in this kind of investment so therefore it has been necessary for states in the core to produce a dynamic and committed approach to innovation, the very opposite of the claims of the neoliberal ideology that has been a part of GFA (Harvey, 2007; Hudson, 2003). By contrast it is the lives of workers and the unemployed that have become far more 'risky' as a consequence of these changes, losing welfare support, health and safety protection, job security and often the ability to feed themselves and their families. In chapter six, we outline how the experience of the International Domestic Workers Network is a prime example of the vulnerability of workers to such forms of exploitation and also of their ability to organise with a view to transforming their working conditions. As Eder notes, over 1 billion people, one third of the world's working population, are unemployed or underemployed, living precarious lives (Eder, 2002).

Corporate Propaganda and the Colonisation of the Public Realm

At the same time corporations have introduced new forms of propaganda amongst their workforce to manage these changes and encourage people to conform to the dictates of neoliberalism. In the workplace new systems of behavioural management have become the norm, all attempting to individualise and separate workers from unions and collective action: human resources management, total quality management, flexible working practices, have all been designed in ways that effectively reduce the power of unions to organise, mobilise or even recruit (Guest, 1987; Snell, 1992; Elger & Smith, 1994; Thompson & Ackroyd, 1995; Guest, 1999; Croucher & Cotton, 2009; Fairbrother, 2000; Bratton & Gold, 2007). These strategies have been effective in many corporations in fragmenting the workforce and undermining unions and are allied to the idea that there is a new form of individualism that renders the necessity for collective action and representation redundant. This individualism encourages legalistic approaches to workplace problems, which, of course, presuppose that workers have any legal rights to begin with or possess the money needed to defend themselves in courts, something available to a small percentage of the world's workforce (Taylor, 1994; Danford, Richardson & Upchurch, 2003, pp. 1–10; Colling, 2009). Many unions have taken this route towards providing a service for individuals, culminating in the promise of the possibility of legal support for court actions against employers. Case work has transcended organising and mobilising activity in terms of importance for unions in the core in particular (Ewing, 2005).

More realistic and representative of working life under neoliberalism is the 'hire and fire' culture that is now global and a consequence of the deregulation of much of the global economy and the removal of regulations that might provide important protection for workers (Elliot & Atkinson, 2009). Unsurprisingly massive global job agencies have emerged to fill the need for the regulation of this massive temporary and casualised workforce, with major firms operating globally and able to help discipline the vast army of cheap labour pitted against each other in a desperate struggle to survive, that GFA has produced (Staffing Industry Analysts, 2013). That is the essence of the risk society for most people, employed or not.

Supporting this ideological offensive by corporations has been the spread of the consciousness industries into all areas of daily life. Where corporations confront unions or workers they are able to call upon an array of PR firms or specialists in union-busting to advise on tactics and to plant anti-union stories in the media to turn public opinion against workers (Clawson, 2003; Logan, 2002, 2006; Freeman & Rehavi, 2008; Walsh, 1988; Beder, 2002 and 2006). At the same time corporations have extended their brand and image into all areas of life from sport to politics, education and to health care (Klein, 2000; Beder, 2006). The strategic aim of these consciousness raising strategies is to build a benign image of corporations and to render them as *natural* institutions of everyday life in the mind of the consumer. It is also to increasingly colonise public life so that there can be no space or event free from identification with corporate power (Lewis, 2013). Again, as Orwell noted, if the language available to us is the language of the powerful we will often lack the linguistic tools necessary to oppose or challenge their power. In the same way the expansion of corporate propaganda into all areas of public space only strengthens this power symbolically, denying the possibility of social space outside of corporate control. The public square becomes the privately owned shopping mall and, for example, childhood becomes an extension of corporate life as evidenced in such developments as the remarkable Girls Intelligence Agency (GIA, as in CIA) (GIA, 2004). The GIA is a club for girls (sic) from the age of 8 to 29 (sic) to join, sponsored by corporations, who are recruited as 'secret agents' in order to hold parties and provide reports for the firms as to the consumer tastes of their friends. GIA now boasts over 40,000 secret agents who hold regular parties at which the brands and goods of their clients are tested and the information fed back to the corporation. This includes such companies as Nestle, Procter and Gamble, Lego, Warner Brothers, Fox and Johnson and Johnson. Brand loyalty is a process to be started at as young an age as possible.

This need to colonise public space and private thoughts has led corporations to quickly establish teams of researchers to study and respond to developments on social media such as Twitter and Facebook, surveying and monitoring behaviour as well as adverse criticism by consumers or even worse, employees, so that the company can move quickly to protect themselves, using special online tools such as Social Mention, Tweetdeck and Hootesuite (O'Conner, 2013). By comparison, as Eric Lee comments, unions have been slow and resistant to respond to the impact of the internet and social media and the possibilities they might generate for them (Lee, 2000, 2013).

In addition we have seen the proliferation of forms of Corporate Social Responsibility (CSR) charters that pledge companies to all manner of missions and humanitarian actions, all of which provide good publicity and at the same time help to promote consumer identification and loyalty to the corporate brand. It is also apparent that for companies the budget for CSR is a small price to pay when compared to the money that they save from tax cuts and tax avoidance that have become the norm under global neoliberalism. These are, of course, taxes that might otherwise have been used to pay for the same public services that people need and that are deemed to be no longer affordable by national governments. They are no longer affordable, of course, because the same national governments have shifted the burden of taxation onto the middle classes and the poor and off of the shoulders of corporations and the rich, not because there is any natural law of the economy that makes such policies inevitable. On the contrary, these are policies designed to promote the interests of the elites that run and own these corporations (Beder, 2006).

Post-Fordism, Financial Globalisation and the Modern World-System

Allied to these changes has been the growing importance of financial power at the expense of productive capital, the increased and dramatic shift in the circulation of capital and the power of financial institutions to control national economies and effectively undermine democratic control by the public (Hudson, 2005/1977; 2012b; Harvey, 2007; Baker, 2010a, 2010b). As is often noted this financialisation can be measured by the transformation in the flow of capital towards the production of goods or speculation in assets such as land, property and money itself. In 1980 80% of global financial investment went into productive capital and 20% was speculative; these figures have reversed as capitalists generate vast fortunes from unearned income, using financial power to terrorise national governments (those that might raise objections to the destruction of their public services, for example) and similar threats to force unions to agree to a renegotiated role in the industrial system, where they have a meaningful role at all (Hudson, 2005/1977, 2012b). As Ewing notes, increasingly unions have become subordinate partners, at best, to corporations, with many instances of unions accepting recognition agreements in return for helping corporations with their restructuring of the workforce. This kind of development shows how far many unions have fallen in their role as defenders of their own membership, never mind the working class in general (Ewing, 2005; Danford et al., 2003, p. 19; Terry, 2003, p. 494).

The end of the Cold War opened up great possibilities to corporations in the core (primarily North America, Western Europe and Japan) to work with international organisations such as the GATT and then WTO along with core states and political elites to open up previously closed economies to their investment. This had the immediate impact of increasing the available workforce in the global economy and effectively signalling the end of the uneasy compact that had existed in the core since World War II between labour and capital (Hodkinson, 2001). The second wave of globalisation meant that corporate interests could now be advanced in a much more brutal manner and the world's trade unions were unable or unwilling to comprehend this or respond effectively (Moody, 2007, p. 79). The 'death of socialism' was a much mooted part of this period with corporate propaganda gladly able to promote the mantra that there is no alternative to the market and that socialism died with the end of the Soviet Union. These themes were given clearest expression in Fukuyama's well-known thesis on the end of history, which was nonetheless qualified by later work in which he acknowledged the comparative success of Soviet-style industrialisation, an alternate model of state-led capitalism to that found in the core states (Fukuyama, 1992b). A clear alternative was presented to the world's citizens: they could have either free markets or a command economy led by the state–capitalist democracy or totalitarianism. These two choices remain the dominant ideological parameter for elite discussions of global political economy. That there might be other options available falls mainly outside this framework (Munck, 2002, p. 93; Hahnel, 2007; Mason, 2010). That this picture of the history of free trade was not an accurate account of the evolution of state capitalism in the core was beside the point, in the war of propaganda what counts are slogans, images and powerful rhetoric (Scott & Street, 2000; Chang, 2002; Wallerstein, 2011b). What is strategically important is the ability to affect people's emotions, desires and fears.

The reorganisation of work and the corporation has led many commentators to talk about moving into a new age of post-Fordism (Dunn, 2004; Amin, 1995). The implication is that the world has qualitatively changed and old assumptions about the fixed nature of class, status, power and capitalism itself have to be abandoned. Many radicals accept these premises and take them further, arguing that there is in effect no longer any sense in talking about structure, hierarchy and system when discussing the global economy, that capital has become deterritorialised and transnational, constantly moving in search of new locations for investment, that it is fluid and able to permeate all barriers (Waterman, 2001a; Lash & Urry, 1991; Hyman, 2001; Munck, 2002).

But how plausible is this narrative? It is certainly true that capital has become highly mobile again in the second wave of globalisation and that financial markets are now constantly scrutinising government policies, ready to punish those that step out of line with neoliberal dictates (Hudson, 2005/1977, 2012b). It is also true that there are greater flows of people now than in much of the twentieth century, a wave of migration that has helped to restructure society and economies in the world-system (Moody, 2007, pp. 59–63; Solimano & Watts, 2005). In addition firms have greater opportunity to relocate in search of cheaper labour, though this is not straightforward and relocation also involves massive costs to corporations. However, these notions of post-Fordism and the new economy are overstated. Capital may be mobile but it is not deterritorialised. Most capital flows between locations amongst the core states and outside that to the major semi-peripheral countries China, India, Brazil, Mexico and Russia (Freeman, 2002; Danford et al., 2003, pp. 8–10; Hunya & Stöllinger, 2009; UNCTAD, 2014). Most trade is still dominated by regional agreements, reflecting regional free trade agreements such as the EU and NAFTA, but also intra-firm and inter-core (Danford et al., 2003, pp. 8–10; OECD, 2014; OECD, 2002; Dicken, 2010; Dunn, 2004; Van der Linden, 2004; Harrod & O'Brien, 2002b).

Equally terms of trade and terms of work remain hierarchical, established by the core states and the world's major corporations through international institutions such as the WTO. The rise of the BRIC states has begun to unsettle the structure of world trade and of long-standing geo-political assumptions behind it, allied to the relative decline of the US since the early 1970s. This is an important point for the labour movement in that as the world-system moves towards a multi-polar structure of power it opens up spaces for social change and challenges to entrenched forms of political power and economic privilege. The Arab Spring and the Occupy movement, however inconclusive their impact, are testimony to this point. Opposition to capitalism and political dictatorship was underpinned by support from the core states in many areas of the world-system throughout the Cold War period. However, those Cold War structural certainties have disappeared, much in the same way that the assumptions of mainstream unions about the nation-state and welfare systems have been undermined by the impact of neoliberal policies. The emergence of left-wing governments throughout South America over the past 15 years is illustrative of this changing geo-political structure as it reflects the reduced ability of the US-led core to control political processes in the periphery and semi-periphery. Thus we are seeing the emergence of trade links and blocs amongst states in the periphery and semi-periphery that potentially create spaces for the labour movement and other progressive social movements.

At the level of work itself companies have restructured their activities to produce a more flexible system with much work outsourced and temporary but this does not reduce hierarchy and power in the workplace. On the contrary, it intensifies the nature of the exploitation of workers. As has been shown repeatedly since the global economic slumps of the 1980s, companies can make record levels of profit by the mass lay-off of workers (thereby saving on wages) acting as a threat to the remaining workforce to increase their productivity, forego pay rises and abandon attempts to organise unions (Munck, 2002; Rasmus, 2014). This practice has been repeated endlessly and is no doubt a testament to the efficiency of neoliberalism in generating profits for corporations and their shareholders. It is also a clear statement of the fact that neoliberal policies are not based on a neutral economic science but are expressions of class interest in a global class war (Moody, 2007, p. 90; Harvey, 2007). Even the notion that there is no longer any analytic purchase in terms such as core and periphery is overstated (Munck, 2002). In fact global inequalities have deepened dramatically over the past 40 years, sharpening the division between core and periphery and much of the semi-periphery as well as within nation-states.

If the traditional Fordist jobs that were a feature of the core for much of the twentieth century have been relocated to the periphery and semi-periphery, often becoming feminised work as part of this relocation, this does not mean that the principles underpinning Fordism have been abandoned. Routine, systematic work, with tasks mechanised and broken down into the simplest possible components are seen as synonymous with Fordist patterns of work and Taylorist behaviour management. This is also symptomatic of many of the jobs that have arisen in the core to replace the old manufacturing industries, what are often called 'mcjobs', work in call centres, fast food and retail (French & James, 1997; Dunn, 2004; Thompson & Ackroyd, 1995; Kahmann, 2003; Dølvic & Waddington, 2004). This is hardly a brave new world. It is also worth noting that the relocation of many manufacturing industries to states in the semi-periphery has generated and intensified union organisation and often violent class struggle, requiring state violence and coercion to protect corporate interests. China, Mexico, India, Brazil and Russia are all experiencing varying levels of class conflict as workers struggle for better pay and conditions under severe and repressive conditions (Bizyukov & Olimpieva, 2014; Sen, 2014; Buketov, 1999; Chan, 2011; NACLA, 2014; Giri, 2009; Human Rights Watch, 2013). Only Brazil can be seen as anything like an exception here after the election of Lula as the Workers Party's first president in 1998, which led to some modest gains at first for Brazilian workers as well as much subsequent disappointment and class conflict (Jakobsen & Barbosa, 2008; Zibechi, 2014). As Tilly wrote, all nation-states have historically been akin to forms of organised crime, extorting money and obedience from populations in return for protection, so it is little surprise that this pattern has reproduced itself throughout the world-system. While democratic movements have been able to moderate or amend this relationship they have not been able to transcend it (Tilly, 1985).

The Neoliberal State: 'No Banker Left Behind'

The neoliberal state, described by Richard Rosencrance as the 'Virtual state', has been fundamental to the developments that have shaped social, political and economic life in the second wave of globalisation (Rosencrance, 1996). The transformation of the economy to the overwhelming advantage of corporations has seen states take a number of strategic actions to transform themselves and their relationship to labour and capital. It is important to stress that neoliberal principles are always applied selectively and strategically by political elites in the core in ways that they hope will maximise their political and economic strength. Nonetheless there are general trends that have emerged that tend to apply to states throughout the world-system with regards to the rights and entitlements of workers and the labour movement.

First, it has been necessary for the state to intensify its coercive capacity to regulate unions and the labour movement, removing or undermining rights to organise and carry out industrial actions. A 'free market' needs a strong, coercive, and when necessary, violent state willing to attack its own population and communities in defence of the right of corporations to maximise profits at their expense. Second, the state has added to this social conflict by cutting public services for its citizens and at the same time cutting taxation for the rich and for businesses, directly shifting the burden of financing the state's activities onto the middle classes and the poorest sectors of society. In those regions where there is little if any welfare support for working people the state has been able to impose the most draconian and severe punishments (Harvey, 2007; Hyman, 2001; Hudson, 2012b). Third, the state has retreated from long-held commitments to systems of national industrial relations, arguing that regulations need to conform to the requirements of a global marketplace. This has led, in effect, to the abandoning of forms of protection for working people and of agreements with trade unions over rights and recognition. These have tended to be replaced by either voluntary codes of conduct on the part of corporations that have little purchase on corporate activity in reality, or the somewhat more solid International Framework Agreements (IFAs) that commit companies to abide by what are minimum standards in terms of their treatment of workers (Pearson & Syfang, 2001; Stevis & Boswell, 2007; Croucher & Cotton, 2009; McCallum, 2013; Fairbrother & Hammer, 2005). Fourth, it is through political elites that these policies have been advanced and embedded over a period of 40 years, and these political elites have increasingly drawn for policy advice from the ranks of the world's major accountancy firms and financial institutions as to how to reform their national economies. It is most unusual for governments to promote the advice of trade unions as part of their policy deliberations, even less to appoint trade unionists to important roles within government. Thus private banks like Goldman Sachs provide advisors to many of the world's governments on economic policies that directly affect the interests of Goldman Sachs itself, and this is regarded as normal politics, not corruption (Ellis; 2009; Taibbi, 2009; Johnson, 2009).

Thus, political elites and state managers in the core have tended to shift away from the contingent post–World War II compact with labour, revealing themselves more sharply than ever to be firmly allied with the world's economic elites. Even in countries with strong corporatist traditions, such as Germany, these practices are being abandoned (Baccaro, Hamann, & Turner, 2003; Forman, 2013b). The neoliberal state in the core has hollowed out only in a limited sense; it has retreated from directly providing public services whilst at the same time extending its power of surveillance and discipline over their populations. The virtual state has become a surveillance state of almost unimaginable power and scope as the recent expose by NSA whistle-blower Edward Snowden has revealed.

At the same time the increasing geo-political and cultural power of the BRIC states is creating a challenge to the power of the US-led core that is causing much distress amongst political elites. As former US Secretary of State Hillary Clinton acknowledged when she testified before a congressional committee in 2011,

> *During the Cold War we did a great job in getting America's message out. After the Berlin Wall fell we said, "Okay, fine, enough of that, we are done," and unfortunately we are paying a big price for it…Our private media cannot fill that gap.*

> *We are in an information war and we are losing that war. Al Jazeera is winning, the Chinese have opened a global multi-language television network, the Russians have opened up an English-language network. I've seen it in a few countries, and it is quite instructive.*
> (quoted in Lubin, 2011).

In terms of the nature of representative liberal democracy these developments over the past 40 years have reduced the power of trade unions to influence government policy to the point that even elected governments that are nominally sympathetic to labour can now largely rebut the claims of the labour movement as being against the *nature* of global markets, as though capitalist markets are natural phenomena like gravity. Although a stark picture, what we have provided here is a sketch of the realities that trade unions and the labour movement face in the twenty-first century. What then, have been the responses of unions to these trends?

Trade Unions and Globalisation from Below—The Death of the Labour Movement?

The response of the trade unions and labour movement to the second wave of globalisation has, in general, been one of retreat and decline. There have been and continue to be important exceptions to this trend with active and aggressive union movements emerging in undemocratic countries in the 1980s to push for democracy (Brazil, South Korea, Poland) and often drawing upon the tradition of independent unionism in order to do so. Equally in the 1990s general strikes took place in many countries, sometimes serving to unseat governments as occurred in France in 1995 (Harrod & O'Brien, 2002a; Chin, 2008). So the example of trade unions helping to push a different kind of GFB continue to be found and they have been important in opposing even greater neoliberal excesses such as the proposed and subsequently abandoned Multilateral Agreement on Investment (MAI) in 1996. Importantly the campaign against the MAI was an example of unions being able to coordinate their protests with a number of civil society groups and citizens' networks in an example of social movement unionism (Deibert, 2000).

But as is endlessly noted in union and academic literature the overall picture is one of decline with questions being raised as to the future of unions. But why has this decline taken place? There are three major reasons for this and each of them needs to be understood and used to inform how unions need to reform themselves if they are to revive in the twenty-first century.

The 'Iron Law of Oligarchy' was a concept originally coined by Robert Michels but later taken up by C. Wright Mills in his study of US union leaders, which presents it as being a *natural law* of social life (Michels, 1968; Mills, 2001/1948; Greene, Hogan, & Grieco, 2003). The argument here is that, where there is organisation, there is oligarchy, and rule by the elite (or the few). In the context of unions this has meant the development of hierarchical union structures dominated by leadership and full-time professional officials who have tried to control grassroots initiatives in return for securing legitimacy in the eyes of capital and the state and in order to secure their own full-time positions. In particular it led many unions to embrace a corporatist ideology that for capital was always a temporary and contingent relationship that could be abandoned when the time was ripe. This is precisely what has happened in the second wave of globalisation with the spread of neoliberalism as the ideology of GFA, and the union movement has generally lacked the ideological tools needed to address this. In many core states the belief in social partnership is still seen by unions as the goal to be achieved. Elsewhere, as Waterman has noted, many unions in the periphery and semi-periphery remain mired in Leninist ideology and practices, bad nationalism and other forms of reactionary social ideology, almost invariably oligarchic in nature and organisation (Waterman, 2001a, p. 150).

Secondly, the attack and infringement upon working conditions and rights in pursuit of corporate interests has been legitimated or imposed with the help of the neoliberal state. These developments have been central to the crisis of corporate power and the crisis of the labour movement itself. What is clear is that the two are necessarily related; the relative decline of labour power that has led to a crisis of representation for the labour movement throughout the world-system is directly related to the emergence of a transformed capitalist system within which corporations have become increasingly free to pursue profit and ignore the attempts of the labour movement to defend social welfare and workers' rights. As billionaire Warren Buffett has noted this global class war has been driven by political and economic elites through the implementation of neoliberalism (Buffett, 2012). The consequences for the labour movement have been profound, challenging its legitimacy and power, using a mixture of violence, coercion, propaganda and law to bind and suppress the rights of unions and workers (Snell, 2007).

Finally, unions have failed to adapt ideologically to the reality of the changed organisation and strategies of global capitalism (Thomas, 1995b;

Healy, Heery, Taylor & Brown, 2004). As corporations have transformed their modes of organisation and production, work has been feminised and rendered flexible and temporary, with vast new waves of migrant workers emerging from South America to South east Asia and Eastern and Central Europe. Unions have struggled to deal with these trends, often leading to the marginalisation of migrant workers or clashes between older groups of workers and newly arrived migrants, as our case studies illustrate (Standing, 1989; Mies, 1998; Elliott & Atkinson, 2009; Sklair, 2002; Beder, 2002). This is not just a question of tactics or strategies but is a deeper issue as many writers have commented. It is about the future direction of the labour movement and how it relates to broader progressive social movements. It is clear by now that the labour movement needs to work with these social movements to promote common and self-interests. The problem for the labour movement is that so much of its structure and ideology over the course of the twentieth century has been shaped to pursue goals that now appear to be outdated, most obviously, forming alliances with political parties and the state and subordinating their autonomy in return for specific gains for their members. The divisions within the labour movement that have historically undermined its capacity to promote the interests of the labour movement as a whole (gender, nationalism, sectionalism) still stand in the way of the possibility of the emergence of a progressive ideology and practices that will enable it to build meaningful and sustainable alliances with social movements. These divisions work much to the benefit of the political and economic elites who have promoted and gained from neoliberalism.

These factors have been important in undermining unions, bringing together a mixture of changing objective conditions, attack from external actors and self-inflicted wounds caused by adherence to ideologies, practices and modes of organisation that are authoritarian (Leninism, patriarchy, racism) or no longer relevant in the current phase of capitalism (social partnership, corporatism in all its forms including business unionism). However, the oligarchy that Michels and later Mills wrote about is not an iron law akin to a natural law. It is a social law that reflects specific historical conditions and circumstances; it is a tendency amongst social organisations that adopt hierarchical and authoritarian modes of organising (Scott, 1998). There are alternatives to these practices that can be drawn from the libertarian body of ideas within the union and labour movement and indeed from socialism itself. If the union movement is to be rebuilt it needs to engage with these libertarian ideas and find ways to transform their practices.

There are reasons for cautious optimism that unions and the labour movement have begun to address these issues, always lagging behind the changes brought about by capital and the state but nonetheless getting there eventually. In the context of this book these developments have been particularly important as they embrace debates about new forms of union organisation allied with the use of information and communication technologies (the internet and social media) as a means of rebuilding a more libertarian form of unionism. Many writers and union activists have expressed the belief that these communication technologies and social media can help to democratise and radically transform unions, overcoming the problems of oligarchy and conflicts between union rank and file and grassroots and the leadership (Danford et al., 2003, p. 13). Having a bureaucracy is not inherently a bad thing; it depends upon how it is organised and to what purpose. It is impossible to run an effective union or labour movement without some administrative infrastructure to ensure the necessary day-to-day continuity that helps sustain such organisations, something that proved a divisive issue for many syndicalist unions. The central issue is: How is the union to be organised?

Debates amongst the world's trade unions since the end of the twentieth century have focussed upon three main possibilities for future development: global unions, community unionism and social movement unionism—underpinned by a call for theoretical and political renewal for the labour movement (Bronfenbrenner, 2007; Munck & Waterman, 1999). Each of them has their strengths and weaknesses and we will examine them in more detail in our case studies when each has purchase on the examples we focus on. In addition there is also a resurgence of interest in syndicalism as a natural response for many workers confronting the impact of global class war in their daily lives (Dølvic & Waddington, 2004: 26; van der Walt, 2014; Ness, 2014). Here we will set out what these terms mean and what the implications are for trade unions.

Global Unions

There has been much debate about the need for global unions to enable workers to combat a dynamic and global capital (Hogan, Nolan & Grieco, 2010). There have, of course, been global unions for 150 years in the shape of International Trade Secretariats (now Global Union Federations) and the First International was itself an attempt to build such a movement (Cole, 1970;

Croucher & Cotton, 2009; Lee & Mustill, 2013; Lee, 2005b). The GUFs have certainly expanded in terms of their activities and importance over the past 15 years but they remain very small and lacking in resources. They are also frequently in opposition to each other and dominated by national unions, as Dan Gallin notes (Gallin, 2014). The idea of global unions is far from straightforward, however attractive it might be in theory. As Herod notes, it is hard to get unions to cooperate at a local and national level, so the idea of global unionism seems a distant goal (Herod, 2002). What does seem crucial in these debates is the recognition that the division amongst trade unions has historically promoted sectional interests amongst groups of workers and that now where capital, backed by the state and political elites, has been able to wage a highly successful class war against a divided working class and poor, such divisions can only serve to reinforce the power of capital and the state. For Arrighi and Silver the division between workers in the global North and the global South remains the defining issue undermining global solidarity (Silver & Arrighi, 2001). A form of union organisation that transcends sectional interests would seem the minimum requirement for a revived and combative union movement in the twenty-first century. Where GUFs have proven effective is in helping unions to organise along the supply chain to put pressure on employers in different parts of the world and helping to coordinate communication and solidarity amongst trade unions (Croucher & Cotton, 2009; McCallum, 2013; Fairbrother & Hammer, 2005). As Eric Lee of *LabourStart* and others have noted, the internet opens up important opportunities for reviving and developing a new form of global labour internationalism that builds a more lasting solidarity between workers (Lee, 1997; Hogan et al., 2010).

Community Unionism

For some the idea of community unionism is really an old idea brought back to life. As Wills and Simms notes unions were originally small and local, built in and reflecting the interests of those living and working in specific communities (Wills & Simms, 2004). So the concept of community was rooted in both specific geographical terrain but also in a shared meaning and sense of connection amongst the population. The internet has led to many discussions about online communities that have extended to unions and their activities, seeing the emergence of ideas such as the e-union and cyber communities (Kerr & Waddington, 2012; Kollock & Smith, 1999; Greene et al., 2003). As unions evolved and became national bodies so the community link changed and weakened, shattered in many places in the second wave of globalisation (McBride & Greenwood, 2009). So what does the concept mean now for trade unions? The argument is that unions need to organise not just in the workplace but should concentrate on the geographical area in which their members and non-members live and work, drawing upon support from the wider community to aid their activities (Wills, 2001a). For some this need not entail a focus on a specific workplace at all, in contrast with Social Movement Unionism (McBridge & Greenwood, 2009, p. 12; Stewart et al., 2014, p. 12). Rather this means an alliance with community groups within which unions are but one actor amongst several. The assumption is that unions can learn from this process and transform themselves along the way and that there might not be a workplace focus for particular campaigns but one that addresses issues affecting the community, such as threats to the local environment (Banks, 1991). In so doing it also reasserts the view that it is not as easy for capital to relocate many industries as is often argued. Relocation involves significant costs for MNCs and the second wave of globalisation does not guarantee automatic success for capital (Wills, 1998, p. 114). There are also opportunities for unions to use these developments for their own ends.

Social Movement Unionism/Social Justice Unionism

Social movement unionism has proven to be a popular idea as unions have sought to find ways to mobilise and organise workers in vulnerable and precarious occupations such as fast food, cleaning and security. The idea is that unions will work with social movements (human rights groups, environmental groups) in order to work towards wider goals and the resolution of workplace issues. Social movements are viewed as being a network of (often) informal relationships between individuals, groups and organisations who combine to undertake forms of collective action (Johnson, 2000; Dani, 2000; Munck & Waterman, 1999; Kapstein, 2000; Waterman, 2012). Thus it is argued that unions should accept the reality that there are multiple forms of oppression and that they should work with groups in coalitions to challenge them (Healy et al., 2004). The Seattle WTO protests in 1999 brought together a diverse array of social movement groups with trade unions to protest against the specifics of the WTO proposals but also against the destruction of democracy by corporate power, a much broader theme that connects all of these anti-systemic movements. Many of these civil society groups have labour-related interests on which a coalition might be built (Juris, 2008; McCallum, 2013, p. 30; Wilkin, 2000; Waterman & Timms, 2005). Social justice unionism has also emerged in these debates now and it chimes with the argument that unions need to present a picture of a good society that can be built through cooperation, solidarity, mutual aid and direct action on the part of working people, a revived and libertarian form of socialism that rejects the dogmatic nature of authoritarian socialism of the twentieth century (Bliss, 2014).

Syndicalist/Autonomist Union Movements

Ness and a number of others have recorded the resurgence of union movements around the world that have rejected the corporatist/business union model in favour of the libertarian tradition of independent unionism that draws upon syndicalist principles of direct action, self-organisation, solidarity and mutual aid (Waterman, 2001b, pp. 98 –115; Fink, 2014; Ness, 2014; Dølvic & Waddington, 2004). Such movements have adhered to classic syndicalist formulae of workers organising themselves in the workplace, often in open assemblies where possible, eschewing bureaucracy, state regulations and mainstream unions in order to challenge their employers directly. Whether considering the Italian 'hot autumn' and autonomist tradition, the rise of militant and independent unions in Argentina occupying and reclaiming factories, labour protests in Russia, the actions of South African Mineworkers or workers for 'Jimmy Johns' in the USA allying with the IWW to organise coffee shops, the libertarian tradition of independent and militant union action has reappeared in many forms over the past 25 years as the traditional corporatist/nationalist/business union models have collapsed under the combined pressures of transformed capital and the state (Munck, 2002, p. 16; Ness, 2014). The dilemma for these movements is a familiar one, whether to build independent unions outside of the mainstream that will remain true to their principles or whether to move into the mainstream unions in order to persuade colleagues to transform them in a more militant direction, in essence, whether it is possible to transform mainstream unions in a direction that is congruent with the reality now facing workers world-wide.

We will examine these developments in our case study chapters but it is worth noting here that despite much discussion and analysis unions have very mixed records in terms of responding to wider social protests and movements that have occurred over the past decade. The Arab Spring, as it became known, was certainly preceded and made possible by the militant action of trade unions in Egypt, though this is often overlooked in favour of more superficial descriptions of them as 'social media revolutions'. At the same time when protests were taking place in Gezi Park in Turkey against government policies for urban development and a range of issues including freedom of the press and an end to censorship, the unions showed little support and in fact took the opportunity to make a deal with the government, effectively undermining the protestors (Dosemi, 2014). So the picture is uneven and the responses of unions reflect an array of local and global factors.

So the answer to the question as to whether the union movement is already dead must be a contingent one. It is certainly in parlous condition but it has many of the tools that it needs in order to revive and rebuild. As we will turn to in our next chapter, developments in digital media technologies may play a part here, but more than this the labour movement needs a vision about the democratisation of social and economic life that takes control and power away from the tyranny of corporations and the limitations of the state and places it in the hands of workers and communities so that they can build for themselves a good society that will be both free and equal.

· 3 ·

SOCIAL MEDIA, DIGITAL ACTIVISM AND LABOUR MOVEMENTS—WORKER RESISTANCE IN THE NEW PROTEST ENVIRONMENT

As we have seen, media and developments in media technologies—as part of the consciousness industries (Ewen, 2001)—have been important in advancing the interests of corporations and manifesting their power at a global level. The digitization of the global economy and the integration of digital media into corporate practices have profoundly changed not only corporate structures and working conditions but also the possibilities for corporations to manage and circulate information about their own activities in new and innovative ways. There is no question that corporations have been able to take enormous advantage of the possibilities that digital media technologies allow. However, much debate over developments in media has highlighted how some of these possibilities have also extended to social and political actors that seek to challenge or resist the expansion of corporate power and the spread of neoliberal ideology and global capitalism. Although unions and labour movements more broadly have received very little attention in these debates, they occupy a significant role in advancing such resistance. Historically, unions have been slow adapters to the web and the development of media practices within unions has been marked by a long-term and entrenched culture and understanding of resistance that is not necessarily immediately receptive to a digital environment. Indeed, the appropriation of media technologies by unions and worker organisations has been diverse, multi-faceted and certainly not consensual. Attitudes and perceptions of the use of digital and social media amongst labour activists and union officials are often conflicting and contradictory, partly due to the contradictory nature of these technologies in themselves. The nature of digital activism, the relationship between online and offline mobilisation and organisation, the use of social media platforms for resisting and challenging forms of domination and institutions of power are all issues that are of increasing concern in a growing digital economy. From organising strikes amongst Yue Yuen shoe factory workers in China that supply for global brands such as Nike and Adidas to awareness raising and campaigning around the working conditions at Bangladeshi garment manufacturers in Rana Plaza making clothes for the likes of Primark and Benetton, the use of media has become central in debates on worker resistance.

It is clear that as the climate of protest and political activism has changed, alongside developments in communication technologies, traditional forms of political organisation such as trade unions are also going through significant transformations. The developments we are seeing within the labour movement as outlined in the previous chapter, such as global, community, social movement and indeed syndicalist forms of unionism, have emerged in a context of a digitized world-system that marks the second wave of globalization that has also presented new opportunities—and challenges—for the organisation and advancement of workers' interests. The perceived 'affordances' (Gibson, 1986/1979) of digital and social media have played a part in how the possibilities for organising workers and challenging global corporate power might be changing. As we will outline in this chapter, we are seeing this in a number of ways, not only in terms of the creation of platforms to share information and news about workers' struggles and union campaigns that are otherwise neglected in traditional capitalist and mainstream media, but also increasingly in terms of creating widespread advocacy campaigns to put pressure on corporations and political elites. What is more, we see it in new ways of reaching previously unorganised workers and building networks of solidarity amongst workers and organisations. These developments are significant in and of themselves, but as we argue in this book, they cannot be abstracted from broader debates within the labour movement regarding the nature and purpose of unions in the twenty-first century. That is, the role of media and the nature of digital and social media practices within the labour movement needs to be understood in the context of the challenges and dilemmas that are facing trade unions and worker organisations in the modern world-system.

As is further highlighted in our case studies, media practices and the engagement with digital activism and a 'new' protest culture are significant for trade unions and labour organisations in that they tell us something about the direction of the labour movement in the current context.

This chapter will provide an overview of some of the ways in which digital and social media have been appropriated by trade unions and have come to play a part in new (or revisited) forms of worker organisation. In doing so, it will explore some of the debates that mark contemporary media practices amongst workers' movements and forms of protest. In particular, we will look at the different repertoires of digital activism that are emerging as forms of resistance as these media technologies become increasingly integrated into union activities. As we will argue, the development of new protest cultures evidenced with uprisings around the world in recent years that are said to have a central role for social media in particular are significant for how labour movements might move forward. However, the potentials of these forms of protest and resistance for labour movements are also met with significant challenges and concerns regarding the purpose and future of unions in such an environment. These concerns need to be taken seriously and critical debates around the nature of digital activism need to form a central part of how unions and labour activists seek to advance the long-term interests of workers in an increasingly hostile modern world-system.

The Internet and Unions—The Makings of a Global Labournet?

The early adaptations to computer-mediated communications by trade unions were primarily concerned with improving communications between trade unionists, creating networks of exchange across borders and boundaries in various incarnations of 'labournets' (Lee, 1997). As is often pointed out, the adoption of new technology by the labour movement has been an uphill battle throughout most of its history (Waterman, 1992; Lee, 1997; Fitzgerald, Hardy & Lucio, 2012). Sceptical towards disruptive change to existing infrastructures and confronted with the sense of unpredictability and lack of control that advancements in technology can introduce, unions have historically been resistant to appropriating technologies that are simultaneously being implemented by corporations to drastically change the working conditions of many of their members. Even adopting email and creating mailing lists to reach members of the workforce has been a relatively slow development for unions with many rank and file members still not being reached this way today (Buketov, 2014). However, throughout the 1980s and 1990s there were still experimentations going on in this regard within the labour movement. Lee (1997) has illustrated how these early adoptions of the internet became increasingly oriented towards establishing new forms of 'internationalism'. Drawing inspiration from the British Columbia Teachers' Federation (BCTF), which already back in 1981—faced with the problems of involving leaders and rank and file members in decision-making processes and union activities in a geographical vast region such as British Columbia (four times the size of the United Kingdom)—decided to set up portable communications terminals for each of the members of the Executive Committee spread across the province to create a network of electronic message exchange, initiatives to strengthen existing trade union structures through the use of communications technologies began emerging. These developed relatively quickly into discussions about the potential for a 'global labournet' (Lee, 1997).

Although the technological infrastructure was there, developing a global communications network for the labour movement was never going to be a straightforward process. Waterman has written about the failure of unions to advance such a project in those early stages and argues that it probably had to do with ignorance or hostility towards the new technology, organisational conservatism, and a conscious or unconscious strategy of informational deprivation (or limitation) as a membership control device (1984, 1992). These themes are still prevalent today. However, in those early days of the internet it meant that the focus for many unions was to integrate these new technologies into union practices within a framework of centralised control and organisational status quo. As such, the internet debate has largely focused on the internal politics of the labour movement and how to deliver existing services more efficiently without challenging hierarchical structures or threatening union leadership (Fitzgerald et al., 2012; Drew, 2013). Union websites and members mailing lists have proliferated around the world, but for many the 'New Internationalism' hypothesis that the web will strengthen the international labour community still leaves much to be desired (Diamond & Freeman, 2001). The vertical nature of the global make-up of labour movements shapes and creates many of the directional flows of communications between unions and labour activists and the narrative of horizontalism that accompanied the early days of the internet (and continues to accompany the advancement of social media as will be discussed below) did not manifest itself as some labour activists had hoped. Certainly, as Eric Lee points out, the development of some kind of 'horizontal' global labour net did take foot amongst rank and file members, often on the margins, in the form of solidarity networks amongst individual workers and local organisations (Lee, 1997, p. 161; Drew, 2013).

Despite the limited advances in the democratisation of unions and the prevalence of centralised control, developments of new communication technologies did from the outset lend itself to grassroots solidarity and collective activism that frequently by-passed established international trade union bodies and other usual channels of coordination. As has already been mentioned in previous chapters, we saw early signs of this in the 'anti-globalisation' movement or 'global justice movement' (Della Porta, 2005) that ascended on the streets of Seattle for the World Trade Organisation ministerial conference in 1999. These events demonstrated some of the innovative uses that digital media technologies afforded resistance movements. In particular, activists could communicate, collaborate and demonstrate in new ways by aggregating small contributions into a broader movement (Van Aelst & Walgrave, 2004). For some, this came to mean that the movement in some ways could be said to mirror the 'rhizomatic' infrastructure of the internet itself in its fragmented yet networked and connected architecture (Hardt & Negri, 2005). Rather than emerging as one coherent movement with a collective identity and a particular ideological position as might be seen in more traditional forms of organisation in political movements, the anti-globalisation movement or global justice movement emerged as a 'movement of movements' (Mertes, 2004) in which different collectivities and ideological positions, including an important role of labour unions, united around resistance to corporate power. As previously discussed, the early 1990s saw the building of new alliances between labour organisations and new social movements and nongovernmental organisations in response to the onslaught of neoliberal restructuring programmes and free trade agreements. As Drew (2013) argues, the interests of labour activists increasingly coincided with the concerns of other organisations in terms of the environment, social justice, gender or health issues: 'The ability for labor to survive, many began to believe, did not rest on its ability to become a large monolithic force, as in the post-World War II period, but to engage in "Lilliputian Linking" (meaning many small groups fighting together) to find common ground with other causes and build grassroots support.' (108)

In this way, the 'Battle of Seattle' of 1999 came to be a very significant moment in the labour movement's trajectory, particularly in the United States. It illustrated the possibilities of a reinvigorated movement of workers in solidarity with other progressive sectors of civil society, not historically linked with organised labour. According to Drew, this unified show of force was a result of the growth of the many new channels of communication that allowed stories of workplace oppression, environmental disaster, economic injustice, and social power to flow between people all over the world, not constrained or filtered by corporate mass media institutions (2013, p. 121). As we will discuss below, these kinds of efforts continue to be central in discussions on the role of social and digital media in the labour movement today.

Digital Media as Alternative Media: From Indymedia to *Labor Notes*

One of the most important aspects of this interplay between the global justice movement and media technologies became the emphasis on these technologies for a new kind of media activism that could bypass the mainstream capitalist press. Although alternative media has a long and rich history, the ability to set up independent media centres (what became the alternative media network known as Indymedia) during the protests in Seattle in order to report on the movement independently of the mainstream media became key to the repertoires of contentious action available to activists. The slogan 'don't hate the media, become the media' came to epitomize the media practices of the global justice movement and the centrality of producing and distributing own media content rather than having movement activities mediated via a historically hostile corporate press.

Certainly Indymedia highlighted the possibilities for creating own media channels and for using digital technologies to distribute information and content that would otherwise not reach people. This has been a central aspect of how historically marginalized labour struggles have been able to make it into public debate on terms that did not seek to discredit unions and labour activists. The adverse relationship between capitalist media and trade unions has meant that labour activists have always sought to produce their own information about working conditions and labour disputes. Faced not only with a hostile treatment of union activities but more generally an almost complete exclusion of union voices in mainstream media, online platforms have proven to be central to the dissemination of information within and beyond labour movements (Drew, 2013).

Initiatives such as *Labor Notes* in the United States, for example, were created to publicise and debate union activity and workers' actions. Founded in 1979 by a couple of left-leaning union activists in Detroit following a string of large-scale national actions in which militancy amongst union members would often run up against their own union leadership, *Labor Notes* became a space to discuss strategies and lessons learnt that could incorporate rank and file militancy. Predominantly a print-based publication for most of its history, the current editor Mark Brenner outlined in an interview that *Labor Notes* 'has always seen itself as a media and an organising project' that is about more than just reporting on labour struggles and issues that do not get reported on elsewhere: 'We are not just impassionate journalists, we're project workers trying to engage in a form of…advocacy journalism. Here it's not just about being partisan to a particular case, it's also about being connected to the movement that those folks are trying to build and being a part of that and creating spaces for that to develop and mature' (Mark Brenner, editor of *Labor Notes*). In particular, this has been catering to the more radical parts of the labour movement within the US that otherwise have not been made visible. As Brenner notes:

> You are not going to find information about what's happening in your industry even if you are a steel worker…So we provided a really critical avenue for keeping in touch with what's happening, what the unions were doing about it, what activists were doing on the ground, and helping to hold up a model that you could do things differently. Because a lot of people were doing things differently and cutting against the grain and really showcasing those cases.

With the move online, the possibilities for increasing content that would fit this vision proliferated despite *Labor Notes*' slow migration to go digital, which did not happen until 2005. The outlet has now tripled the amount of content they produce just in the last 3–4 years, and now publish across multiple platforms including print, website, and social media. Of course, as is so often the case with online alternative news sites, the interplay between mainstream and alternative media platforms remains a crucial part of how alternative media activities come to engage in public debate. The online world replicates the structure of the offline media ecology in many respects, particularly when it comes to news, and the most frequently visited news websites remain the most established 'traditional' mainstream media institutions (Dencik, 2012). On a good month the site has around 50,000–60,000 unique visitors. This increases significantly if a journalist from the mainstream press sites a *Labor Notes* story, which will drive massive traffic to the site. The outlet therefore often remains marginal as a news site in the traditional sense, but it serves an additional important function within the labour movement as a space for news and discussion that comes to be part of shaping the practices of the movement itself. This is particularly significant at a time when the direction of the labour movement is up for grabs, particularly in terms of the use of radical tactics that have historically been confined to the more militant wing of the labour movement that gave birth to *Labor Notes* as an organisation.

Initiatives such as *Labor Notes* illustrate the long-standing tradition of media activism within the labour movement that has further advanced with the proliferation of digital media technologies. The ability to challenge dominant news agendas that mostly neglect or misinform on significant industrial developments and disputes continue to form a significant part of labour activism, as is further evidenced in our case studies, particularly with regards to marginalized and largely invisible workforces that are frequently patronized when not ignored by capitalist media. However, as *Labor Notes* also indicates, these alternative media platforms struggle to find voice in a still largely unequal digital environment, where big media corporations continue to dominate news agendas and public reach (Fenton, 2010a; Dencik, 2012).

A Case of Numbers: Unions and Digital Campaigning

Where digital media technologies have manifested themselves as particularly pertinent in questions around the changing nature of activism and politics more broadly has been their use for the purposes of campaigning. Often such trends are marked by references to political campaigning and the way social media now plays an important part in elections and political communication in general (McNair, 2010). These trends have been matched by civil society efforts to advocate on particular topics and debates incorporating digital technologies into campaigning efforts. Initiatives such as *change.org* and *38degrees* operate specifically as digital campaigning platforms in which issues are advanced via email lists and online petitions. This forms an important part of the debate on the ways in which politically engaged citizens express and lobby for particular causes within democratic societies today. Such platforms have been heralded as reinvigorating channels of engagement between citizens and decision-makers within institutions of power and allow for campaigns to mobilise faster and wider than previously possible (Lowery, 2013). For labour activists, the possibilities around digital campaigning have been very significant. Not only has it been an important aspect in the wish to build international solidarity and for the labour movement to think and operate as a global movement, but it has also come to be an important avenue for using digital technologies as tools of pressure on employers (Lee & Mustill, 2013). Central to this is the digital campaigning platform *LabourStart*, mentioned in previous chapters, which has come to occupy a significant position in the development of digital media practices within the labour movement as a whole.

Set up by American labour activist and computer programmer Eric Lee in 1998, *LabourStart* developed out of research into a book by Lee on the labour movement and the internet in the early 1990s. This was a time with no websites for unions and very limited online activity amongst labour activists of any kind. Two large British unions, CWU and NSF, now part of UNITE, commissioned Lee to launch an online portal for unions: '*LabourStart* was designed to be a proof of the concept that you can actually do trade union websites that would do news and campaigning and stuff' (Eric Lee, founding editor of *LabourStart*). It was meant to simply be a prototype for larger, more established confederations to emulate and improve on, but revealingly, this never happened and *LabourStart* came to establish itself as the primary platform for news and campaigns related to union activity. This actually says a great deal about the hesitancy and limited engagement with new technologies within the trade union movement. As Eric Lee pointed out:

> Looking at the first days of *LabourStart* in 1998, we didn't run our own campaigns, we just linked to anyone who had done a campaign…But it became clear after a couple of years that the unions were clueless how to do this. Still are…So we wrote a campaigning platform.

LabourStart is funded by a diverse range of unions, but it remains a very small operation with no full-time staff; Eric Lee himself is part-time with most of his income still coming from web-consulting and web-designing for unions, and the day-to-day running of the platform is predominantly done by a part-time intern who recently joined Lee in his London office. The news content on the platform is aggregated from a pool of around 700 unpaid 'correspondents' (content aggregators) and 30 unpaid translators based around the world. Interestingly, however, Lee does not see this as an alternative news outlet in the vein of *Labor Notes*. The average amount of news stories *LabourStart* receives is 250 stories a day, but the bulk of them comes from mainstream news media.

If there is a strike or an industrial action, they will try and publish something that comes from elsewhere, but the material they can gather for this is limited. Often unions will only provide the one press release rather than comprehensively producing their own content as a form of media activism as we have become familiar with through platforms such as Indymedia:

> Unions think we've embraced the website, we don't need to sucker up to mainstream media, we have our own resources. That's exactly what they don't do. Unions are the ones who are most likely to read a print newspaper or watch the 9 o'clock news. Because of their age and their culture. So obviously unions should have their own media but they don't know how to write. (Eric Lee, founding editor of *LabourStart*)

Focus has therefore shifted predominantly to digital campaigning, learning and taking inspiration from platforms such as *38degrees*, *Change.org* and *Avaaz*. In fact, these platforms are increasingly used by labour activists to advance causes related to workers' rights. In the UK, for example, *38degrees* has been campaigning with support from unions around so-called zero-hour contracts, targeting retail companies such as Sports Direct that overwhelmingly use these kinds of contracts for their staff. However, for the labour movement the internet's 'economy of eye-balls' (Fenton, 2010b) in which campaigning becomes largely a numbers game is very problematic. Getting large numbers of people involved in a campaign is not necessarily a form of success if it does not lead to actual change on the ground. In fact, the proliferation of digital campaigns and the trend to aim for viral-friendly causes that will engage (however superficially) large numbers of people in one way or another has pushed the threshold for the number of people participating in digital campaigns up, making it increasingly difficult to be effective. As Eric Lee pointed out:

> My understanding of success is always facts on the ground. Did the lockout end? Did the strike end successfully? Did they get a contract? I don't care if they did that with a 100 messages or 100,000 messages. And it's getting harder in a sense. It used to be that a 100 messages to an employer would freak them out. Now, bottom-line is thousands, many thousands. So in a sense it is almost getting harder to do.

This dilemma reveals some real limitations to the participatory possibilities that digital media technologies are said to have provided in communicating causes and campaigning for actual change. In a context in which such technologies allow for vast numbers of people to add their 'voice' to campaigns, getting 'heard' has become one of the internet's biggest paradoxes. That is, as Couldry (2010) puts it, finding a way to make 'voice' matter. This pursuit has become entrenched in a political economy centred on numbers that often obscures relevance and importance, and one that frequently favours a decontextualised and sometimes abstract cause that is free from the shackles of securing an observable and concrete outcome (cf. Meikle, 2014 on the Kony 2012 campaign). This makes it a challenging terrain for unions looking to use digital campaigning to achieve better working conditions for workers by settling disputes and enforcing contracts. This is not to say that it has had marginal impact; there is much evidence to suggest that digital campaigning within the labour movement has seen a great number of successful outcomes, pressuring companies to pay higher wages, improve conditions, or reinstate fired labour activists (Lee & Mustill, 2013). What is more, it has been greatly significant in efforts towards global unionism and building solidarity networks across community groups and social movements. However, it is to argue that the architecture of the digital media economy in the broader context of corporate power also significantly limits the potential for digital campaigning, particularly that done in the interests of sustaining broad, collective grassroots labour activism.

Social Media, Movements and 'New' Protest Cultures

In fact, an increasingly prominent part of debates on digital media and political activism has shifted from a focus on the participatory potentials of single-issue online petitions and campaign mailing lists to looking at the role of media technologies in fostering and shaping new types of social movements that culminate around protest and direct action. Events in recent years have advanced debates around the relationship between digital media technologies and forms of activism at a significant speed. Initial claims about the mirroring of movements in the fragmented and 'rhizomatic' nature of the internet have been replaced by the rapid development of social media and the emergence of 'spontaneous' protests and uprisings that are said to have been made partly possible by the increasingly participatory nature of social media. Events such as the Arab Spring, the Indignados, Occupy, and more recently Gezi Park in Turkey and the Free Fare Movement in Brazil, have led to an explosion of research in the field of digital activism and the affordances of social media for 'new' types of protest movements. Much discussion has concerned itself with the ways in which social media provides new opportunities for political activism, for people to organise and mobilise in new and easier ways at lower costs. Castells (2009b; 2012) has been at the forefront of this debate, advancing an ongoing argument about the shifting nature of power in a 'network society' that sees communication tools as being central: 'power relies on the control of communication, as counterpower depends on breaking through such control.' (Castells, 2009b: 3) The rise of digital media technologies and social media, or the rise of 'networks of mass self-communication' as he describes them, offers new opportunities for autonomous communication between individuals and groups that can facilitate precisely such counterpower. The movements of recent years, he claims, can be explained by the material support of social networking sites and the internet more broadly that support a new type of political participation, a participation that is based on horizontal networks, on political autonomy, leaderless organisation, and boundless solidarity (Castells, 2012).

Bennett and Segerberg (2012) have presented a slightly more complex picture of this interaction by focusing on how these digitally enabled political protest movements engage in a form of 'connective action' that stands in juxtaposition to the 'collective action' of traditional forms of political organisations such as political parties or trade unions. Such 'connective action' is marked by personalized, individualized and technologically organised processes that come to replace the requirement of collective identity framing or formal organisational structures that usually require a lot of resources for membership. As Diani has noted in this regard, networks are not just precursors or building blocks of collective action: they are in themselves organisational structures that can transcend the elemental units of organisations and individuals. These organisational structures made up of digital communication, in turn, are much better suited to contemporary forms of political engagement (Bennett & Segerberg, 2012). Indeed, the opportunities that these technologies have facilitated for political activism to flourish have been explored across a range of both scholarly and media discourse (cf. Shirky, 2008; Mason, 2012; Ghonim, 2012), sometimes even heralding platforms of social media as the defining feature of uprisings as in the BBC documentary series on the Arab Spring called *How Facebook Changed the World* (Kemp, 2011).

These accounts celebrate social media platforms as new (mainstream) spaces for political activism that are inclusive and accessible to majorities and that have moved online activism from the technological margins, appealing previously to radical ghettos of media activists and political groups, to everyday platforms of communication and exchange (Gerbaudo, 2014). These platforms are seen to allow for ordinary members of the public, in particular the ever-elusive 'youth', to share information, communicate and organise events outside of the peering eyes of the state or corporations. The power of these social media technologies is said to lie in the spontaneous and unpredictable ways in which networks of protest and solidarity can emerge. In fact, Paul Mason has tried to explain the particular functions of different social media platforms in the spread of recent revolutions in the past few years:

> Facebook is used to form groups, covert and overt – in order to establish those strong but flexible connections. Twitter is used for real-time organization and news dissemination, bypassing the cumbersome 'newsgathering' operations of the mainstream media. YouTube and the Twitter-linked photographic sites— Yfrog, Flickr and Twitpic—are used to provide instant evidence of the claims being made. Link-shorteners like bit.ly are used to disseminate key articles via Twitter. (Mason, 2012, p. 75)

Inevitably, more critical accounts have accompanied and followed such discourse, foregrounding not only broader historical and social developments in any explanation of protests (Curran, Fenton, & Freedman, 2012) the significance of face-to-face interaction in mobilisation (Juris, 2012) and shared physical space (Gerbaudo, 2012), but also the problems with assumptions around autonomy, horizontalism and connectivity that surrounds the narrative of social media protests (Gerbaudo, 2012; Barassi & Fenton, 2011; Cammaerts, Mattoni & McCurdy, 2012; Fuchs, 2012b). Although concepts such as 'connective action' provide a detailed and considered framework for analysing how 'new' protest movements differ in nature to traditional forms of political organisation, there is a danger of attributing too much of the analysis to social media and digital media technologies. What is more, as further outlined in chapter seven, there is a significant neglect of important dynamics of digital media by basing the framework on an economic logic of participation and sharing. Rather, questions around actual freedom and autonomy of communication are being fore-grounded as algorithms and surveillance have come to be the primary agents of the digital economy (Fuchs, 2012a; Andrejevic, 2014; Leistert, 2015). Instead, these technologies are affecting political imagination and practices in quite contradictory ways that speak to a very complex and convoluted emerging protest environment. As Fuchs (2012b) has argued, the media—social media, the internet and all other media—are contradictory because we live in a contradictory society. As a consequence, their effects are actually contradictory, they can dampen/forestall or amplify/advance protest or have not much effect at all. And the media, in turn, stand in contradictory relation and power struggle with not only each other, but also with politics and culture and ideology that also influence the conditions of protest.

The complex media context that surrounds contemporary forms of resistance and protest has also been part of the debates on the transformations, challenges and opportunities that face labour movements today. This is an interesting moment to look precisely at this relationship between protest, social media and workers' organisations, because organised labour is at a significant moment of flux. As political activism has developed and diversified in shape, structure and content, so unions have had to increasingly consider how to stay relevant and effective in the current climate of resistance. As outlined in previous chapters, labour movements are currently confronted with real tensions around the direction they need to go in order to best represent the interests of workers. Unions have had to reconsider their distribution of resources and efforts and transform the nature of worker resistance in a way that can more adequately respond to the challenges of the modern world-system. The promises of social media for reinvigorating political activism therefore come at a crucial moment and the emergence of 'new' protest movements in recent years have certainly played a part here. Unions have had to reflect and reconsider the ways in which mobilising and organising collectively can best be achieved.

Social Media and Transformations in the Labour Movement—Building a New Unionism?

In particular, the move to consider organising workers outside the workplace and outside of collective bargaining agreements, as outlined in previous chapters, has gained increased significance in light of developments in social media and recent popular uprisings. Initiatives such as AFL-CIO's *Working America* and SEIU's *Fight for a Fair Economy* set out to describe a revised, more flexible, vision of how to mobilise low-income workers who cannot get union recognition in their workplace. With a significant increase in low-wage precarious labour, unions have actively been considering how to build more flexible types of membership that are focused on community affiliation and communicated at home—online—rather than the workplace. This has meant an increased focus on community organising and a concerted effort to broaden mobilising strategies and tactics. As Freeman (2013, p. 46) states, 'the spread of low-cost Internet-based information and communication tools gives [labour activists] inexpensive ways to mobilise, organise demonstrations and campaigns, and connect workers outside of the work places where employer opposition can defeat all but the strongest union organising drive.'

Although this is in line with debates regarding contemporary forms of protest cultures as discussed above, the actual (social) media practices of labour movements are far more complex and contradictory. New forms of labour organisations that challenge traditional corporatist models of trade unionism are certainly emerging. Movements such as Occupy have been part of a move towards broader society-based labour organisations that target broad economic issues, such as income inequality and living wage as highlighted in our case studies on cleaners and fast food workers. We have also seen the rise of occupation-based or immigrant community centred labour organisations such as worker centres and alliances, for example, those made up of janitors or cleaners (as is explored in chapter 4) that aim to support low-wage workers mostly from immigrant communities. Or we are increasingly seeing employer-based labour organisations that are formed to deal with individual employers such as OURWalmart or the Starbucks Workers Union (as discussed below), often seeking to be independent unions, that illustrate ways in which workers can exert influence on employers to improve working conditions outside of collective bargaining agreements. The labour movement is being shaped by these new forms of organisation and is moving in a direction that might increasingly try and take advantage of new forms of communication and social media at a pivotal moment of social experimentation in worker representation (Freeman, 2013).

However, as outlined above, unions have been historically slow at adapting to shifting technological environments and the concerns that have emerged out of debates on social media and 'new' protest movements are certainly prevalent within organised labour as well and take on further complexities in the context of union structures. This goes beyond long-standing criticisms of the threat of new media technologies to centralized decision-making and hierarchical structures within labour organisations. The different and often contradictory attitudes and forms of engagement with social media amongst unions and labour activists speak to a number of key themes in our understanding of the relationship between social media, digital activism and labour movements.

The predominant way in which unions have sought to engage with social media has been as an extension of existing communication strategies. That is, social media practices have often become integrated as an extended communication tool of existing information or as part of broader advocacy campaigns and public relations strategies. This is part of a trend within many mainstream trade unions to focus resources on the professionalisation of communications instead of on organising. We see this particularly in our study of the fast food worker protests in the United States in chapter five. Social media, in this context, is less about spontaneous organising or protest mobilisation, but becomes used as an extension of traditional media relations with the possibilities of more immediate and direct channels of communication. For many of the labour activists we interviewed, this has actually led to an over-emphasis on media management in the advancement of worker resistance. As Mark Brenner, editor for *Labor Notes*, said:

> Most of the time I've been a union activist, most unions haven't had a strategy…and after losing spectacularly in key battles people start to get savvy: the media matters a lot in how a strike is perceived…The problem is that the pendulum has swung too far in the other direction where people start to think that that's how we're going to solve things, if we get press, and they keep forgetting the fundamentals that we win what we want from the company by our power vis-à-vis their power and if we can't build enough power to get what we want from them, we're not going to get it. And yes, the media plays into that power because it's not just our power, it's what the company thinks our power is, what their perception of our power is not unrelated to what our actual power is, and in the end even if they actually underestimate our power and our power is greater, that's all to the good, fine, we'll shut them down and they'll be fucked and we'll win.

In other words, as we illustrate in our case studies, there is a worry that understandings and definitions of worker power are being reformulated in the context of this new protest environment. The notion of digitally enabled activism has, within the context of trade unionism, not been translated into a restructuring of the labour movement as much as a greater emphasis on (digital) media visibility. Rather than using digital media to mobilise industrial power in new ways, therefore, the focus has been on building symbolic power by enhancing pressure through public image campaigns:

> I think people have been much more obsessed with how do we use the media, and stunts to get media, and they've used it as a crutch instead of actually organizing, instead of building real commitments, solidarity, awareness, even just the basics as to why does this matter to the membership. (Mark Brenner, editor of *Labor Notes*)

Often the emphasis on media in this regard is seen at the expense of actual organising as resources and energies within unions are finite. This is not to say, however, that there is no appreciation for the possibilities that developments in media technologies have provided in terms of creating struggles over public image that can be used as a powerful tool. An interesting example of this is the Starbucks Workers Union, predominantly active in the United States, but gaining significant grounds in both the United Kingdom as well as in Latin America. The Starbucks Workers Union formed in 2004 in New York City as an affiliate of the Industrial Workers of the World (IWW) and is informed by libertarian syndicalist unionism. What is significant about the Starbucks Workers Union in this context, however, is the way in which it creatively engaged with the brand of Starbucks to pressure the company into improving working conditions. This has partly been made possible by the trend amongst companies like Starbucks to engage in socially responsible branding in which the running of the company is linked to some form of ethical guidelines as discussed in the previous chapter. This emphasis on the branding of companies has been exacerbated by the development of social media and the pursuit of companies to use these technologies to advance as 'social brands', pertaining to 'listen' and 'respond' to consumers (Jones, 2012).

For a company like Starbucks, this type of branding strategy has made them enormously successful, but it also leaves them vulnerable to critique. In addition to disruptive direct actions that form a central part of the IWW's philosophy (such as unionists entering the store at peak hours to buy drinks and then paying for them one penny at a time to slow down business and to highlight issues around the emphasis on 'speed of service' within the company over and above the well-being of its workers), the Starbucks Workers Union managed to engage media and damage the Starbucks brand by highlighting the poor working conditions of barristas. Calling a press conference in front of one New York City Starbucks store next to a giant inflatable rat to draw attention to the problem of rodent and insect infestation in many of the Starbucks stores, for example, created additional pressure on a company that has made corporate social responsibility and concerns with environmental and workers' rights a central part of its 'social brand'. As one of the barristas who started the initiative and is now a full-time labour activist said: 'we wanted to unpack some of the hypocrisies of the brand. (Daniel Gross, founder of Brandworkers). Engaging with media from the very beginning, through both their own media Starbucksunion.org as well as corporate media and traditional outlets, allowed for the union and campaign to create excitement, to put pressure on the company and for it to spread to different stores. Of course, Starbucks would never admit to conceding to the actions of the Starbucks Workers

Union, but during the initial years of the Starbucks Workers Union when it was particularly active in the United States, workers received increases in pay and a big victory for the union was the official recognition of Martin Luther King day as a holiday, meaning that workers would be paid time and a half for working on that day:

> that was a tremendous victory for us…emotionally…for the very right for free association which is the right that fast food and retail workers are fighting for. And then the extra money, believe me, was very welcome as well. (Daniel Gross, founder of Brandworkers)

However, it is important not to attribute the strength of the Starbucks Workers Union entirely to its media practices. According to Daniel Gross, far more important aspects are to be found in the self-organisation and solidarity amongst workers to break through corporate control. In fact, concurring with the discussion above, he was keen to stress that there has been an over-emphasis on the role of counter-PR:

> I think it's overstated. Such a huge topic. Naomi Klein wrote a great book about this idea, everybody talks about it, everybody is obsessed with it. It's a tool. But that terrain, the company will always have an advantage. Because most of the media is owned by large corporations and companies are large corporations, they are an advertiser, they have ideological interests in common, they have big advertising and marketing budgets. (Daniel Gross, founder of Brandworkers)

What is more, as Eric Lee of *LabourStart* pointed out, these forms of media practices are limited to corporations who have pursued a media presence around this kind of 'social brand' that Starbucks is emblematic of. This still excludes many big corporations:

> The reputation of companies like Nestlé and Coca-Cola, I can't contribute to tarnishing their reputation, it's so tarnished already, which is actually a very serious problem. With a company like Nestlé we can't campaign against them. You can't campaign against Nestlé for sacking some workers in the Philippines or something. This is a company that kills babies, nobody is going to care about that. We can't campaign on that. (Eric Lee, founding editor of LabourStart)

There is of course also a broader point to be made about this, alluded to above, with regards to the purpose of unions in concentrating resources on counter-PR strategies. As many of the labour activists we interviewed highlighted, this is all part of the shift in unions away from organising and advances unions less as agencies representing the interests of workers with the use of labour as a bargaining mechanism and more as pressure groups seeking to advance workers' rights through advocacy campaigns. As Daniel Gross (founder of Brandworkers) stated:

> any group can generate PR, an environmental group can generate PR against Starbucks. What's the unique power of workers? Well, it's their role as folks who build or produce or distribute a product or a service.

Even within the Starbucks Workers Union the focus in recent times as it has tried to re-establish itself, particularly in New York City, has been on building relationships on the shop-floor rather than dedicating resources to media strategies, digital or otherwise. As one of the barristas currently involved in organising Starbucks workers in New York City (and therefore anonymised) said in an interview, this is now about building 'everyday unionism'. That is, resources and time are put in to creating solid relationships of trust and solidarity within the workplace that allow for workers to feel supported and part of a collective effort to improve working conditions—in the vein of what might be considered traditional organising. Of course, this also means that it is a slower and less visible form of movement building than what might have come to be expected in relation to how social media is transforming forms of resistance, which has created a new kind of protest 'temporality' (Barassi, 2015; Kaun, 2015).

Bringing Organising Back in through Social Media

It would be a misconception, however, to conclude from this that media practices, and perhaps particularly an obsession with social media practices, somehow cancel out organising practices altogether and that the only answer is to keep to traditional forms of organising, regardless of the frustrations with a protest temporality that strides against contemporary times. Still marginalized within the labour movement, there is some evidence of ways in which social media is being used, not simply as part of a (professionalized) communication strategy, but as an actual organising tool. Of particular interest here is the OURWalmart campaign in the United States that has illustrated ways in which social media might be incorporated into worker resistance, not necessarily with a focus on advocacy alone, but as a way to complement traditional forms of workplace organising of workers. As the world's largest publicly traded employer, with over 2 million employees across the world and net sales of over $140 billion in 2013 (Fortune, 2014), Walmart has inevitably been the target of various anti-corporate campaigns over the years. Labour activists have been involved in campaigning against Walmart's business model and labour practices for many years in various iterations, such as Wake Up Walmart and Walmart Watch, often critiquing from the outside. However, in 2011 a new campaign was initiated with a very different strategy that sought to make worker organising the foundation of the campaign, establishing a minority unionism model under the banner of OURWalmart. What is interesting about this campaign within this context is the way in which social media were incorporated into actual organising strategies. Due to the sheer size and number of workers that Walmart employs, the issue of reaching and penetrating a critical mass of the workforce has been a long-standing hurdle to organising such massive corporations. However, social media proved itself to be useful as an additional tool in reaching and organising workers, particularly because such a large number of people would identify themselves on social media platforms as Walmart employees. This data allowed for the possibilities to engage with Walmart workers directly without having to enter the workplace. As a key organiser for the campaign explained in an interview,

> when we were gearing up and we were working on reaching out and doing real traditional worker organizing in the United States which is really about cold calling, inviting people at home, sitting down, talking to them about organisations, bringing people to meetings, we launched in parallel a process where we were using Facebook to reach and survey and get into dialogue with workers as well. (Andrea Dehlendorf, Assistant Director, *Making Change at Walmart*)

A key aspect was to conduct simple surveys via social media about working conditions at Walmart to initially engage workers and build a list of people who might want to get more involved in the campaign. As a tool for reaching people, this proved very effective and allowed for the collection of a great deal of data about Walmart employees and their experiences working at Walmart. However, the real organising strategy of this social media engagement came through the creation of online groups of Walmart workers to share experiences and create dialogue. These have proliferated around particular issues, such as the discrimination of pregnant women, LGBT rights, or the Walmart Latino group. In some ways, these online spaces came to be additional 'field' operations to offline and workplace organising that equally needed to be engaged with and managed as platforms for organising. Indeed, the ability for Walmart workers to share experiences and stories with each other away from the workplace and in spaces they, at least, regarded as private (the challenges of this perception are further discussed in chapter seven) has been a central aspect of how the OURWalmart campaign has been shaped. It has so because the *sharing of stories* became the starting point for further actions outside of the social media realm. Importantly, an organiser was hired in a role that ended up being called 'online-to-field' in order to ensure that activities did not simply remain within the online spaces, but that people who were active online were organised into on-the-ground action:

> We…started doing these leadership summits, where we would actually bring people together. So we'd call hand-raisers, so people who indicated through a conversation online, taken some action, that they really wanted to do more. We'd bring them together, we'd do a leadership retreat and then give people the skills to then go back and start to organize in their home areas. (Andrea Dehlendorf, Assistant Director, *Making Change at Walmart*).

An interesting use of social media for the labour movement, therefore, is to use the 'sharing' ideology that underpins much of digital media developments (also problematized in Chapter seven) for the purposes of organising, rather than simply as an extension of communication strategies. This notion is also what underpins recent initiatives such as the project *Stories of Solidarity*, a social media platform that is designed for precarious workers to share experiences and stories about their working conditions, to establish relationships with each other and with labour activists. As one of the founders of the project explained in an interview, the nature of employment today, particularly in low-wage work where work is often precarious, is such that people do not have normal hours and frequently work in isolation, and there are few opportunities available for workers to get to know one another, create social contacts and share information. Creating spaces where it is possible for workers to communicate and create relationships have therefore become increasingly pivotal in any form of worker organisation:

> We called organisers and said what is it you need? Is there anything that you need that would be useful in your work? (…) the common denominator amongst many of these on the ground organisers is it would be great to have a place where workers could share stories, because stories is one of the ways that people communicate in a way that is accessible and in a way that people can connect to. (Jesse Drew, academic and co-founder of *Stories of Solidarity*)

Of course, creating spaces for the sharing of stories goes beyond worker organising and also incorporates some outward media-targeted communication in that these stories may also form part of the communication of campaigns to media sources and the public to enhance understanding and present particular narratives of workers' experiences. However, engaging with social media practices with organisation at the centre does shift our understanding of media activism as it is frequently discussed. It does so by using media technologies not necessarily for increasing visibility or garnering media attention, but rather for the purposes of building relationships and solidarity that can be mobilised into on-the-ground activity, not so dissimilarly from how we might understand 'traditional' organising.

Although incorporating social media practices for worker organising rather than digital campaigning and extending communication strategies might become increasingly prevalent within the labour movement, it remains a relatively limited form of activity for a number of reasons. Partly it links back to a historical tradition within organised labour of quite passively engaging with new technologies. However, a broader point may also be made regarding a prevalent reluctance amongst unions to overhaul hierarchical and bureaucratic structures that would allow for a certain lack of control over communication and activities organised by workers themselves. As Drew (2013, p. 126) has argued, there is a widespread perception amongst labour activists that effective use of new communication technology is dependent on the will and ability of organised labour to transform its organisation into a democratic, grassroots social movement of workers built from the ground up, rather than the top down. Although rank and file reforms may be seeing a resurgence and conditions are in place for extensive social experimentation of worker organisation, such radical transformations within the labour movement as a whole may still be quite a way off, as we have outlined in previous chapters. Such a transformation does not come about from technological developments per se, but requires much broader changes in institutional culture that is able to look backwards in order to move forward.

Conclusion: Digital Media and Defining the Future of Unionism

The use of new media technologies for campaigning and political protests in recent years has illustrated some important aspects about the possibilities as well as the challenges of digital activism in the modern world-system. Although little attention has been paid to the role of unions and workers' organisations in recent social revolts, there are certainly lessons to take from this for the labour movement more broadly. The manner in which institutions of power such as large corporations and state governments have jointly advanced the use of digital technologies in ways that undermine and threaten workers' rights and conditions advancing GFA has been met by significant efforts of using some of these technologies for resistance and advancing GFB. They have become an increasingly important part of union strategy and vision. However, as digital media technologies come to shape and permeate contemporary protest environments, labour activists need to engage with and understand the context and uses of digital activism.

The spread of social media does provide workers' organisations with certain transformative potentials. In particular, we can see how these technologies have a part to play in trends towards global unionism, community unionism, social justice/social movement unionism, and even libertarian unionism. This has meant that unions have had to become more flexible with types of membership and act in coalition with different types of groups and associations alongside innovative uses of social media in order to reach an increasingly precarious and individualized workforce. They have also had to incorporate activities of contention that challenge global corporate power outside corporatist or business union models by engaging with a relatively social media saturated 'new' protest culture that favours immediate direct action and highly visible symbols of solidarity amongst workers on a global scale.

However, debates on social media and 'new' protest movements have also highlighted some concerns with unproblematic readings of digital activism. It is important not to turn to these technologies as an automatic 'fix' for the current challenges that are facing unions and labour organisations. In interviews with labour activists, the concerns that have been expressed about the current emphasis on social media in contemporary protests are not unwarranted. This is not just about questions of control or keeping hierarchical structures in place as is often, rightly, the accusation towards unions and their hesitance towards the adoption of new technologies. Certainly, some of these issues run through the history of unions and prevail still today. However, some concerns about the use of social media also speak to some of the limitations we have seen with recent protest movements. Labour organisations need to be careful about not assuming that technologies necessarily empower and that power necessarily resides in communication. The 'ephemeral' nature of social media might also be seen to undermine or distract from more grounded and sustained practices of organising and building relationships and trust. Social media platforms particularly lend themselves to quick and relatively low-cost actions that place primary emphasis on visibility and immediacy. Many commentators have talked about social media activism as 'clicktivism' or 'hash-tagism' in which action remains limited to the fast sharing or clicking 'like' on a post but does not go beyond that. Dean (2009) has taken this argument further and argued that not only is this often a pretty limited political act that is likely to get drowned out in the sheer volume of online noise that digital communications have produced, but it may in fact stunt or directly disempower political mobilisation. What we have developed, she argues, is a 'technological fetish' in which we allow for technology to act in our stead and thereby enable us to remain politically passive: 'We don't have to assume political responsibility because…the technology is doing it for us.'

Using social media to spread the word about a campaign or to try and increase online presence around a particular issue can certainly be very useful for unions, but if it becomes the main emphasis there is a risk that labour organisations find themselves primarily in the role of pressure groups, shouting alongside many others, at the expense of organising workplaces and genuinely empowering workers to advance their own interests. Of course advocacy has its place in labour activism, and social media has an important part to play here, but there needs to be a broader overhaul of union structures for these potentials to be as effective as they could be. For example, as we outline in our case studies, it is often a few individual experienced social media coordinators and communication experts who become the main actors and disseminators of information for any one social media campaign. Even as these campaigns expand and start having rank and file workers involved, digital activism remains in the hands of a selected few who have enormous power over the nature and development of the movement—and often it is done under the guise of horizontalism that we associate with these platforms in which there is a sense that it is the voices of workers being heard.

Although social media lends itself to advocacy, amplified visibility and fast and short-term (media) events, the use of social media for actually organising workers still remains marginal in how the labour movement thinks about digital technologies. For this to develop, it requires a shift away from looking at social media as an extension of communication and public relations strategies and think about it as part of organising efforts—although by no means at the expense of other forms of organising.

The point is that the way that social media gets used will also tell us something about what kind of unionism we think is the future of the labour movement. If unions make social media their main focus and make that focus about visibility and advocacy primarily, they risk neglecting the solid relationships that are necessary to sustain any campaign or organising drive over time. And they risk limiting unions to an advocacy group that relies on media spectacles to put pressure on political and corporate elites. This is certainly a useful dimension to advancing workers' interests but it tends to be short-term and ephemeral in nature and can sometimes back-fire and alienate workers who have not been sufficiently consulted about campaigns, or put workers at risk by leaving them vulnerable to retaliation by employers without the necessary support in place to protect them. Direct action may be an increasingly key component of unionism as unions are faced with decreasing membership and broken political partnerships as most political parties, certainly in core states but also in the periphery and semi-periphery, have embraced neoliberalism as status quo. However, what debates have highlighted is that such direct action needs to emerge out of an organised workforce and cannot be coordinated solely as a social media stunt. Communication power is an important dimension of contemporary understandings of power and no one has exercised this form of power more forcefully than the transnational capitalist class in order to advance their interests. But it is not the only form of power that shapes the world-system of today. The labour movement at large needs to remember and reinvigorate confidence in what makes their power unique in the modern world-system, and, as we will now turn to in our case studies, the answer to that is not going to be found solely in developments in media technologies.

· 4 ·

THE GLOBALISING OF THE JUSTICE FOR JANITORS MOVEMENT

The impact of the Service Employees International Union's (SEIU) *Justice for Janitors* (JFJ) campaign has been perhaps the most powerful symbol of union resistance to GFA over the past 30 years. Pioneering what its proponents regard as a more sophisticated and powerful model of union organising, JFJ has morphed into a global organising format that has led the SEIU to build global partnerships with unions in 25 nation-states as well as with the Global Union Federation (GUF) ITU (Forman, 2013a). The reasoning behind this is simple and was expressed by former SEIU president Andy Stern who argued that to fight globalised capital, unions had to go global and build alliances with each other around the world (Aguiar & Ryan, 2009). And this, in essence, is what the SEIU have tried to do.

The success of the SEIU model of organising has been built around a multi-layered strategy that places the struggle for workers on different planes: media, workplace and civil society. Andy Banks goes so far as to argue that the SEIU broke all the rules of organising and became a hybrid organisation, part union and part community group (Banks, 1991, p. 17). As we noted in chapter two, the public realm that most workers inhabit, particularly in urban areas, has become a site of continual corporate propaganda whether in everyday forms such as advertising, newspapers and television or as manifested in the spread of corporate funding of cultural and social activities from sport and the arts to education and health care. It is in this environment, one that presents the corporation as a largely benevolent and democratic institution, which unions have to compete for public support. The SEIU JFJ campaign learnt this lesson well and used a variety of tactics to mobilise sympathetic media coverage for their campaigns (what McCallum calls 'symbolic power'), and this strategy and these tactics have spread to similar campaigns around the world, such as the Justice for Cleaners Campaign (J4C) that has emerged in Europe, South Korea and Australia. Indeed, so successful has the SEIU strategy become that there is now an International Justice Day for Cleaners and Security Guards (15th June), supported by UNI Global Union (GUF) (Chin, 2005; Erickson, Fisk, Milkman, Mitchell & Wong, 2002, p. 548; McCallum, 2013, p. 53; Tattersall, 2007, p. 162; Albright, 2008, p. 68).

This chapter will set out the rise of JFJ and the SEIU's global reach before analysing the impact of these strategies and tactics on the related Justice for Cleaners campaign that emerged in London in the noughties. The ongoing J4C campaign is important because it illustrates many of the issues facing trade unions and the labour movement in the twenty-first century: dealing with transformed working conditions in which much labour is temporary, sub-contracted, vulnerable and non-unionised; addressing the impact of new waves of migrant workers into the local community and labour market; trying to find ways to get around state imposed anti-union legislation that has been a part of GFA and the neoliberal political agenda, as set out in chapter two, and the extent to which mainstream unions that have historically embraced forms of corporatist, business or nationalist trade unionism can now reinvent themselves to deal with the realities of the state and capital in the twenty-first century (Waterman, 2005). The J4C campaign in London gives us provisional answers to all of these questions. In particular the J4C campaign encapsulates the four main possibilities for union renewal in the twenty-first century that we addressed in chapter two: global unions, community unionism, social movement unionism and the revival of syndicalist-style independent unionism.

Going Global? The SEIU Organising Model

The JFJ movement organised by the SEIU emerged in the USA in the mid-1980s against the backdrop of rapid union decline under the first Reagan presidency. The attack on striking air traffic controllers (11,000 sacked) in 1981 leading to imprisonment and the televised display of chained air-traffic controllers on their way to court sent out a stark message that the neoliberal counter-revolution was well underway. Behind the soft rhetoric of consumer choice and free markets was the coercive state acting to intimidate those unions that sought to resist the attack on the workplace and society (Lehman, 2012). As the hegemonic state what happens to industrial relations in the USA has important implications for the rest of the world, both in terms of the attempt to impose a neoliberal agenda on society and the ways in which it has also been resisted.

By the mid-1980s many of the traditional patterns of post–World War II US union recruitment and servicing of members had been dramatically transformed. In the building and maintenance sector that incorporated janitors and cleaners the industry underwent a rapid wave of mergers leading to the establishment of major multinational corporations that have dominated the market. Small and medium-sized, often family-based firms remain significant in the market for cleaning services but in relative terms their political and economic power is far less than that of the major corporations (Aguiar & Ryan, 2009). As part of this reconstruction of the industry cleaning corporations and the businesses hiring their services undertook a series of changes that reconfigured the organisation of the workforce, intensifying the competitive nature of an industry with tight profit margins (Waldinger et al., 1996, p. 3).

First, services that had been traditionally kept in-house were contracted out to the lowest bidder. This presented unions with an immediate organising problem. Who was to be the target of any potential industrial action? The cleaning corporation's HQ (which might not even be in the USA), or the building where the cleaners worked? The law made it clear; unions were not to target the owners of the building as they were not the employer of the cleaners. The question then became, how to organise protests and industrial actions that were still effective and legal (Ness, 2011). Second, the cleaning corporations took advantage of a new wave of mainly Latino migrants into the US, a characteristic of the second wave of globalisation, to undercut the pay and conditions of existing workers in the industry who were largely Afro-American. This was a classic employer's tactic of dividing and controlling the workforce, drawing upon Marx's 'reserve army of labour' and playing up and building racist fears in the existing community about jobs being lost to immigrants. Third, many of the immigrant workers were not unionised, afraid to join a union, unaware of their rights, spoke little or poor English and were classified by the state as being 'illegal'. This last point is a good illustration of the power of the state to control populations not just by material force but ideationally too. The categorisation of people into migrant/citizen, legal/illegal, is a construction of modern nation-states that serves to divide populations and control the flow of people (Waldinger et al., 1996; Moore & Watson, 2009; Erickson et al., 2002, pp. 546–547; Robinson, 2006). It serves, in practice, to reinforce hostility between communities, as was seen amongst the US janitors in the 1970s and 1980s, in a race-to-the-bottom in terms of pay and conditions (Waldinger et al., 1996, p. 7). Historically many unions have had major problems dealing with waves of immigration as they have been caught between commitments to solidarity and brotherhood and in practice adopting a hostile response to migrants in an apparent defence of the immediate interests of existing members (Ness, 2011). The IWW in the USA was the first union to espouse a clear commitment and practice of accepting all workers but this remained a relatively unique position for many years. The IWW aimed to organise the entirety of the working class including those employed in precarious or casualised jobs and the communities in which they lived. Its influence though has far outstripped its membership and achievements (Simms, Holgate, & Heery, 2013, p. 40).

At this time the SEIU building and maintenance division was in serious decline and under the leadership of President John Sweeney moves were made to find a new strategy that could enable the union to deal with the transformed nature of capital, the state and work (Waldinger et al., 1996). The case of JFJ illustrates clearly the relationship between GFA and GFB, both of which are essential to an understanding of the transformed nature of work and industrial relations in the twenty-first century. The circumstances facing janitors encapsulated a central characteristics of the transformation of labour-state-capital relations in the second wave of globalisation: temporary, vulnerable and flexible patterns of work; short-term, part-time or casual contracts; the use of migrants to undercut unions and established communities; the replacement of unions with new forms of soft and hard management in the form of Human Resources (HR) and Total Quality Management (TQM); a revised industrial relations framework that takes away workers' rights and sees the state act vigorously to protect corporate interests. Despite the appearance of being independent the reality is that HR departments have very little autonomy of senior management in public and private sector organisations and as such they are an extension of management (van Wanrooy et al., 2011, p. 12).

However, the story of JFJ and related campaigns is the story of workers and their unions trying to find ways to fight back against GFA, drawing on diverse and often contradictory tactics including those associated with the traditions of bureaucratic unionism, community unionism, social movement unionism, global unionism and on the margins, syndicalism, to raise the profile and defend the interests of workers in a way that sought to build a wide and lasting coalition of support from civil society, communities and other unions (Ness, 2014a; Erickson et al., 2002). On the ideational level the period of the second wave of globalisation also saw an increased concentration of corporate media ownership that has created hierarchical and structured patterns of media (broadcast, print and radio) ownership that have shown themselves to be largely hostile and unsympathetic to unions and workers' rights (Waterman, 2001b); Herman & McChesney, 1998). In addition to this the specialised sections of the consciousness industries also became more important to corporate strategies in this period, including the use of PR firms to promote corporate image in the media and public realm, the rise of corporate social responsibility as a concept and practice to illustrate corporate largesse (as opposed to a more traditional type of ruling class paternalism), the spread of anti-union busting firms who are able to advise firms on strategies for destroying unions and in practice blacklisting workers, all of which have been a part of the JFJ and JFC story. In the UK corporations have worked with the police and UK border authorities to target groups of militant cleaners and organisers in the hope that they will be deported back (O'Reilly, Hearn & Bergos, 2011; Simms et al., 2013, p. 142).

Unions were originally born in specific communities, and were an integral part of them. That aspect of being a part of and accountable to a wider community has been lost for many unions as they have become professional organisations aiming to recruit and maintain their status in relationship with the state and capital. So on a broader level union decline is also a reflection of the ways in which unions have tended to evolve over the twentieth century, into organisations that have less meaning to their members than, for example, their membership of the local church or the community in which they live. Class identity is not always sufficient to mobilise workers to act and nor is it synonymous with a desire to join a union; motivations for trade union activity are more complex. Rather class identity is never just a product of the workplace but is also embedded in patterns of cultural life found in communities (Moore, 2011). Rebuilding this relationship with the community is partly what the idea of community unionism is about, building a new meaning to the idea of being a member of a union. This is not a far-fetched or impossible goal as it is precisely the strategy that London Citizens and similar groups, influenced by the Industrial Area Foundation (IAF) type strategies started in Chicago in the 1960s by Saul Allinsky, have followed (Johnson, 2000; Fitzgerald & Hardy, 2010; Holgate, 2009). Indeed it is what the SEIU have aimed to do with the JFJ campaigns: face to face meetings, home visits, member intensive organising and the revival of inactive locals (Rudy, 2004). Some UK unions (Unite, Unison, GMB) have also sought to build a community strategy but thus far with limited success or lasting commitment. Unite, for example have a Community Membership Department and 9 community branches in the UK. Despite this critics go so far as to argue that there is no real interest in community unionism or social movement unionism in the mainstream TUC unions in the UK (Holgate, 2013a; Simms et al., 2013, p. 170; Wills, 2001, p. 465).

The Evolution of JFJ Strategies and Tactics: The SEIU Organising Model

The roots of the JFJ campaign are in a conscious decision by SEIU leadership, under the guidance of John Sweeney and then, after 1996, Andy Stern, to build the union up through new strategies and tactics. The bigger strategic aim, certainly under Stern, was for the SEIU to become the national union for janitors whereby all contracts for janitors nationwide would be negotiated at the same time when due for renewal. This would transform the capacity of the union to bargain and negotiate with employers from a situation whereby contracts have been traditionally renewed at irregular intervals and locally, much to the disadvantage of workers (Erickson et al., 2002). In addition this also meant the SEIU attempting to change the nature of the AFL-CIO, the main US union federation, so that it, too, became committed to organising, and in particular organising workers in previously unorganised industries. The SEIU JFJ victory in Century City, Los Angeles, in 1990 became the union flagship. The workers' action led to cleaners suffering brutal assault by the police (leading to the popular slogan 'yes we can' with its echoes of the future Obama presidential campaign adverts) (Waldinger et al., 1996; Erickson et al., 2002). The JFJ campaign became the torch bearer for a revived US trade unionism, attracting the attention of UK film director Ken Loach in his movie *Bread and Roses*, and influencing unions around the world. One outcome of the SEIU campaigning has been the emergence of what has become known as 'the organising model', which embraces a number of themes: organising workers by industries and not crafts, getting workers to participate meaningfully in campaigns, spending more money on organising workers and less money on electoral politics, with the idea that it will enhance the power of the union movement to influence politics through its collective strength (Forman, 2013a). But how have the successes been achieved?

The first development in SEIU strategy was to devote time to research and planning. This was driven in part by the recruitment of university graduates into the union to serve as researchers who would study patterns of ownership and control of corporations with a view to establishing a plan that would clarify where corporations were vulnerable and to what kind of union tactics. So attempting to understand the nature of the modern corporation and the political, economic environment in which it was evolving was critical for the SEIU. Specifically the SEIU mapped the patterns of growth and development in its target industries and their relationships to other industries along the supply chain, targeting industries that were tied to specific places. It also planned well in advance for strike action, recognising that this would often be a long-term struggle over many years (Rudy, 2004; Erickson et al., 2002; Tattersall, 2007).

But so, too, was an understanding of and sensitivity to the media and the need to secure public support for campaigns. As Rudy comments this led the SEIU's JFJ campaigns to orchestrate crises in the local community in order to draw political actors into the dispute; at the same time this enabled the campaign to create an audience amongst the local community (Rudy, 2004, p. 135). Using focus groups, interviews and questionnaires to gauge public opinion, aping in practice the marketing strategies of corporations themselves, were key tools for the SEIU (Erickson et al., 2002). By this time these marketing strategies had become commonplace in political culture, illustrating the increasingly complex and co-determining relationship between political and media culture in the late twentieth century (Moloney, 2000). Within the SEIU these trends were accelerated under the leadership of Andy Stern after 1995, who was himself a university graduate of a solid middle class upbringing.

One major factor identified early on by SEIU researchers was to focus on industries that could not be easily off-shored, such as cleaning, janitors, maintenance workers, security staff and long-term care (Tattersall, 2007, p. 161). The reasoning here was that one of the strategic advantages enjoyed by capital in the second wave of globalisation was that it could easily move capital and certain forms of production around the increasingly inter-linked global economy.

However, not all jobs could be moved in this way, and those that were local, national or regional could more easily be defended by unions.

Nonetheless the union's strength was ultimately dependent upon recruiting and organising workers in the workplace and so the second strategic change under the SEIU was to devote as much as one third of their resources to organising (Stern, 2006, p. 63). The key tactic was the use of militant action to force employers to agree to their demands rather than following the established legal process set out in the National Labour Review Board regulations. These campaigns often culminated in mass acts of civil disobedience and subsequent arrests to further publicise the campaign and to place the authorities in the morally dubious position of imprisoning low-paid workers (often migrant and female) and defending rich corporations (Rudy, 2004). In specific cases the tactic of spreading protests around the USA and beyond in support of striking workers often proved to be very effective, and a way of avoiding state regulations prohibiting secondary action (Erickson et al., 2002; Clawson, 2003, pp. 99–100). This was a huge shift in the way that the union sought to act. Organising was often something that officers did apart from their real work, which was recruiting, casework and representing workers in collective bargaining. To prioritise organising was a radical move and even now much research in other unions shows how marginal and little valued organising and organisers are. Indeed organisers in general (and for the SEIU) are often themselves symptomatic of modern working culture: overworked, under-paid, on short-term contracts and paid by results as though on a piece-rate (Forman, 2013b; Simms et al., 2013; Simms & Holgate, 2010).

In terms of its impact there is no doubt that the SEIU has grown significantly since the mid-1980s and this was a primary strategic goal under John Sweeney's presidency. Much of its growth has also come about through a related strategic initiative: mergers with other unions. Many mainstream unions in the USA are highly decentralised in ways that often work against their member's interests as they become local fiefdoms that are dominated by cliques who become an oligarchy in the local union's structures (Fitch, 2006). The SEIU have aimed to overcome this as part of their goal of becoming one big union under central leadership and mergers are part of this strategic direction, eliminating what they regard as small and weak unions that undermine the possibility of national bargaining (Moody, 2007, p. 185; Savage, 2006).

As SEIU organisers have emphasised, success has been determined by the involvement of workers in the campaigns. The janitors themselves had to be central to the campaigns and this has brought about some positive developments for the SEIU and unions in general with women eventually coming to take important roles in the movement including leadership, overcoming familiar patriarchal obstacles in the process. Thus local 399 was set up with a team consisting of 2 organisers, 1 researcher and 1 services sector representative. This team and the local developed a model for organising that included building relationships with the local community and a media-friendly strategy that would maximise positive exposure for the JFJ campaign. In the local itself it led to the creation of a steward's council, regular meetings for JFJ members and supporters, an educational program aimed at non-union competition in order to help unionise the entire janitor workforce in an area. That said, as Cranford reports, it is also the case that women in the JFJ campaigns have also had to contend with familiar patriarchal obstacles to their union involvement (Banks, 1991; Cranford, 2007; Aguiar, 2004).

An active membership has been vital to the JFJ movement as the campaigns themselves have often been long-term, lasting several years before victory could be achieved. To sustain such a long-term commitment can only happen when the workers directly involved believe in the project and union itself, they come to feel that the union is theirs. One of the major points of contention within the JFJ campaigns is, in fact, the extent to which the campaigns are controlled by the union hierarchy or the workers on the ground, as we will see later. To this end the JFJ campaigns have rested upon not just the workers but their families, too, as the campaigns have reached out into the wider community. This has been a very important development as it is frequently family commitments and child-minding that fall onto the shoulders of women unionists who have to curtail their union commitments to take on these tasks (Cranford, 2007).

A third strategic shift for the SEIU was to focus on a geographical space rather than particular workplaces (Tattersall, 2007, p. 161; Clawson, 2003; Moody, 2007, p. 187). The point of this was to help overcome the problems caused for union activity by the fragmentation of the workforce and the transformation of terms and conditions under corporate restructuring in the 1980s. To focus on one employer or building was a problem for unions as the employer could simply switch contracts when it was time for renewal in the face of persistent union opposition and turn to a non-unionised workforce working through another service agency. This corporate strategy works across many industries and has often encouraged unions to agree to no-strike deals with employers in return for recognition, effectively leading unions to police their own membership on behalf of employers in so-called 'sweetheart deals', which the SEIU have also embraced as a way of dealing with internal dissent and competitor unions (Stern, 2006; Erickson, 2010).

The way around this problem of fragmented patterns of ownership and employment for the SEIU was to focus on a geographical space and to target all employers at the same time. Thus the Century City campaign in LA focused on the area and all janitors working there. The idea here, as Stern has explained, was that you could pressurise all employers to agree to pay the living wage for their staff at the same time so that any loss of earnings was shared amongst them rather than penalising just one employer. This tactic has proven to be effective in many instances and has been taken on by Unite in the J4C in the UK (Stern, 2006, p. 58; Wills, 2008, p. 313). It also connects to the idea of community unionism that is part of the JFJ organising model that the target for union campaigning and organising is to mobilise entire communities and the spaces within which they live and work, rather than persist with the traditional model of focusing upon a static and fixed workplace. Thus the success or failure of a campaign will often depend upon the extent to which the workers involved can build alliances with wider community and political actors including churches, students and other trade unions. The campaign in Houston in 2006 is a good example of this as it was waged in a Democratic Party dominated town and in the face of hostility from the local Democratic Party who disparaged the JFJ campaign (Lerner, 2007). Thus as Stern has said the SEIU will work with politicians of *all* parties if they are prepared to work with the SEIU (Stern, 2006, pp. 93–94).

Tactically JFJ has had to find a way to work around stringent legal constraints that severely restrict the kind of industrial action that a union can undertake, taking what Cranford calls 'creative legal action' (Cranford, 2007). A popular approach within JFJ has been to mobilise public support through protests that embrace music, guerrilla theatre, petitions, leafleting and through Unison the use of colour (purple) to maximise the visibility of the often described 'invisible workers'. This tactic has become very effective and taken on by many unions in other countries as a way of trying to name and shame employers who pay their staff poverty wages. It also helps to galvanise workers and create solidarity among them as they fight their battles.

Coupled with this has been the practice of taking control of and reorganising locals to direct them in a way that conforms to nationally determined goals and practice. Some locals have now become huge within the SEIU, a source of friction for critics, and when there are significant problems locals have been taken into trusteeship with local officials suspended and external officials from the union's Washington, DC headquarters sent into reorganise the local. This connects with the aim of the SEIU to professionalise organising and make it a distinctive role in the union. Organisers can be and are sent into locals to help organise and run campaigns, or more controversially where the leadership views it as necessary, to place a local under trusteeship while it is rebuilt (Savage, 2006: Moody, 2007, p. 188).

An innovative media strategy has been important to the JFJ campaigns and finding ways to gain sympathetic coverage has been important. In part this has meant trying to shift the debate around low-paid work, something that has become easier over the years as the dramatic rise in inequality and poverty in the USA has become apparent and a major political issue. To attract the media requires organising public events that will interest them and here the SEIU have been innovators including organising protests at the country club of an employer, encouraging cleaners to give evidence at shareholders' AGMs and launching campaigns to decriminalise illegal immigrants working in the sector (Clawson, 2003, pp. 100–103). To win the battle with the employer the SEIU had to understand the nature of the modern corporation and the media. In the JFJ campaign it meant understanding the nature of the building services industry. As Steven Lerner, then organising director of the SEIU building services division, said, 'the most important thing to understand about the industry is that in most cases janitors do not technically work for the owners or managers of the buildings they clean' (Banks, 1991, p. 21). Thus organising a building will not work as the building manager will put the contract out to tender and take non-union labour—hence the need to organise the whole community and not just the workplace.

For Stern the goal was to create a win-win environment in which the union and the corporation would build a new partnership for the twenty-first century to promote America as a nation over their own sectional (business/labour) interests. In order to achieve a position where such a negotiation was possible it was crucial that the union could build up its power. Thus for the SEIU it is quite clear that seizing power is the rationale for their activities as without power you cannot achieve your goals and you cannot force the employer and the state to consider a new kind of partnership with the union and the wider labour movement (Stern, 2006, pp. 20–21). Everything that adds to the power of the union, that enables it to move towards becoming One Big Union, is to the advantage of the membership. Such has been the momentum generated by the SEIU that it has led to the emergence of the Change-To-Win federation with the International Brotherhood of Teamsters and the United Farm Workers who have broken away from the AFL-CIO who, they argued, were too slow in executing much needed reforms, especially a commitment to organising. The aim for the new federation was to increase union membership and reduce the number of unions through mergers as well as prioritizing industry-wide organising. The assumption here is that the fragmented nature of US union history has seriously weakened unions. Thus as the SEIU achievements have taken on the form of a modern union mythology so the union has sought to extend its reach beyond community and social movement style unionism to global union organisation (McCallum, 2013, p. 48).

The appeal to mainstream unions of the SEIU and its organising model was reflected in its ambitions to build global alliances. To this end the SEIU set up a Global Partnership Unit in 2004 to establish contacts and coordinate activities with unions in a number of other countries, sending its own organisers from its headquarters in Washington to the UK, Canada, Netherlands, Germany, Australia and elsewhere to advise unions on how to revitalise their activities (Connolly, Marino & Lucio, 2012; Aguiar & Ryan, 2009; Tattersall, 2007, p. 155). The strategic aim was also to try to change the way in which European unions, in particular, were evolving with a view to transforming their outlooks into one that was more congruent with the SEIU and the realities of twenty-first century capitalism. This did not mean that the SEIU organising model was a simple universal template that could be applied anywhere and indeed it generated resistance from within the SEIU Canadian health care workers section who felt that the aggressive tactics adopted by the model might undermine their relatively good relations with the main employers in Canada (Aguiar, 2004). Whilst many unions and confederations have talked about the need for global unions in the twenty-first the SEIU have sought to make this a part of their development, alongside the increasingly prominent activities of the GUFs. The JFJ campaign run largely by migrant Latino workers in Houston, Texas in 2006 is a good example of this. It brought fierce and violent attacks from the state and business and was ultimately faced down by the striking and imprisoned workers who were able to draw upon a network of global support that led to demonstrations in support of their actions world-wide. As Warnecke argues, transnational collective action is already a reality and reflected in, amongst other things, global campaigns such as that organised through the GUF, the IUF, against Coca-Cola and Nestlé (Garvey, Buketov, Chong & Martinez, 2007; Bronfenbrenner, 2007, p. 58; Lerner, 2007; Warnecke, 2007).

London Calling: The Rise of the Justice for Cleaners Campaign

'We just want to be treated with respect and dignity, to be treated like human beings'
('Maria', London cleaner, 2014)

The transformation of the City of London in the 1980s was driven by the policies of the neoliberal Thatcher governments as well as the emergence of an increasingly dominant financial capitalism (see chapter 2). London's transformation in the 1980s was dramatic as old industries, factories and warehouses were closed and either gentrified or turned into flats or cultural outlets aimed at middle class professionals (May et al., 2007). The rise of the power of the City of London in this decade was promoted by government policies and state support that liberalised and deregulated the financial services industry in the UK as the first act of the first Thatcher administration in 1979 (May et al., 2007, p. 153). This shift in regulation and competition has, of course, been a crucial turning point in global capitalism, repeated in the USA and then across the major national economies, fuelling the boom and bust cycles that have hit different national economies and regions over the past 35 years. In London itself there was a significant movement of working class communities who had traditionally been rooted in the inner city who were able to sell their homes to a new rentier class of landlord. These landlords were either wealthy professionals from the City itself or drawn from the ranks of middle class and working classes who were able to take advantage in the 1990s of new forms of buy-to-rent mortgage coupled with the general deregulation of the rented sector. These trends helped to reorganise housing across the city and much of the Home Counties around London (Mullins & Pawson, 2011; Hamnett, 2003; Butler & Robson, 2003). The movement of these working class communities away from central London into neighbouring counties such as Essex, Kent and Hertfordshire saw them, in turn replaced by new waves of migrant workers in the 1990s from South America and Africa and in the noughties from Central and Eastern Europe. Migrant workers now make up over 35% of London's working population (May et al., 2007, p. 158). This enabled landlords to recreate the slum dwellings of the nineteenth and early twentieth century, ably described by Jack London in his classic, *The People of the Abyss*, cramming multiple impoverished families into what were built as single-family dwellings and thereby helping to inflate the housing market across London and the southeast of England (Heyes, 2009; London's Poverty Profile, 2007; House of Commons, 2011).

Thus the reorganisation of London and the construction of a new division of labour in which migrants provided many of the essential services, doing the dirty and difficult jobs for poverty wages, was in part a way to undermine unions and increase profits in an industry where margins were very tight, just as had occurred in the USA. At the same time it saw the destruction of manufacturing industries to be replaced by service industry jobs, which are much harder to organise and easier to casualise. For many of the migrants their poverty pay was still enough for them to send money home to families and dependents in the periphery and semi-periphery, where conditions were even worse (May et al., 2007; Datta et al., 2007; Moore, 2011, p. 140).

But what were the dominant experiences of this new wave of cleaners forming London's essential low-paid workforce? First, racism has been one of the defining characteristics of the modern world-system, and its complexity is illustrated in the case of migrant workers moving into London throughout the past 35 years. Racism is embedded in political and popular cultures and manifests itself in the rhetoric and policies of all major political parties, even when they are nominally committed to anti-racist policies. In the case of cleaners in London, racism manifests itself in the experiences of working and everyday life. It is the primary experience of many cleaners, transcending class (Hearn & Bergos, 2011; Wills, 2008). At work they are subjected to degrading and humiliating treatment by managers and in many instances supervisors too. 'They talk to you like you are stupid, as though you cannot understand anything, said Maria, a Polish cleaner we interviewed who works at a London university (Maria, London cleaner). As one union representative pointed out,

> These cleaning companies want to employ migrant cleaners as they can drive down wages, deny them sick pay, holiday pay, and generally treat them like shit. But on top of that they make no effort to even try to understand migrant workers, they don't speak their language and use their lack of English against them, claiming "we told them clearly what the position was", knowing full well that the cleaners don't necessarily understand the realities of their rights at work. This is a racist tactic used by cleaning companies to cut back on the already meagre wages and terrible working conditions these cleaners face ('James', Unison trade union representative, London).

This point about managers using tricks to unlawfully deduct wages from staff is a common one in the cleaning industry (Hearn & Bergos, 2011, p. 72).

Racism serves to divide workers and scapegoats migrant communities, often playing on the fears of many older white UK born cleaners who told us that, 'we don't really talk with them' ('Sarah', cleaner in a London university). Until the J4C campaign unions had been ineffective in addressing this divide amongst London's workers. In one example of a protest that occurred at West London University the generalised nature of the issues being confronted by cleaners very quickly brought together cleaners who had previously been largely confined to ethnic groups in order to deal with their common problems. This included Polish, Somali, White UK and Sierra Leonean cleaners. The fears that different ethnic groups amongst the cleaning workforce might have towards each other can be overcome, at least temporarily, in the context of a commonly held grievance and conflict with the employer. Militant action can provide the basis for solidarity that a union is able to build upon.

The migrant cleaning workforce have also been described repeatedly and accurately as an *invisible community* in the midst of London (Cohen, 2014). They are invisible as for many of the cleaners work commences at 5am and finishes at 9am, or they are working on an evening shift after other workers have finished, so they have little opportunity to meet other workers in the city. Some cleaners who have been working at institutions for a long time and have been transferred across to the their new employers (technically this is called being TUPE'd [Transferred of Undertakings (Protection of Employment) Regulations 2006] in UK labour law) have been able to cling onto contracts that enable them to work more sociable hours, such as 3pm to 6pm. But where this does take place these cleaners are under great pressure to change their contracts so that they too can be rendered part of London's invisible economy. Strategically this working pattern makes sense for the employer and the client as it minimises the possibility of the cleaners having time to talk to other workers or even to meet union officials.

The cleaning profession reflects wider trends in the global economy towards the feminisation of the workplace (Caraway, 2007; Mies, 1998; Lutz, 2008). Employers gain from this trend as historically women have been under-represented in the union movement and subject to discrimination not only from their employers but also from their male workmates (Cranford, 2007). The feminisation of work and the wave of migration into London in this period has enabled employers to use a range of familiar sexist and racist arguments to justify low pay for migrants and women in particular including the view that certain ethnic groups are 'only fit for cleaning' and that women are naturally suited to cleaning jobs and therefore it is not a skill that needs to be rewarded by higher pay ('Maria', London cleaner).

The movement of migrants into the London economy, by far the most important part of the UK economy, also coincided with the restructuring of many industries, which led to the casualization of working practices. For cleaners this places immense pressures on them not to join a union lest they be victimised by the employer, a familiar experience for many cleaners who have sought to stand up for themselves and their workmates (Datta et al., 2007). The hire and fire economy of the cleaning sector depends upon a steady stream of migrant workers who are willing to endure hardship and abuse in return for pay that they can send to families and dependents in their country of origin.

Cleaners have been subject to all manner of verbal, physical and sexual abuse from managers including police arrests and detention of cleaners suspected of being illegal immigrants. Such tactics of intimidation are often used to break a group of workers trying to build a union. In addition cleaners have been subject to both physical violence at the hands of managers and security staff, usually for attempting to argue for their rights. In one instance a pregnant cleaner was hospitalised and underwent a miscarriage after abuse from her managers. More normal is the pattern of everyday intimidation by managers, site managers and supervisors, who will use their authority to try to scare cleaners by using tactics from shouting abuse to attempting to mock and humiliate them in front of their peers. As one cleaner told us, 'our manager, she shouts and swears at us, she treats us like criminals. If we say anything back we are the ones who get in trouble' ('Anna', cleaner London University). The aim of these patterns of intimidation is to keep the cleaning workforce subordinate, divided and atomised, a feminised workforce often subject to the patronising dictates of male (and female) managers who dismiss them on all manner of sexist and racist grounds.

The last experience, which is most symptomatic of the reality of everyday life for cleaners, is that of poverty. The London economy is built on a vast pool of low-paid workers of which cleaners are one vital component. Many cleaner, are parents, often single, living lives of great deprivation in the most expensive city to inhabit in Europe (Hearn & Bergos, 2011, p. 66).

So it is against this backdrop, these conditions, a social pattern established over a period of 30 years, which led to the rise of the London Living Wage in 2001 and Unite's Justice for Cleaners campaigns that emerged after 2005. The status of migrant workers has been at best negligible and at worst the lowest part of UK society during the second wave of globalisation. This reflects the way in which status has become ever more important at the expense of class identity, however much the two are interrelated (El-Ojeili, 2012, p. 106). The status of migrant workers and cleaners has been reduced to less than that of an equal citizen and as a scapegoat for general decline in the pay and conditions of workers across London. Finding means to overcome hierarchies of status and to reinstate social solidarity with migrant workers is in part what the J4C campaign has attempted to do.

London Citizens, Unions and the London Living Wage Campaign

The origins of London Citizens can be traced back to the US and its powerful tradition of radical grassroots community organising, associated with Saul Alinsky. The ethos of these groups is one of self-help and direct action and they are part of the strong American libertarian grassroots tradition, reflected in the motto associated with Alinsky's Industrial Area foundations (established in 1940) 'never do for others what they can do for themselves' (Holgate, 2009; Alinsky, 1989; Horwitt, 1989).

Following on from and influenced by these ideas the aim of London Citizens is to strengthen civil society in relation to the market and the state on the belief that a healthy democracy requires the three sectors to be in balance with each other. On the relationship between social justice and the market the West London Citizens organiser told us that:

> We are saying that we have a market economy and where employers are able to pay a living wage to their lowest paid they should do so. There is a moral obligation to do so. It is worth noting that firms who introduce the living wage also benefit from it as it improves staff morale, performance, and so on. So there is a business case argument for firms to introduce the living wage. But we think there is a basic moral imperative to do so. If you are a profit-making firm in this country you also have moral responsibilities. And if you ignore this we will bring the issue to the public and you have to answer for them (Stefan Baskerville, senior organiser West London Citizens).

The first appearance made by what has now become the nation-wide Citizens UK was in 1989, before the setting up of its first formal branch in Bethnal Green in 1996, The East London Community's Organisation (Telco). Its aims are straightforward, espousing a non-ideological outlook and political neutrality: the Citizens movement aims to promote social justice and to mobilise and organise communities as opposed to markets and the state in order to defend the former as an autonomous realm of free citizens. To this end the Citizens movement aims to train community leaders and support the initiatives of its members in promoting social justice and the common good. In this way it has the explicit aim of transforming the UKs political culture by teaching the art of politics to its members so that they can bargain and negotiate more effectively with powerful elites on behalf of their communities. The key to this is to target the reputation of the powerful in order to force them to negotiate. If not community unionism, then, Citizens, see themselves as a civil society community organising group for all citizens (Holgate, 2013a, 2013b; Alberti, Alberti, Holgate, & Tapia, 2013; Baskerville & Stears, 2010; Wills, 2008).

It has now grown into a nation-wide movement (Citizens UK, of which London Citizens is one part) that although still dominated by London has branches in Nottingham, Cardiff, Glasgow and Birmingham. In London alone its reach is impressive with over 230 affiliated organisations with each possessing at least 1000 members. The Citizens movement aims to build a sustainable and permanent foundation. Its impact has grown immensely over time so that before the last UK general election and London mayoral elections all major candidates were invited to speak before the London Citizens Assembly to an audience of 5000 members. No major political figure can turn down such invitations without inviting criticism from the movement whose links to the broader communities in which members are situated are part of a wide and growing network. The movement has member institutions across society but is mainly dominated by churches of different denominations. Alongside this it has also recruited university departments, major corporate institutions, schools, G. P. surgeries, think-tanks and housing associations. Its community organising activities complement the idea of community unionism and the importance of this for the J4C campaign has been apparent with London Citizens working with major UK unions (Unison—public sector—and Unite—private sector) as part of the campaigns in London that extended successfully into London universities (Holgate, 2009, 2013a and b; Wills & Simms, 2004; Wills, J., Datta, K., Evans, Y., Herbert, J., May, J., & McIlwaine, C., 2009; Hearn & Bergos, 2011; Kirkpatrick, 2011).

The main initiative behind the London-based J4C campaign has been the concept of the London Living Wage (LLW), which has shifted the terms of the debate about a living wage amongst the UK's political elites. In 2001, influenced by the SEIU JFJ campaigns in the USA, The East London Citizens Organisation chapter of what is now Citizens UK (Telco) called for the setting up of a *living wage* that would guarantee a minimum quality of life for all citizens. There was also an additional *London living wage* (LLW) that would take account of the cost of living and working in the capital city. The initial protests were focused on the HSBC bank and the Canary Wharf area and a number of East London hospitals in support of low-paid cleaners and security staff and they included a number of direct action tactics that had become powerful tools in the SEIU JFJ campaigns, including occupying a branch of the HSBC on Oxford Street; the public shaming of chairman Sir John Bond at the 2002 AGM when Telco activists who had bought shares in HSBC took the opportunity to demand action on low pay in the meeting; drawing upon the support of the musician Billy Bragg to promote the LLW campaigns as part of his nationwide tour and a number of public rallies and marches to keep the issue in the public mind. Initially trade union involvement in the campaigning was limited but the public sector union Unison commissioned its Family Budget unit to work out what a living wage for London might consist of and made a donation to the Telco campaign (Holgate, 2009, 2013a and b; Hearn & Bergos, 2011; Wills et al., 2009; Holgate, 2009, pp. 52–53). At the same time Professor Jane Wills produced a report for Telco called *Mapping Low Pay in East London*, which was important in laying the framework for the debate about living wages that followed (Wills, 2001b). This led to an alliance of sorts between Telco and Unison around the common issue of poverty pay and its impact on the East London communities (Holgate, 2009). By 2004 London Citizens (including Telco) were working with both the Transport and General Workers Unions (now Unite) in the private sector in Canary Wharf and Unison in the public sector in East London hospitals and had begun to attain victories with Barclays Bank signing up for the LLW for its cleaners in Canary Wharf and cleaning company OCS agreeing to pay its HSBC staff in Canary Wharf too. In addition London Citizens pushed the issue firmly onto the broader political agenda by calling upon the candidates for London mayoral elections that year to endorse the LLW campaign. The successful mayoral candidate Ken Livingstone agreed and the Greater London Authority established a living wage unit in 2005 to set the rate for the LLW annually (Hearn & Bergos, 2011).

This campaign has had great appeal both inside and outside London with other cities in the UK seeking to take on board the idea of a living wage. Many employers have begun to seek accreditation from the Citizens Living Wage Foundation (established in 2011), which would act as a form of brand recognition for the employer and which means a guarantee to all staff working for them that they will earn at least the LLW (Baskerville, 2014). This building of alliances with institutions in order to influence social change is at the heart of Citizens UK strategy, and assumes that a win-win outcome is possible for all parties—workers gain the LLW, employers gain an ethical brand identity. There are now over 1000 LLW accredited employers in London (Baskerville, 2014).

The London Citizens movement has sought to use a variety of methods in order to achieve its goals, which are in a way congruent with the goals of the SEIU. Citizens UK want to increase their power so that they are in a position to negotiate with political and economic decision-makers. To do this they use a variety of mechanisms to put pressure onto these groups of elites and have been prepared to undertake long-term campaigning to do so. Echoing the SEIU position, London Citizens emphasise the need to be in a position to negotiate with economic and political elites in order to establish a balance between the market, the state and civil society—to place communities, solidarity and the idea of the common good back onto the political landscape. Thus their campaigning methods will involve a mixture of such things as mediated and media driven public events to win public support and media attention, such as organising a red tent protest outside city hall in 2007 against then mayor of London Ken Livingstone's failure to live up to promises made to London Citizens in 2004 (Stefan Baskerville, senior organiser West London Citizens). The most important aspect of their work, however, remains face-to-face organising. Many low-paid workers are involved with London Citizens including those in the various strands of the J4Cs movement and they relate to London Citizens in a way that is quite different to how they relate to their unions. As Baskerville of London Citizens and Watson of trade union Unison concur, 'we can't win without the cleaners, that is basic'.

A common criticism of unions raised in interviews with both cleaners and the London Citizens is that the unions have manifestly failed the cleaners, as *Observer* columnist Nick Cohen has argued (Cohen, 2014). So the Citizens movement has succeeded because it reflects the areas of its members' lives that give them meaning and a sense of solidarity: religion and their community (Wills et al., 2009; Holgate, 2013a). It is more than a little ironic that the practices and language of those who devote their energies to the Citizens UK movement, whether paid or as is the case for the majority, voluntary, echoes the language of the union movement at its strongest. However, there is clearly much resistance in sections of the UK union movement towards working with what they see as a faith-based organisation such as London Citizens, despite the strong Christian tradition in the UK union movement (Holgate, 2009, 2013a; Watson, 2014).

In 2005 Unite launched a *Justice for Cleaners* campaign, which was a result of its relationship and work with the SEIU and aimed to unionise cleaners in Canary Wharf, the City of London and the House of Commons. This included Unite seconding assistants from the SEIU JFJ campaigns to assist in its activities. By 2009 the JFC campaigns had secured agreements with major cleaning companies including ISS, OCS and MITIE for the LLW, a sizeable victory for the campaign (Alzaga, 2011; Hearn & Bergos, 2011; Simms et al., 2013, pp. 62–65; Holgate, 2009). Nonetheless the relationship has proven to be a mixed success in London in terms of developing community unionism. As Unison branch secretary at London Metropolitan University Max Watson told us in an interview about his experiences of working with London Citizens,

> We wanted the management to meet a cleaner and a security guard who would tell them what it is like to survive on less than living wage. Part of the strategy was to get outsourced workers to the meeting, not just the usual negotiating team as the managers are fed up of hearing my voice. When London citizens arrived for the meeting they said here is our agenda and here is how we are going to run things. We had to say to them, we do know what we're doing. There wasn't much discussion between us or negotiation on tactics and what goes on the agenda; they came in with a template to show us how to organize. We had to say we've affiliated to you in order to work with you, not for you to tell us how to do things, we have initiated this meeting. You did not come to us asking us to support your campaign. I don't think they got that. (Max Watson, Unison branch secretary, London Metropolitan University).

Watson was not a hostile critic of the Citizens movement but he noted that their methods did not chime with his experiences of the approach of unions. By contrast the view of London Citizens is that the unions are bureaucratic, conservative and slow and that they use the need for democratic decision-making by endless committees as an excuse and justification for not acting (Stefan Baskerville, senior organiser West London Citizens). Indeed, as Holgate argues, the reality is that the mainstream unions have the veneer of being representative democracies but the reality is that in practice members are not active and do not control their unions in any meaningful way (Holgate, 2009). Rather than revealing an alliance of equal partners, as community unionism aspires to do, it seems more accurate to view the relationship between London Citizens and the trade unions in terms of two institutions struggling to assume the position of leadership of a campaign. The major UK TUC unions remain wary and antipathetic towards the Citizens movement, most obviously because they fear it encroaching onto their 'territory' (Wills et al., 2009, p. 447; Holgate, 2009). But what about the cleaners themselves? How has this movement evolved?

Justice for Cleaners—From Community to Social Movement Unionism?

The JFJ and J4C movements illustrate the ways in which an idea transcends its origins and takes on new meaning in the hands of different groups of actors. Inspired by a top-down union organisation (SEIU) and taken up by UK unions with a similar organising structure (UNITE and Unison) the J4C in the UK moved beyond the control of the unions or the London Citizens movement and was taken up by groups of cleaners who sought to organise themselves autonomously through groups such as the Latin American Workers Association (LAWA) and also through small revolutionary industrial unions in London such as the IWW and the IWGB. This splintering of the movement is seen by critics such as Max Watson as undermining working class unity (Watson, 2013, 2014).

The counter view to this is that for those cleaners who wanted to be free to act to promote their interests without being controlled by what they saw as a union bureaucracy and officials this was logical progression towards autonomous, grassroots and worker self-organised unionism that connects with the syndicalist tradition (Broder, 2010; Kirkpatrick, 2011). Both the IWW and the IWGB are small and minor unions in UK industrial relations but they also aspire to be a form of social movement unionism that draws upon links with other groups and organisations and involves people who are not formally members of the union. As Salerno argued, the IWW has always born the hallmarks of a social movement rather than a union in any conventional sense, in part because of its social vision to change the world for the benefit of all working people (Salerno, 1989).

The campaigns illustrate the fact that cleaners are not victims in need of help from external actors but are capable of organising themselves in ways that are militant, grassroots democratic and participatory. The J4C campaign in London is a complex and shifting coalition of unions, communities and social movements, often antagonistic, but that serve to illustrate very sharply the nature of the debates about the future direction of the union movement along the lines that we have set out in preceding chapters: community unionism, social movement unionism, global unions and the syndicalist tradition.

Organising the Unorganised? From the Virtual to the Real World of J4C

The rise of the J4C in London at the beginning of the twenty-first century coincided with a debate and ultimately a decision amongst the major TUC unions in the UK to devote resources and energy to organising, inspired by the SEIU organising model. In 1996 the TUC opened its own organiser academy (based on the AFL-CIO organising institute) to train professional organisers straight from university in a move that also aped the strategies of the SEIU (Forman, 2013a; Heery, Delbridge, Salmon, Simms & Simpson, 2002, pp. 42–50; Simms et al., 2013; Kirkpatrick, 2011). Not all affiliated unions signed up to the TUC academy, however, with *Unite*, *Amalgamated Engineering and Electrical Union* [AEEU], *Union of Shop, Distributive and Allied Workers* [USDAW] and the *General, Municipal, Boilermakers and Allied Trade Union* [GMB] preferring to establish their own organising centres, with Danford et al. arguing that this was because of a desire to retain control over organising and possible rank and file militancy (Danford et al., 2003).

The SEIU organising model placed great stress on identifying workplace leaders; a reliance on planned organising campaigns; the use of mapping in the workplace; identifying identity issues and grievances around which to organise; using action to mobilise the workforce and membership; to publicise victories effectively and to attempt to reach out to and organise the unorganised. The embrace of this organising model very quickly ran into the realities of British trade unionism where organising was seen as secondary activity on the part of union officials and reps, a general lack of trade union activists after the 15 year decimation of the union movement and a general antipathy from the union leadership, fearful no doubt of losing control of their bureaucracy and authority (Heery et al., 2002).

But the question that the J4C movement raises and is indeed reflected in the different strands of the movement remains: Organising for what? For many unions organising is an instrumental practice, a toolbox of tactics for recruitment not allied to a wider social vision of the kind that we have argued is essential for the transformation of unions and the labour movement in the twenty-first century (Simms & Holgate, 2010; Waterman, 2001b; Gorz, 1999).

Throughout this book we have argued that the labour movement is central to any rational and humane solution to the global crises facing humanity in the twenty-first century. In order to address these issues the movement needs a vision of social change that is capable of mobilising people in support of its classic goals of solidarity, democracy, mutual aid, cooperation and self-organisation in order to build a better world. What the J4C campaigns in London illustrate is the nature of the ongoing tensions with the union and wider labour movement about these different trajectories. The J4C campaigns in London show that unions remain locked in ideological debate and conflict on the answer to this question. The methods used in the J4C campaigns have been a mixture of traditional forms of organising and new virtual methods to build public support and to attempt to use different media as a means of challenging corporate power.

Virtual Organising Along the Supply Chain—Networks of Resistance

As we discussed in chapter three, many claims are made about the impact of the internet on the possible revival of the trade union movement, including the view that it can strengthen union democracy, increase worker participation, extending reach and recruitment, limit union bureaucracy and help to coordinate global union activity. There is no doubt some merit to all of these claims and they are illustrated by many of the experiences of the JFC campaigns in London. Technology and social media have been instrumental in helping the J4C/JFJ campaigns although what is revealed in the experiences is that this is a tactical development that is still very much at an early stage of use. London Citizens, for example have only just begun to use Twitter and in the past year appointed their first ever media officer. The use of digital media forms has aided union activities in a number of ways as the JFC campaigns have made clear. In terms of organising activity they enable unions to build a communication infrastructure at national and local levels. This can, in theory, enhance the ability of local union branches to organise their activities through their grassroots membership, though the extent to which this potential is realised will tend to be determined by the nature of the local branch officials. In addition digital media have aided the organisation of activities through the coordination of protests, whether in the form of public rallies or 'email bombs', both of which have been a feature of the JFC campaigns.

Finally, digital media also enable unions to challenge media representations of issues and corporate public relations by trying to present alternative narratives to the media. This latter point is no doubt the most difficult to realise given the relative levels of resources open to unions as opposed to the corporations they regularly have to confront. Nonetheless, as London Citizens organiser Stefan Baskerville made clear in interview, there has been a fundamental shift around the issue of the living wage and poverty pay in London that has been driven by the impact of JFCs allied with the LLW campaign.

The use of emails by unions remains very uneven and despite the fact that some writers have argued that emails have a power to reinvigorate participation and help democratise the union movement this assumption is far from straightforward (Freeman & Rehavi, 2008; Diamond & Freeman, 2001). The J4C movement has relied on email in order to try to coordinate activities and sustain networks of activists across unions, activist and migrant communities. This proved particularly important for LAWA in sustaining its activities through regular email bulletins to help mobilise its network of solidarity around London (The Commune, 2009). But there are familiar problems here in terms of issues such as the fact that not everyone, even now, uses email or a computer and that unions are not always able to commit themselves to translating materials into as many languages as are reflected in their membership. Given that cleaners are amongst the poorest paid workers in London it is not surprising that many are not online at all (Max Watson, Unison branch secretary, London Metropolitan University). However emails also have a more combative use for unions and can be used, along with phone calls, to institute email and phone blockades (email bombs) of offending corporations or senior managers. This strategy, which has been used in the J4C campaign, involves coordinated emails to flood organisations' strategic departments with questions about the treatment of cleaners. The idea is to bring a section of a company to a halt and raise the costs for the company of allowing low pay and abuse of their cleaning staff. Such a tactic can be directed at the cleaning company itself (usually one of the big corporations in an industry dominated by ISS, Sodexho, MITIE) and/or against the client of the service agency as occurred with HSBC and various London universities (Van Laer & Van Aelst, 2009; LibCom, 2011).

Both in terms of building solidarity and in order to create powerful narratives, digital media platforms have been crucial to the J4C campaigns in enabling them to bypass the mainstream media in order to get the stories of cleaners direct to the public. In particular, digital media platforms have been used for revealing the personal biographies of cleaners not only to humanise the so-called invisible workforce but also to illustrate the diverse array of talents and experiences shared amongst the cleaning community, with many cleaners in the UK being political exiles or refugees. The story of Consuela is a good example of this, via the website *Migrant Voice*, which exists to provide a platform for migrants in the UK. A former lawyer in Colombia who was threatened with death if she did not flee the country; she has been unable to practice law in the UK and has chosen to work as a cleaner to support her family (Migrant Voice, 2014). The web pages can also promote solidarity with those involved in the J4C campaigns who suffer victimisation from employers for their activities. This has been the case for many ranging from Unison reps at London Metropolitan University through to Colombian workers who were victimised by their employer the Willis group (Broder, 2010; Raw, 2014). Blacklisting and victimisation are primary weapons for employers against union activists and the web has been used effectively to raise the profile of those targeted. Web pages have importantly enabled migrant groups moving into the UK to gain information and solidarity with each other and unions (Fitzgerald et al., 2012). At the same time many unions now use blogs as a way of informing their members and, ideally, the wider public about their activities.

The emergence of social media has been perhaps the most important virtual development in the J4C campaign as it provides an ongoing and real-time update of events as they are unfolding. Facebook activism is now a well-recognised phenomenon and more or less ubiquitous for building networks of solidarity and promoting the cause of the cleaners affected (Castells, 2012). The advantages of social media as a platform for J4C are clear: it is quick, easy and automatically connects you to a network that can add to your level of support. Importantly it also raises concerns for corporations who are very sensitive about their public image that invariably presents them as family-centred and caring employers, despite what is often the reality of their actual practices. As one cleaner told us of her experience being a single-parent employee of a major cleaning agency, 'when my baby was ill they said if you don't come to work you won't have a job' ('Alenka', London cleaner, 2014). The reality of corporate social responsibility propaganda can be revealed with brutal clarity through social media and force corporations onto the defensive. It is an important factor in adding moral and political pressure from communities, not just workers, on corporations and employers who abuse the cleaners not only with low pay but inhumane working conditions and treatment

(Holgate, 2009, p. 63). Smaller unions such as the IWW and IWGB have used video footage to run their own version of protests that provide detailed and alternative coverage to the limited accounts found in the mainstream print and broadcast media.

As we have discussed in chapter three, social media platforms such as Twitter are seen by many as being synonymous with the rise of new forms of networked social protest that Mason, amongst others, view as a reflection of an increasingly individualist modern culture (Beck & Beck, 2001; Bauman, 2006; Mason, 2013). Indeed, Ward and Lussoli argue that the impact of the internet not only encourages an individualistic culture but also undermines trade unions, civic associations and political parties (Ward and Lussoli, 2003). But this individualism is not simply or only of the neoliberal kind, which according to Mestrovic encourages an asocial narcissism and anomie rather than compassion for others (Mestrovic, 1994). Instead Beck, Bauman and Mason, in their own ways, all argue that the new individualism lends itself to forms of solidarity and moral action. Thus, Twitter attacks against corporations and employers can have a wider moral and political basis, derived from a sense of social justice, as has been used by, for example, the London Citizens to publicise low-paid staff at Tesco's. As Baskerville told us in an interview,

> We have been using twitter to mobilise support for an online petition asking Tesco's to pay the living wage. We got more than 30,000 signatures from people who signed a petition and then received an action pack which enables them to insert a fake shelf label in a Tesco store, which said pay your staff a living wage. People can print out a copy of the label, take it into the store, take a photo and tweet it, adding a message: just saw this in your store. That's fun and gives people an opportunity to do something, to participate. We are beginning to innovate in this area. It is more suited to this instant individual participation, where people have relatively weak ties in what is a loose network. I view it as a useful campaigning tool (Stefan Baskerville, senior organiser West London Citizens).

What is evident in the case of the J4C campaigns is the extent to which these activities are underpinned by the emergence in civil society of a network of inter-linked individuals and groups who are critical of or opposed to existing structures of power. Networks are important though in a sense union solidarity has always been, in part, a network that transcends specific geographical locations. They have proven to be particularly important in the ways in which migrant communities in London have sought to defend themselves, drawing upon classic libertarian principles of self-help, mutual aid and direct action to engender group solidarity (Però & Solomos, 2010, p. 2). But virtual networks are increasingly important as they enable protestors such as the J4C campaigns to globalise their activities and generate international support. This can extend as far as organising solidarity protests in other countries in support of cleaners in London, something that was organised by the UK Solidarity Federation in support of cleaners protesting at a London University. A network can enable the careful planning and development of a wave of activities and protests that connect workers across an entire industry rather than within a single workplace, potentially raising the costs for employers. This relationship between networks, structures and the world-system is part of the ongoing struggle over GFA and GFB.

So the virtual form of protest and mediated activism has certainly been an important tool for the J4C campaigns and explains something about the ways in which individuals and groups are organising their protests in the twenty-first century.

Organising for Real

The reality is, though, that the J4C campaigns ultimately depend upon more traditional union methods in alliance with these virtual tools in order to build campaigns that will win. They cannot be a substitute for workers participating in or leading their own fights. As we have argued in the previous chapter, the virtual is important to the extent that it becomes a part of the real world of union activity. By this we mean the extent to which digital technologies enable unions to carry out their activities in ways that enhance the power and goals of their membership. Clearly the use of digital technologies by unions is still at a very early stage of development but the JFC campaigns have shown that the virtual can enhance the power of even the most marginalised groups of workers to challenge the ways in which they are exploited and abused.

All of the groups that we interviewed stressed the fact that face-to-face organising remains the most important part of any campaign. Building trust and solidarity takes time and commitment and cannot be bypassed through mediated or virtual forms of solidarity. Social media and emails can be conduits to face-to-face organising but they cannot replace it. One thing that became clear in the course of this research was that the strength of a campaign would often come down to the individual union branch involved and the commitment of the activists there. In social theory this is an issue of structure and agency in that the structure of a union can be viewed in terms of its organisational logic (the extent to which the union encourages centralisation or decentralisation of its activities); the nature and organisation of decision-making within the union, particularly with regard to taking industrial action; the degrees of autonomy of grassroots activity to resist hierarchical and bureaucratic control; and the strategic goals of the union, such as its relationship to political parties and its view of the state as an institution for promoting its interests.

These structures tend to place certain limits on the activities that the union will undertake, encouraging some choices rather than others and instilling a culture that shapes the ethos of the union. But we need to be careful not to reify these structures; they can and do evolve and change and often leave spaces for activity on the part of local union branches that might be seen to be in conflict with the overall strategic goals and practices of the national union leadership.

Nonetheless public support has been an important factor in London's J4C campaigns and this has required the development of a media strategy on the part of the unions involved and London Citizens. To win media attention it is necessary to present them with something that they can print, transmit or broadcast. The J4C in London has been effective in part because it has often been driven by its strong Latin American community support to engage in popular protests outside targeted employers that include live music, speeches and leafleting along with the use of vibrant colours and flags to present a very visible form of public dissent. These activities also lend themselves to useful online material to publicise the campaigns. They are also backed up by other forms of public protest including the use of petitions (online and real), occupation of the workplace and hunger strikes (Lee & Mustill, 2013).

Despite the importance of these media strategies, taking industrial action, from strikes to actions short of a strike, remains the main weapon in the J4C campaign. Despite the strong and aggressive anti-union legislation in the UK it is possible for an organised and motivated workforce to successfully take industrial action as the J4C campaigns have shown. Cleaners for the RMT on the underground, Unison at London SOAS University and the IWW at John Lewis department store on Oxford Street have all voted for strike action and as a consequence won their claims against the employer (Hearn & Bergos, 2011; Kirkpatrick, 2011).

Being able to build alliances amongst a variety of civil society groups has been crucial to the J4C campaigns. As we have seen London Citizens is itself a highly effective coalition of diverse institutions but the J4C campaigns have also brought together student groups, anti-immigration control movements such as *No Borders*, anti-sweatshops movements such as *No Sweat* and anarcho-syndicalist groups such as the *Solidarity Federation*. The point about these relationships is that they create a loose and decentralised network of solidarity that is able to support the central focus of the movement, the actions of the cleaners themselves (The Commune, 2009; Broder, 2010; Kirkpatrick, 2011).

Evaluating the JFJ/JFC Movement

In terms of securing the practical and realistic goal of the London living wage for cleaners (and other groups of low-paid workers) the J4C campaigns have been a significant success for the union movement in London, drawing sympathetic media coverage and public support as well as seeing the emergence of nascent community unionism. Ongoing and recent victories at London SOAS (2014) as well as other London universities only underline this point. However, as the movement has spread across London it has also diversified into different groups. There is no single or unified J4C movement; there are many.

What the London J4C campaigns illustrate is the way in which innovative methods (virtual and real) have enabled invisible workers to become visible and to use the media in a way that enables them to construct broad-based alliances within communities and more widely, building some level of public support. There are elements of global unionism in this in that the SEIU organising model and JFJ campaigns are the inspiration for much of these activities, however thinly drawn the connection may be in the minds of those involved in London. There are also clearly both elements of community unionism in the activities of London Citizens and to some extent in the union activity of Unite and Unison, though as noted earlier this has proven to be problematic for the unions in practice. The spread of the campaign into much smaller unions such as the IWW and the IWGB links with Waterman's idea of social movement unionism that connects disparate social movements around the themes of social justice and social change. It also brings back into the labour movement, in a small but significant way, syndicalist ideas of direct action, solidarity unionism and worker-led industrial action. The appeal of this should not be overlooked as it is the radical direct action tactics that have won cleaners many of their victories and that are influencing JFC campaigns in other countries such as Finland (Justice for Cleaners, 2013).

Indeed, the recent Carr report (Carr, 2014) commissioned by the Coalition government was concerned precisely with revived union militancy in the UK including the actions of the JFC campaigns.

The SEIU inspired JFJ and J4C campaigns have had a significant impact on the possibilities of unions organising workers in insecure and often previously unorganised workplaces. In the London-based J4C campaigns many of the strands of the SEIU strategies are apparent, both its strengths and weaknesses. Dealing with the strengths of the SEIU model first we can note that the most obvious point is that the strategy has proven to be effective; it brings victories to workers though there are questions as to how sustainable they are, with McCallum arguing that the victories were determined not by mobilising the public or the media alongside the workers but because the victories were cheap for employers to settle (McCallum, 2013, p. 57; Simms, et al., 2013, pp. 151–152). The second area of innovation has been around the media itself, in all of its formats. The JFJ and J4C campaigns have grown increasingly media sensitive and have skilfully mobilised public support through the careful construction of counter-narratives that expose the reality of life for low-paid, most often migrant workers in major cities such as London. In particular the use of the internet and social media has proven to be a cheap and easily used tool for disseminating information, reports and enabling easy contact between the often fragmented networks of supporters of the J4C campaigns (Broder, 2010; Juris, 2005; Lee & Mustill, 2013, p. 111). Crucially the JFJ/JFC campaigns also show that it is possible for unions to organise the unorganised in the new global economy. To this end the SEIU global alliances have sought to promote this view around the world and in effect present a global organising model that can be taken up, adapted and applied in different countries.

There are, however, fundamental weaknesses in the JFJ/J4C movement that relate to the issues that this book addresses. These are reflected in the unfolding of the London JFC movement and its spread across the city. The first weakness with the model is one that connects the SEIU with Unite in London: the tension between democratic control by rank and file union members as opposed to centralized control by the union leadership (Moody, 2007). The SEIU has received a great deal of criticism for its centralisation of power and decision-making into the hands of a leadership that have placed the acquisition of power as its goal. For example, this led to a split in the union in California and the establishment of a new union, the National Union of Health Workers, who raised the important question about the SEIU organising model: Organising for what? For the NUHW power is not an adequate answer, there has to be a vision of social transformation at the heart of the model if it is to inspire people and create the belief in the possibility of a better world. For the NUHW the wishes of the workers on the ground are more important than the ambitions of the union leadership, which remain, as Stern made abundantly clear, business unionism: the pursuit of power to enable union leaders to negotiate a new partnership with the state and capital and the rejection of class struggle (Aguiar & Ryan, 2009, p. 98; Forman, 2013b; Stern, 2006, pp. 59, 66–67; Simms et al., 2013, p. 12). As Erik Forman notes, turning organising into a professional activity and inserting centrally directed professional organisers into union campaigns does not transform the culture of unions and does not encourage grassroots activity, which must surely be the basis for any sustained union revival. It merely treats organising as a technique without any need to transform the nature of the union (Clawson, 2009; Simms et al., 2013, p. 43; Forman, 2013a, 2013b).

These criticisms are substantive and complex and illustrate the broader themes that we have focused upon in this book. The future of the labour movement is being debated and built through the practices of workers in countless struggles around the world. As it stands the JFJ campaigns in the UK illustrate a point made by Simms et al., which is that the mainstream TUC unions prioritise their relationship to the Labour Party and corporatism over wider issues of social justice (Simms et al., 2013, p. 170). The JFJ/J4C campaigns illustrate different elements of the four dimensions of possible union renewal that we have focused upon: global unionism, community unionism, social movement unionism and syndicalism. Within these movements there are competing tendencies towards more authoritarian and more libertarian possibilities. How these campaigns evolve will be fundamental to the way in which the labour movement reconstitutes itself in the twenty-first century.

· 5 ·

FAST FOOD FORWARD—FROM INDUSTRIAL POWER TO PUBLIC IMAGE

As we have argued in this book, we are seeing trends of new and revisited forms of unionism emerging, particularly amongst low-wage workers movements. The developments and initiatives within the Service Employees International Union (SEIU) that were outlined in the previous chapter with regards to the janitors/cleaners campaign are indicative of the movement of experimentation we are currently witnessing in labour organisation. The janitors/cleaners' campaign set out some fundamental shifts in how previously unorganised sectors might be incorporated into broader community and social movement related campaigns, and the possibilities for more society-based movements of worker resistance as we have seen with the advancement of the living wage campaign in the UK. Moving towards such forms of worker resistance allows for a significant role to be played by media, and particularly new media forms, as a way to create wider networks of solidarity within and between communities and groups. These trends have been revisited again, also in relation to the SEIU, in the context of the fast food workers movement that kicked off in the US in 2012. As we will see in this chapter, the fast food workers movement has moved the debate about the changing nature of worker resistance along as it has situated labour movements within the continuous narrative surrounding 'new' protest movements, particularly the Occupy movement, by foregrounding direct action, social media, and wider questions regarding social injustice (income inequality, systemic racism and sexism, immigration). However, we will also see the challenges of such developments in the context of mainstream trade unions that remain hierarchical and business-oriented in structure, severely limiting the potential for community and social movement unionism, and least of all a genuine shift towards grassroots-driven independent unionism.

In 40 years the fast food industry has grown from a $6 billion industry to more than $170 billion in annual revenues in the US alone (Bernstein, 2011). There are about 3.5 million fast food workers in the United States. Importantly, almost half of those jobs were created in the past decade and no industry has created more jobs in the US since the financial crisis in 2008. As we have outlined in previous chapters, this is indicative of a broader trend in developed economies, with the US in the lead, of rebuilding economies as low-wage economies, alongside a minority of very high-wage jobs creating a stark 'job polarisation' in the US labour market (Boehm, 2014). Big classes of low-wage workers now work in very precarious working conditions with few entitlements and rights—and are largely non-unionised. This growth in the industry has also seen a significant change in the demographic of the fast food workforce. Traditionally, fast food work was carried out by high-school students or graduates, looking for part-time and temporary work to supplement other primary incomes in the household. That has changed. Today, workers in fast food restaurants are usually over the age of 20, often bringing up a child and in as many as 68% of cases they are the main wage-earner in the family (Allegretto et al., 2013). At the same time as the demographic of precarious low-wage sectors has changed, wages for the bottom 70% of the wage ladder have either stagnated or declined in the past decade (Mishel & Shierholz, 2013). The current federal minimum wage is $7.25 an hour, which comes to an annual income of about $15,000 for full-time work. The median pay for core front-line fast food jobs is $8.69, with many jobs paying at or near the minimum wage. Benefits are also scarce for these workers; an estimated 87% of front-line fast food workers do not receive health benefits through their employer (Allegretto et al., 2013). This is therefore a sector of the US workforce that has been going through significant changes and growth that are increasingly symbolic of economic developments in the global North and that provide a context for understanding the emergence of social unrest and protest. Rallies and strikes amongst fast food workers have become part of a broader struggle for economic and social justice in the United States and globally, revealing high levels of tension around issues of inequality. The research carried out for this chapter focuses on the United States and the city of New York, particularly. Fieldwork was carried out in New York during December 2013 where most of the interviews were conducted (some of which are made anonymous here upon their request) and where participant observation was carried out during a fast food workers strike and rally on December 5th, 2013. The analysis presented here is therefore predominantly based on impressions gathered from this period of the struggle and less so on events that followed this period, although later developments have been considered. However, it should be remembered that, at the time of writing, Fast Food Forward and the fast food workers movement is still very active and going through significant developments that cannot all be captured here.

The campaign for higher wages for fast food workers started in early 2012. As was indicated with the Justice for Janitors/Cleaners campaign outlined in the previous chapter, it marks an important moment for organised labour within the United States and more widely as it signifies a changing approach to not only organising, but also to the question of what unions and unionism is for in the modern world-system. The fast food industry has historically been sidelined in the trade union movement as too difficult to organise with not only a high turnover of mainly young staff, but also a corporate structure based on individual franchises that limit the ability to negotiate with an overarching employer for collective bargaining agreements. As has become a familiar story with global corporations, the giants of fast food outlets are organised around a multitude of hierarchical management layers and decentralized operations that allow for very effective control of employees but absolves any central body of responsibility. However, as outlined in previous chapters, big unions, especially in the United States, have been rethinking the framework within which they are pursuing the advancement of workers' interests and the fast food worker strikes need to be understood within this context.

The driving force and primary funder of the fast food campaign has been the SEIU, one of the largest unions in the United States. In the last few years it has experimented with different models for organising, in particularly with regards to low-wage workers. The *Fight for a Fair Economy* initiative that was launched by the SEIU leadership in 2010 was indicative of the pressure unions have felt to change strategies and tactics in the face of increasing corporate power and a weakness in union representation. For SEIU this has especially meant a shift to focus more on communities, more on creating alternative forms of labour organisations, and a focus to work more with different political and social actors within a broader framework of so-called social movement unionism. According to some, this has also meant a shift in focus from unionizing particular groups of workers with a hope to represent them in collective bargaining agreements towards a focus on grassroots political organising with a broader social justice agenda. The fast food strikes are seen to be an example of precisely such a shift (Weissman, 2014). Therefore, it is an important case study because it has largely been described and understood in ways that relate it to a new form of unionism that draws influences from the protest practices of recent uprisings and is looking to form part of a broader ecology of resistance and activism.

Along with this, much emphasis has been placed on the role of media in facilitating and nurturing this form of unionism that draws more on Occupy than traditional trade unionism (Sanburn, 2013). Indeed, a key feature of the movement has been its heavy media presence, both in terms of social media, blogs and digital campaigning as well as its untypically extensive, positive, coverage in what may be considered 'traditional' capitalist mainstream news outlets. This chapter looks at these media practices of the movement in the context of its development and examines the ways in which they may be seen to be a feature of a new kind of worker resistance that adheres to the principles of social movement unionism. What is particularly interesting about the fast food strikes is, in fact, the extensive use of professionalized public relations in the shaping of the movement. What this chapter illustrates is the way in which this also extends to the incorporation of social media not only for campaigning, but also with regards to the way the movement has come to define itself and its organisational structure. The (social) media emphasis of the fast food workers movement illustrates not only a possible shift within the labour movement to locate power in public image rather than industrial power in response to the widely perceived crisis in unions but also, importantly, to distance worker resistance from traditional mainstream unions towards, at least the perception of, a more grassroots-driven, community-focused form of social justice movement that can adhere to more 'authentic' forms of resistance against corporate power.

Big Unions and the 'Outsourcing' of Organising

SEIU is one of the biggest unions in the United States with around 2 million members, focusing mainly on workers in the health sector, public services and property services (including janitors and food service workers). The organising of fast food workers has historically been sidelined and dismissed by unions due to not only the franchise structure of many fast food companies that makes it difficult to organise across any one company, but also the precarity of the sector and high turnover of (young) staff. However, with the changing demographic and growth of the sector, along with rising inequality, conditions for mobilising this workforce have been gradually emerging. SEIU has been the primary funder of the campaign, and spent in excess of $10 million on the initiative in its first year alone (Gupta, 2013). Rather than this organising coming directly from the union, with SEIU members approaching fast food workers, the organising drive was pursued via a number of community groups that SEIU funded to mobilise workers in the community around wage issues. As we have discussed in previous chapters, engaging with community groups in this way is not a new development as such, but it is certainly indicative of a trend within the labour movement in the United States to find alternative ways of organising than the traditional union steward and shop-floor organising model that still dominates Europe. This includes working with groups and associations that over time have become more entrenched in low-wage worker communities through routes other than unionisation. The main organisation that SEIU has been working with in the fast food worker campaign is the community organising group New York Communities for Change (NYCC). This organisation was created out of what used to be known as the Association of Community Organisations for Reform Now (ACORN), which used to be the largest community organisation in the US of low and moderate-income families. Created in 1970 by activists Wade Rathke and Gary Delgado it reached, at its height, a membership of 500,000 people and worked across hundreds of chapters. However, following accusations of criminal activity and mismanagement of its resources resulting in withdrawal of its main funding sources, ACORN eventually filed for liquidation and closed in 2010. Out of this emerged a number of new community organisations, one of the most prominent being NYCC, which was established by the New York affiliation of the association and particularly Jon Kest who also helped found the Working Families Party in the late 1990s (Urbina, 2010; Fox, 2012).

Working with community groups and other forms of associations is part of the move towards alternative ways of understanding the nature and role of unions that has been expressed by many parts of the labour movement. It speaks partly to the vision of a kind of social movement unionism that, as we have argued, fits the protest ecology of contemporary times. However, this can be approached in many different ways and, as we outlined in the previous chapter, some commentators have raised some scepticism towards the ability and will of big mainstream unions like the SEIU to pursue such a framework for action in a genuine move towards social movement unionism. Rather, as we have suggested in this book, this calls for bigger structural overhauls that reject the corporatist/business union model. For example, labour historian Immanuel Ness remarked in an interview that rather than representing a form of social movement unionism, what we are witnessing in instances such as the fast food campaign is unions 'contracting the organisation of workers to other organisations'. That is, rather than working with different groups in a collaborative effort to organise workers through a variety of different avenues, unions are seeking to absolve their organising practices and rather contract and 'outsource' this activity to other kinds of organisations. There are different reasons for this. Partly, unions are pursuing this due to the restrictive legal framework that they operate under within the United States, which restricts their ability to engage in union-type activity without having elections. Working with community groups and other types of worker organisations therefore provides a way in which unions can be separated from any legal liability for organising workers. However, according to Ness, the use of other organisations for organising also signifies a lack of ability within unions to actually engage in genuine organising: 'there is a sense that these other people can do it better' (Ness, labour historian). From this perspective, the use of community groups in the fast food campaign is not a move to community or social movement unionism as commonly understood, but rather a form of outsourcing practices: 'here we see an example where people are referring to new forms of worker organisation and they are a new form in the sense that they are practicing the same thing that businesses do, multinational corporations, where they find some kind of supply chain; in this case, who are the best organisers' (Ness, labour historian). The turn to community groups amongst unions, therefore, may be a more multifaceted development than extending cooperation and broadening the labour movement to incorporate community and NGO activism as community unionism or social movement unionism might suggest. Rather, it may also be a reflection of the challenges that unions are facing in connecting with people and engaging with organising practices, either due to restrictions and lack of resources being invested in supporting good organisers or due to historical reputation and perception of union mismanagement and bad practice.

For the fast food campaign, SEIU involved community groups by funding NYCC organisers to engage people in low-income communities, where fast food workers are particularly prominent. According to 'John', an NYCC organiser involved in the campaign, this was initially done by petitioning people on issues relating to affordable housing and 'stop and frisk', a police practice in which police officers are allowed to stop and search people without warrant or prior consent (Bostock & Fessenden, 2014). Both of these issues are particularly pressing in lower income communities in New York and 'John' described the petitioning process as essentially "an attempt to collect data." The next stage then included using the data collected on people from the petitions for rounds of phone-calling to try and structure a straightforward call for higher wages: 'there was actually a phone rap printed off for all of us to work off with questions like, we found that most people don't think they can find better housing unless they make more money; would you agree with that or disagree with that? That's a no-brainer' ('John', NYCC organiser). In this way, it was possible to formulate a campaign strategy around an increase in wages. These initial data collection activities would then be followed up with meetings with fast food workers in and around their workplaces by community organisers they had been in touch with on the phone and in this way the campaign developed into what may be regarded as a movement, although as will be explored below, defining it as such is contested.

The demand for higher wages became the primary focus, although as a union, SEIU had an interest from the outset to also use this campaign to unionise this growing workforce that had previously been so difficult to organise: 'From the very outset the goal was to unionise fast food workers and get them $15 an hour and a contract.' ('John', NYCC organiser) However, by engaging workers through community groups and around issues of affordable housing and increased wage demands, the mobilisation of workers came to be seen as part of a community drive rather than as a union drive. As the organiser pointed out, 'the word union was sort of a last resort, we weren't really allowed to mention the word union at the very beginning. It wasn't until sometime late Spring that we started talking about unionisation' ('John', NYCC organiser). As alluded to above, this speaks to a recurring theme in the campaign, one in which unions are seen to carry too much 'baggage' to be able to organise and mobilise workers and are therefore kept in the background: 'SEIU as a name has a lot of baggage attached with it' (Arun Gupta, labour activist). Indeed, as 'John' from NYCC suggested, the use of community organisers and the decision to contract NYCC was part of a vision of the campaign to make it seem like a more spontaneous movement, 'to give it more authenticity that it was this grassroots campaign that sprung out of this necessity' ('John', NYCC organiser). As will be explored further below, this message became central to how the movement entered public debate and the media practices employed to promote the campaign.

Alongside other community and social groups such as MaketheRoad and United NY, faith leaders and local politicians, NYCC, funded and guided by SEIU, created the New York chapter of the campaign under the name Fast Food Forward, which has become its most recognisable name nationally and internationally. This organisation, although largely funded by the SEIU, is an informal coalition that has some similarities to a worker centre, which are 'community-based mediating institutions' that provide support to low-wage workers, operating outside of union structures (Fine, 2006). The demands of the campaign have been clear and concise: fast food workers should get paid $15 an hour and have the right to organise without retaliation. During the period of research, it was difficult to ascertain exactly what the strategy for unionisation was and although some organisers suggested that Fast Food Forward would eventually be established as an 'independent union', the predominant view within the labour movement has been that any unionisation would be through and within the SEIU. Indeed, 'John', the organiser from NYCC, said 'all the organisers I worked with, we were confused as to what that would look like, how it would work, and what it would mean.' However, unionising fast food workers has revealingly become a subsidiary concern to the wage demand, which has been the main focus of the campaign and has broadened the movement to a movement for a general increase in minimum wage under the banner and hashtag #Fightfor15. Although fast food workers remain the most central group to this demand, it has made the campaign a struggle for low-wage workers across American society and beyond, epitomized by the move of most online information and resources related to the campaign onto a digital campaigning platform called *Low Pay Is Not Ok* that is dedicated to low-wage labour more broadly.

New Tactics: 'Flash Strikes' and Non-Unionised Worker Resistance

The first action of the campaign took place in November 2012 in New York with a one-day strike action with around 200 people. This was then followed by further similar actions in other major cities such as Chicago, Washington and Los Angeles in Spring and Summer of 2013 building up to a large coordinated one-day strike action across 60 cities (according to organisers), which took place on August 29th, 2013 to coincide with the anniversary of the civil rights march in Washington in 1963. Timing the event in this way became part of a developing discourse surrounding the fast food workers as symbols of contemporary social injustice in the United States that especially resonated in mainstream media. The action received relatively widespread coverage and sympathetic editorials in most of the elite newspapers. For example, in the *Washington Post* an editorial stated:

> Of all the commemorations of the March on Washington, the one that will best capture its spirit isn't really a commemoration at all. Thursday, one day after the 50th anniversary of the great march, fast-food and retail workers in as many as 35 cities will stage a one-day strike demanding higher wages. Sadly, the connection between the epochal demonstration of 1963 and a fast-food strike in 2013 couldn't be more direct. (Meyerson, 2013)

The August action was then followed by an even bigger action on the 5th of December, 2013 with a coordinated one-day strike, taking place across 100 cities, that at that point was described as the largest strike action in the history of the fast food industry. Subsequent, bigger, actions have followed and at the time of writing, there have been eight of these national one-day strikes since November 2012, including a very large one on September 3rd, 2014 to coincide with Labor Day in the United States and a broader strike alongside other low-wage workers on December 4th, 2014, that also coincided with widespread protests regarding institutional racism following grand jury decisions to drop charges for two separate killings of black men by white police officers.

What is significant about the fast food workers' actions is that they have been described as 'socially organised' (Helmore, 2013), emerged out of a 'broad coalition of unions, local community organisers and members of the clergy' (McVeigh, 2013) collectively supporting these non-unionised workers engaging in direct action. Epitomizing much of the commentary and news coverage of the strikes, an article in *The Guardian* stated:

> These are not union-sponsored protests, [Professor Arne Kalleberg] points out, but socially organized protests. "Frustration has been building for a long time", he says, "and this is spontaneous, non-union activity by people who are increasingly frustrated by the system, and it's catching on." (Helmore, 2013)

In this way they are seen to draw more on the spirit and organisational structures of the wave of 'new' protest movements and uprisings that have emerged in the last few years, such as the Occupy movement, than traditional trade unionism. In fact, one of the main organisers of the campaign, John Westin, has been widely quoted in the media as saying that the strategy of using aggressive one-day 'flash strikes' rather than the traditional union approach of filing federal grievances was directly influenced by Occupy Wall Street: 'Confronting power more openly and publicly and directly…that came straight from Occupy.' (quoted in Feuer, 2013) Indeed, building on broader existing narratives that came out of Occupy in the framing of the movement, both in terms of language and tactics, has been central to how the protests have entered public discourse. For example, the use of the 'human microphone' in which the crowd will repeat the words of the speaker during protests outside fast food shops have a close symbolic association with Occupy Wall Street, and the use of slogans during the fast food workers rallies such as 'Whose Streets, Our Streets' or 'Banks Got Bailed Out, We Got Sold Out', widely used during Occupy Wall Street, have further strengthened this association. Moreover, speeches and statements on the days of action would frequently refer to the 1% and the 99% that the Occupy movement popularised as a way of highlighting social and economic inequality (for a discussion of the 99% slogan during Occupy cf. Juris, 2012) and some posters would carry the words 'Occupy Fast Food' as a direct reference to the popular movement. This has been incredibly successful, as fast food workers have in this way become the new media symbols of the continued struggle against corporate greed and stark inequality. As mentioned above, evidence of this is the way in which these events have continuously received a significant amount of media coverage—and sympathetic media coverage—marking them out from how labour movements have historically been treated in capitalist media. For example, a *New York Times* piece stated:

> Victory for the lowest-wage workers will have a positive impact on wages for everyone…well-intentioned people often ask me what they can do to help improve our food system. Here's an easy one: When you see that picket line next week, don't cross it. In fact, join it. (Bittman, 2013)

Similarly, an article in the *Washington Post* argued:

> The protests have the benefit of putting low-wage workers in the media spotlight, a place they're almost never found in a world more interested in the antics of Miley Cyrus and Donald Trump. (Dionne Jr., 2013)

What is more, the fast food strikes have come to be seen as a significant influence on policy changes at both local and national levels. The United States has seen an increase in minimum wage in several cities following the protests; in SeaTac, Washington they even went for the $15 wage-floor that some attribute to the Fightfor15 campaign (cf. Dean, 2014). In President Obama's State of the Union address in January 2014 he announced he was going to raise the minimum wage of federal workers to $10.10 encouraging corporations to follow suit, singling out particularly the plight of fast food workers (O'Connor, 2014). And in early March 2014 McDonald's filed its annual report to the US financial services regulator where it particularly highlighted a pressure to increase wages based on recent actions. In the report, the campaign was identified as a risk, emphasising:

> [T]he impact of campaigns by labour organisations and activists, including through the use of social media and other mobile communications and applications, to promote adverse perceptions of the quick-service category of the IEO [Informal Eating Out] segment of our brand, management, suppliers or franchisees, or to promote or threaten boycotts, strikes or other actions involving the industry, McDonald's or our suppliers and franchisees. (McDonald's Corporation, 2014)

These developments speak to a very effective campaign in many regards and the recognition that the demand for higher wages has received amongst media and political elites has led to widespread views of the fast food protests as a 'stunning success' for organised labour (cf. Weissman, 2014).

Fast Food Forward: 'A March on the Media'

The orchestration and impact of the fast food worker protests illustrate a significant shift in the tactics of traditional trade unions such as SEIU. The use of community organisers, direct action and Occupy discourse speaks to a different kind of focus for unions than organising workers in individual workplaces with the aim to represent them in collective bargaining agreements. Rather, the fast food worker protests indicate that big mainstream unions are moving away from organising altogether, and are rather looking to work with groups who operate outside the workplace to reach workers. What is more, they are willing to make use of tactics that are historically associated with the more libertarian wing of the labour movement such as direct action, self-organisation and protests with non-unionised workers. What has also been significant with the fast food worker protests has been the strategy to exert pressure, not by organising fast food franchises, but by building a broader advocacy campaign around the minimum wage through extensive engagement with the media in a variety of forms. The media focus has been a central aspect of the campaign as noted in an interview with a social media coordinator for the campaign who said: 'That was their top priority, to make everything media focused' ('Judy', social media coordinator, #Fightfor15). Engaging extensively with media has come about partly from the deliberate professionalization of union communications by hiring expert public relations companies for the campaign. The most prominent of these has been Berlin Rosen with its extensive experience in political communications, particularly for the left and US progressives. It is credited with a key role in the successful campaigns for Democratic New York mayor candidate Bill de Blasio in 2013 and Eric Schneiderman's run for New York State attorney general in 2010. The hiring of Berlin Rosen has been supplemented with other smaller PR companies working on the campaign, such as technology and social movement specialist Purpose, which prides itself on managing communications for movements looking to pursue social change. This is in addition to 'spending a significant amount of money making sure that they had professional photographers, professional videographers, professional social media people, all kinds of people.' ('Judy', social media coordinator, #Fightfor15). The PR aspect of the campaign has been hugely significant for not only how the campaign has been covered in media, both mainstream and alternative, but also for how it is being viewed within the labour movement. That is, the extent to which the media focus has created a veneer of social movement unionism that is not underpinned by a genuine movement. The use of one-day 'flash strikes' has been part of a strategy to primarily garner media attention: 'Every time we had one of these events, afterwards we would have a meeting where we would rate how effective the marches were and the press conferences, and the main organiser, the thing that he always was focused on was the media, how was the media perceiving what we were doing.' The same organiser went on to explain, 'he would have a thing called "what's the media moment?" that would be the moment where we want all the cameras to stand around in a group and take pictures and have the right spokesperson say the right thing at the right time' ('Judy', social media coordinator, #Fightfor15). As such, organising strikes in this regard was less about harming the business of fast food directly through industrial action as a traditional trade union tactic. In fact, these strike actions have included relatively small numbers of people compared to the industry and it has led some people within the labour movement to regard the campaign as motivated not by organising fast food workers, but rather by targeting the media: 'The whole thing is not really about exercising power, it's about stunts which attract media attention' (Stu Melvin, labour activist). What is more, these events have been tightly managed by union officials, organisers, and public relations professionals in order to ensure a clear and concise message that is particularly media friendly:

> [I]f your whole point is not to fight the boss by gaining material power, the whole point is to fight the boss by gaining media attention, then your message has to be sophisticated and clear and follow a good communication word strategy. And to do that, professionals have got to do it, the workers are going to mess it up because they're all going to say different stuff because workers have different opinions – shock horror. So SEIU are massively micro-managing it, or in fact, SEIU's PR company are massively micro-managing it. (Stu Melvin, labour activist)

This sentiment was supported by one of the organisers involved in the campaign who made this very revealing statement:

> They took basically what was a marginalized workforce and instead of organizing those workers into an actual union, into the SEIU, they used these workers as sort of media tools for their larger campaign. And I say this mostly because in my experience from working with them they haven't attempted to actually form these workers into a union, they've just worked with the workers to the extent that they train them as spokespeople. Beyond that, they didn't really guarantee them any more protection than with these strikes making sure they got their jobs back if they were fired for striking. ('Judy', social media coordinator, #Fightfor15)

During participant-observation at the strike action on December 5th, 2013 in New York City, this tight management of the message of the campaign and the creation of the event as a media event was particularly noteworthy. A few designated fast food workers were put forward to speak to media as well as researchers, the crowd was made up of a large number of organisers and supporters that all knew each other with few 'outsiders' present that may have joined spontaneously, and the message was clearly focused on wage inequality rather than unionisation with chants such as 'we can't survive on 7.25' (referring to the federal minimum wage at the time of the protests). Indeed, few of the fast food workers asked during the action seemed aware of the nature or purpose of a union. As mentioned above, the media event was created through symbolic gestures that tied the protests to the plea for addressing wealth inequality that emerged out of Occupy and by creating a spectacle with one-day small protests scattered across cities and, in the case of New York City, culminating in Foley Square (where the Occupy movement also partly located itself) with a rally. These tactics made one organiser describe the campaign as 'a march on the media', in contrast to a march on the boss (quoted in Gupta, 2013).

As part of this, the extensive social media activity surrounding the protests and rallies of the fast food worker movement has been central in how the actions have been perceived and how the campaign has been shaped. Organising the campaign around one-day flash-strikes provided an easy route for how social media could be used to maximise impact. In particular, this has concerned the enhancement of visibility and an attempt to underpin the narrative of the movement that has been advanced by campaigners. Hired social media co-ordinators for the campaign engaged in practices such as creating 'Twitter rallies' in which groups would create a list of tweets related to the campaign (e.g., 'RT if you couldn't survive on $7.25 #riseupny #fastfoodfwd #washny #minwage') for followers to tweet in the lead-up to protests. One of these social media coordinators for the campaign explained how on the day of the one-day strikes she would complement this with an initial meme with a picture of President Obama, for example, and an accompanying quote to be shared on Facebook throughout the day, and she would then write tweets throughout the protests with statements from speakers and workers to build a spectacle around the events:

> [social media use] was mostly for publicity and for support…after a while we realized that it was effective to have a powerful image or a powerful graphic or meme or something to post at the beginning of the day…and to have people share it throughout the day. And actually we had paid Facebook ads and we had specific posts paid for which is something Berlin Rosen took the lead on and that made it more visible and had a higher reach throughout the day. ('Judy', social media coordinator, #Fightfor15)

Partly this is done to inform people of events and to facilitate the mass aggregation of individuals in concrete locales and mobilising what Juris (2012) refers to as 'crowds of individuals'. However, given the distribution of several meet-up events taking place simultaneously, limiting the crowd aspect of the protests, a far more important use of social media platforms has been to amplify the event online for public visibility. This has become a key part of how activism is approached via social media, where the onus is on a culture of sharing and viral distribution. These technological affordances of social media platforms lend themselves particularly to spectacle events, such as protests and rallies that are visually engaging, immediate and temporary. 'Flash-strikes' epitomize particularly this type of activism. Although the number of fast food workers on strike and present at the protests has not been that big, the spectacle of flash-strikes in which different groups of individuals congregate at different fast food outlets and then combine in a public square to stage a rally has been easily amplified by specific (professional) individuals distributing images and text via social media platforms. In this way, social media practices within the movement have been incorporated into its broader public relations campaign and can predominantly be understood as an extension of the professionalised communications strategies that have been a key feature of Fast Food Forward and #Fightfor15.

Social Media and the Creation of Narratives

Alongside the creation of online visibility as part of garnering media attention surrounding the one-day flash strikes, social media practices have been significant in slightly more nuanced ways for the fast food campaign that are less discussed in debates on (social) media and contemporary forms of resistance. The user-generated content that is one of the defining features of social media platforms has led to much analysis of the ability for users to share their own interpretations and understandings of events that concern them. Often this has heralded social media platforms as places where news and analysis that remain excluded from 'mainstream' news outlets due to perceived control and interests that permeate traditional media institutions can be shared and distributed. Certainly, online advocacy for raising the minimum wage as part of the fast food campaign through the sharing of news as well as research reports funded by Fast Food Forward and NYCC on issues relating to the lives of fast food workers and costs to American taxpayers have been key to social media practices. However, this has been supplemented by more innovative 'click-bait' or 'like-magnets' that rather than targeting government policy, have specifically targeted the fast food industry, looking to 'damage' major brands, in what might be considered a form of counter–public relations. As we have discussed earlier in this book, a key feature of contemporary corporate power has been to take advantage of the 'consciousness industries' to extend corporate branding to all aspects of everyday life. This has also simultaneously made corporate practices more 'visible' to consumers who seek to highlight instances of corporate injustice and abuse. Such strategies have emerged out of the fast food and Fightfor15 campaign where active monitoring of corporate activity online has provided opportunities to ridicule certain content and action on social media. In particular, the fast food giant McDonald's has carried the brunt of this by having its resource advice site, McResourceline.com, widely shared on social networking sites for its questionable financial tips to its work force. Advice such as breaking meals into pieces, resulting in 'eating less and still feeling full' and suggesting low-wage over-worked staff take two vacations a year to reduce stress became obvious points of ridicule in the context of the campaign that highlighted the low pay and working conditions of its employees. The digital campaigning group *Low Pay Is Not Ok* also created a short comedic video, easily liked and shared, that used the financial budgeting advice offered by McDonald's to its employees, highlighting that even McDonald's own budget advice made it clear that it is not possible to live on the salary that fast food workers receive. Engaging in these forms of counter-public relations aimed at 'damaging' fast food brands has been an interesting part of the campaign as it illustrates the multifaceted terrain of 'mediated visibility' (Thompson, 1995) and, again, speaks to the emphasis that has been placed on public image as a form of resistance to corporate power.

We also see evidence of this management of public image in debates around how the fast food workers movement has emerged. Despite the fact that most organising tactics that were employed by the community groups contracted by SEIU adhere to what we might think of as 'traditional' organising practices, such as using petitions, phone-calling, and going to workplaces to approach and engage with workers face-to-face, campaigners have been keen to advance a narrative that suggests that social media has been the pivotal instigator of the protests. During participant observation at the protests in New York City on December 5th, 2013 it became clear that most of the fast food workers had become involved in the strike actions through these more traditional practices rather than 'new' forms of digital organising of workers. In fact, the organising and mobilising of fast food workers has been a fairly minimal, and problematic, part of the campaign altogether, which has also attracted criticism from within the organising team and the labour movement more generally. As one activist noted:

> It appears there is a lot of turnover with the workers. In other words, say in a city you have 200 workers that go out on strike and then three months later 300 workers go out on strike. It's not that you have 200 and have added a hundred. It may mean that they have 50–100 left and a lot have fallen away and you have added a lot more. And when you have high turnover among both organisers and workers,

> you're not going to be able to have any sort of shop or organization. (Arun Gupta, labour activist)

This issue of turnover was backed up by one of the organisers from NYCC as well: 'Say there were a hundred workers last year who went on strike, I would be shocked to find that there are 30 of them who are still involved.' Partly such issues in organising are rooted in the long-running and intensive fear-mongering and union-busting techniques that corporations like fast food companies have engaged in for years, making workers very scared and fearful of taking action with the risk of losing their jobs. However, importantly, it also speaks to the lack of empowerment and control that fast food workers may have felt within the movement.

Working with and involving community groups in such a context actually provides more than perceived better organisers, they are also able to crucially increase numbers at protests and rallies, making actions look bigger and the number of workers striking appear greater than what is actually the case. This was highlighted by an organiser:

> Especially if you are talking about grassroots organisations, membership is huge, and being able to draw on these different organisations when you have a rally or you have a strike. You can say, well look, we have about 300 people but only about 70–80 of those people are actually fast food workers. ('John', NYCC organizer)

Although solidarity actions and the bridging of both workers and non-workers during industrial action is a proud and long-standing tradition within the labour movement, in the instance of the fast food workers, the overwhelming discrepancy between the spectacle and the reality of the involvement of fast food workers has led some critical voices to describe the movement as a 'virtual movement' (Arun Gupta, labour activist) in which appearance trumps what is happening on the ground.

Despite the lack of actual organising, and certainly the lack of organising via social media, and the very tightly managed development of the campaign by the SEIU, a very different narrative has been constructed about the fast food workers movement in public debate and this phenomenon warrants some discussion. As outlined above, much coverage of the campaign in the mainstream media has referred to its 'socially organized' construction, its grassroots-driven nature, and a general spontaneity surrounding its emergence. As already mentioned, we can think about how the use of community organisers and the creation of a coalition of supporting groups has been part of creating such a narrative. Indeed, pursuing an organising strategy that substantially incorporates community and informal groups has been useful in distancing union 'baggage' and institutional bureaucracy from the campaign and affiliating it instead to the recent waves of 'new' protest movements that are widely perceived to be more spontaneous, horizontal and grassroots-driven than more traditional forms of political activism such as trade unionism (as discussed in chapter three). This was also the sentiment expressed by one of the organisers in Washington, DC:

> I think [SEIU] wanted to give the image that this is a worker-driven campaign and that they are not actually pulling the strings but that it's the workers who have taken the lead and taken the initiative to start the campaign and then continue to take the lead and I think the SEIU is just essentially using that as a way to give the campaign an air of credibility. ('Judy', social media co-ordinator, #Fightfor15)

As part of this narrative that links the fast food protests to the sort of discourses that surround 'new' protest movements in terms of its movement infrastructure and tactics there is a significant role attributed to social media. Despite the absence of social media from the organising stages of the initiative, organisers and PR consultants for the campaign have been keen to advance the argument that social media has been the driving force behind the spontaneous mobilisation and organisation of fast food workers. A public relations officer involved in the campaign said in a phone interview that 'this is the way most workers have come to us' (Daniel Massey, public relations officer at Berlin Rosen). Although the social media spectacle created around the 'flash-strikes' has certainly made the actions more visible in a way that would have aided mobilisation and awareness amongst fast food workers that the campaign was developing, organisers who were interviewed consistently said that predominantly, the fast food workers who were involved had initially been approached in and around the workplace by organisers, and, moreover, they are small in number. This is also consistent with fieldnotes made during participant observation at the December 5th rally where the fast food workers present had mostly become involved in this way. Rather, social media activity has more been an extension of public relations and communications strategies than an organising tool, used predominantly by dedicated communications officers for the campaign and not fast food workers themselves as is common in the trade union movement. In fact, a social media coordinator for the campaign made a pertinent point when she described how social media became a tool to create a particular narrative about the nature of the movement: 'we basically used Twitter to make the scripted things that workers were saying seem spontaneous' ('Judy', social media coordinator, #Fightfor15).

The fast food worker protests have entered public debate in an incredibly effective and uncharacteristic way in comparison to previous labour movements, which has partly relied on a narrative of spontaneity, horizontalism and grassroots political organising that may to a certain extent be more of a myth than representative of the actual emergence of the movement. Part of this narrative has also come about through the focus on social media, not just by public relations and communications officers for the campaign, but also by mainstream media who have been keen to situate the actions within a longer narrative of 'new' protest movements in which social media is seen to be a driving force. What such a social media narrative has allowed for is to grant the movement a sense of legitimacy and credibility. This speaks to a 'new authenticity' of protest that is partly created by the broader discourses surrounding social media's role in the mobilisation of movements, evidenced particularly in journalistic biases towards social media as an 'authentic' voice in times of crises (Dencik, 2015; Chouliaraki & Blaagaard, 2013; Allan, 2013). For example, Williams, Wahl-Jorgensen and Wardle (2011) found in their focus group research with audiences of BBC user-generated content that the high audience approval for the inclusion of amateur content is linked to a perception of it being authentic, more 'real' and less 'packaged' than news produced solely by journalists. This perception of increased realism is closely linked to the idea that such news is more immediate and that it adds drama and human emotion to a cultural form that is often understood to be dry and distanced from 'ordinary people'. Interestingly, Williams et al. (2011) found that this 'perceived authenticity' of user-generated content is highly valued by journalists and, in the case of reporting news, it is strategically used by journalists to enliven conventional news reports and construct the *impression* of authenticity.

As seen with the case of the fast food campaign, this perceived oppositional framework that contrasts social media platforms with other forms of organisations and communication networks that are deemed to have institutional structures in place that distort or manipulate activity according to interests and agendas may also have significant relevance in our understanding of contemporary forms of resistance. Partly, perhaps, due to journalists' own interest in it, a discourse around social media and protests has emerged that suggests not only that social media is integral to the organising and mobilising of people, but also that movements that are closely associated with social media activity are somehow more horizontal, more inclusive and participatory, broadly free from top-down institutional agendas and interests, and as such ultimately more 'authentic'. As Couldry (2013) has argued, social media companies and commentators have jointly advanced a 'myth of us': the generating of the idea that platforms like Facebook underpin a kind of natural collectivity. In this myth, media institutions seem to drop out from the picture altogether and, rather, 'the story is focused entirely on what "we" do naturally, when we have the chance to keep in touch with each other, as of course we want to do' (Couldry, 2013). In this way, the institutional frameworks that surround social media platforms are removed from the equation. As we have seen in this chapter, such 'disappearance' of institutional frameworks also extends beyond media institutions. In the case of the fast food worker protests, the extensive use of social media by organisers and union officials around the protest days has been part of building a narrative of social media as a key driver of the campaign that has been advanced in conjunction with a broader marketing strategy to present the movement as spontaneous, worker-led, and importantly, not directly affiliated with traditional trade union institutions. The heavy social media presence in the fast food worker campaign has helped give the protests a sense that they have emerged out of workers themselves taking action and speaking out for better working conditions and that they, therefore, have been organised outside of bureaucratic, hierarchical union frameworks that carry historical baggage and are associated with much narrower strategic and political interests. Rather, mediating the movement through social media platforms grants the protests a sense that they are more autonomous, grassroots-driven, and ultimately, more 'authentic' than traditional trade union movements. This has proved strategically very successful in the sense that the campaign has been able to garner significant sympathetic media coverage and fast food workers have entered public debate as a symbolic voice against social injustice within the United States. However, it raises questions regarding the organisational infrastructures of such a movement and it reintroduces long-standing debates regarding prefigurative politics and the 'co-optation' of tactics associated with libertarian principles without broader structural changes in how unions position themselves in relation to state and capital. The fast food worker protests in many ways speak to the extensive union consideration of how resistance to corporate power needs to be approached in the context of the modern world-system and the place of trade unions in this. The success of the campaign in terms of policy changes and media attention, which has grown subsequently to the period of research, has been contingent on this restructured approach to worker resistance. It does, however, also introduce some important questions with regards to the sustainability of such a movement beyond media attention and towards long-term worker control that suits the spirit of its created narrative.

Conclusion

The development of Fast Food Forward and the growing Fightfor15 campaign for higher wages among fast food workers represents a key moment within the labour movement, particularly in the United States. In many aspects it speaks to an unprecedented period of social experimentation within organised labour in response to growing global corporate power and the emergence of a new culture of protest and resistance across society. The initiative to mobilise and organise fast food workers in the United States has been structured around a prominent role of community and grassroots groups to carry out one-day 'flash-strikes' that have been promoted and funded by the SEIU, one of the biggest trade unions in the United States with a long and complicated history. This has allowed for a very successful campaign in some respects that has been favourably incorporated into public debate as a continuation of recent 'new' protest movements, especially Occupy, in which fast food workers have become the new symbols of inequality and social injustice, especially in the mainstream media, rather than instigators of industrial action in the hands of big trade unions out to promote institutional interests and agendas. In fact, relatively few fast food workers have been part of the campaign and rather than seeking to organise individual fast food shops or particular workplaces, union officials and organisers have sought to advance workers' interests by embarking on a very successful advocacy campaign targeting policy on wages. Indeed, behind closed doors, SEIU officials themselves have outlined that the power of the campaign lies in public image, not in industrial power (SEIU official, personal communication).

The emphasis on investing in professional public relations for the campaign speaks to this focus on public image and the media practices of the movement is testament to the multifaceted and complex ways developments in media technologies relate to these kinds of 'new' forms of worker resistance. In many ways, the relationship becomes rather contradictory. Social media activity grants a kind of visibility to the protests that is based on quick and short-term actions that have a tightly managed message in order to target media and political elites. Simultaneously, the use of social media also allows for a narrative of spontaneity, grassroots organising and deinstitutionalisation to emerge that affords protest movements a sense of 'authenticity' in broader society. Along with this, the (social) media emphasis of the fast food workers campaign, with regards to not only PR and activist uses but also with regards to the broader construct of narratives, come to illustrate some pertinent tensions and negotiations within contemporary labour movements and amongst labour activists about the nature of worker resistance, and the role of unions, in the current context. If practices of social media become an increasingly important part of resistance movements, but are primarily concerned with visibility and advocacy, this tends to favour fast and short-term actions of spectacle, and this risks neglecting the solid relationships that are necessary to sustain any campaign or organising drive over time. What is more, it may turn unions into a kind of pressure group that relies on (social) media spectacles to put pressure on political and corporate elites rather than relying on broader social solidarity networks and industrial power. As one of the fast food organisers replied whilst reflecting on whether the campaign could be considered a success:

> As far as the campaign's goals, it was successful, that the main goal they were fighting for was a minimum wage increase for federal contract workers…I think as far as actually achieving tangible workers' rights and better conditions, that wasn't achieved at all through this campaign. I think that can only happen through workers' self-organisation and through forming into unions. ('Judy', social media coordinator, #Fightfor15)

Direct action may be an increasingly key component of unionism as unions are faced with decreasing membership and broken political partnerships, but the question is the extent to which such direct action emerges out of an organised workforce rather than a social media constructed 'virtual' form of protest movement. This, then, becomes not so much about a move to social movement unionism, but rather about whether unions should redefine themselves as non-organising bodies that put their resources into advocacy campaigns on issues of social justice more broadly that affect their members. As Weissman (2014) enthusiastically argued, the fast food workers strikes should not be seen as an effort to improve conditions for a particular group of workers or an attempt to unionise particular workplaces, but are more appropriately understood as spearheading a broader living wage movement. For Weissman this may be considered a 'stunning success for organised labour', but it also raises a fundamental question regarding the purpose of unions in the twenty-first century.

· 6 ·

THE DOMESTIC WORKERS MOVEMENT—CONNECTING INFORMAL LABOUR

The organising of domestic workers is celebrated as one of the biggest success stories of the labour movement in recent years. Despite the age of the profession, domestic workers have historically been operating on the margins of the global economy, excluded by national labour laws, government policies and trade unions. Data on the size of the workforce are difficult to collect due to the high degree of informality of the sector, but estimates suggest there are at least 53 million domestic workers worldwide, not including child domestic workers, and this number is increasing steadily in developed and developing countries. Eighty-three percent of them are women (ILO, 2014). This workforce has been the backbone of global corporate growth in the last 30 years by sustaining 'global cities' (Sassen, 1991) through the fulfilment of tasks and duties at low cost such as cleaning, cooking, child-care, and nursing, not otherwise sufficiently supplied by the state. Such services have enabled sections of the middle classes and the growing 'transnational capitalist class' (Sklair, 2002) to work longer and flexible hours away from home in the interest of capital. Keeping this labour informal has meant that the contribution these workers are making to GDPs often goes entirely unrecognised.

Over the last few years, however, there have been significant developments towards formalising this 'invisible' workforce within a union framework, pushing domestic workers out of the shadows to become recognised globally as workers. In particular, the domestic workers movement highlight the advancement of global unionism within the labour movement as discussed in chapter two and the role that global union federations (GUFs) might play in advancing workers' rights in different national contexts. The adoption of the Domestic Workers Convention (C189) by the International Labour Organisation (ILO) in June 2011 and the establishment of the International Domestic Workers Federation (IDWF) in October 2013 marked the international formalisation of a growing global domestic workers movement. This movement is emerging out of a largely informal network of organisations and groups that are deeply entrenched in long-standing migrant community networks and solidarities. It is characterised by a prominent role for non-governmental organisations (NOGs) and associations that have been at the forefront of engaging with these marginal communities around discourses of human rights, legal and physical protection, and female empowerment in conjunction with GUFs and an appeal to international solidarity. The individualised and 'hidden' nature of domestic work, with workers (predominantly having migrated from elsewhere) working for an individual employer within a household, has in this regard significantly shaped the ways in which this movement has been able to develop. It therefore represents a unique set of challenges within the global labour movement and illustrates the multitude of ways in which worker resistance is manifesting itself in the contemporary world-system in relation to state and capital.

The media practices of this domestic workers movement are contingent upon these particular features of the workforce and their working conditions, and are symbolic of how, alongside developments in digital media technologies, unions and labour organisations are becoming integrated into increasingly complex communication networks that cut across formal and informal groups and communities. This chapter will outline some of the recent developments in the organising of domestic workers globally, before exploring, in particular, the ways in which social media practices are being incorporated into the broader mobilising and organising of domestic workers in the part of the world where most domestic workers can be found, namely South east Asia. Based on interviews conducted during fieldwork in the region in July 2014, the chapter will focus on two contrasting contexts for organising domestic workers—Hong Kong and Singapore—where there has been a long tradition of employing migrant domestic workers to support the economy, but with very different policies and regulations for how domestic workers are able to mobilise and improve working conditions. In particular, the migration of Filipino workers within the region occupies a significant history in how domestic work has come to be known and practiced in both Hong Kong and Singapore. This community is crucial to understanding the nature of the domestic workers movement within these contexts. As will be outlined in this chapter, what is of particular interest is the way in which digital and social media in both Hong Kong and Singapore has been advanced as part of a prominent NGO advocacy presence within the campaign for better working conditions, but has had limited use in organising and incorporating actual domestic workers themselves into a strong collective movement. Rather, most engagement with social media amongst Filipino migrant domestic workers remains as an extension of transnational family communication networks; largely individualised, largely informal, and largely outside the sphere of activism. These practices, however, illustrate the extent to which migrant domestic workers are embedded in everyday online communities. Through common experiences this can express significant virtual forms of solidarity, but they are often disconnected from broader acts of struggle to empower and advance the interests of domestic workers within the framework of workers' rights and organised labour. Rather, these acts remain in the hands of a small group of leaders, union officials, and overwhelmingly (male) human rights campaigners drawing upon a model of global unionism as a strategic tool to put pressure on national governments.

From 'Helpers' to 'Workers'—A Global Campaign

One of the primary struggles of the domestic workers movement has been the recognition of this sector as actual *labour*. As is familiar within long-standing debates on gender politics, work within the household rarely gets recognised as actual work (Waring, 1990). This also extends to migrant women employed within households that have been predominantly referred to as 'maids' or 'domestic helpers', continuing to form part of a depoliticised language that surrounds domestic workers. Indeed, Tom Grundy from the Hong Kong Domestic Helpers Campaign said in an interview that they deliberately use the term 'helper' for search-optimisation purposes as it is the one most frequently used in debates on domestic work. These discursive choices are indicative of the position of domestic workers within the global labour market. The regional organiser from the International Domestic Workers Network (IDWN), who goes by the nickname Fish, explained that often employers 'do not feel that they are employing a worker' (Fish, regional organiser at IDWN). Moreover, a large part of domestic work takes place in the shadow economy. One reason is that the employer and the domestic worker both save paying taxes and social security benefits; another is that the domestic service sector has become a key market for migrant workers who often have limited chances to enter the formal labour market without legal status or without recognised formal skills (Heimeshoss & Schwenken, 2011). In the United States, an estimated 23% of those in private household employment were unauthorised immigrants in 2008 (ibid). Wages are usually low with some households simply providing food and board in exchange for domestic work. This is a problem of compulsory live-in employment for domestic workers in many parts of the world, including Hong Kong and Singapore.

These circumstances also mean that in many countries, domestic workers are not included in national labour laws. In Hong Kong, domestic workers are covered by the employment ordinance, which is rare in Asia. However, as migrant workers they find their protections often undermined by the immigration ordinance, which is an informal way to exclude domestic workers from labour-related laws. That is, regulations and protections in place for workers in general may often be undermined by regulations regarding immigrants that remove these protections for migrant workers, most of whom are domestic workers. What is more, some legislation seeks to explicitly exclude domestic workers, such as the recent ordinance on the minimum wage, which is said to be counted in terms of hours and therefore not applicable to the nature of domestic work (Fish, regional organiser at IDWN). In Singapore, as in many other countries in Asia, domestic workers are not included in employment law and labour related policies altogether, lacking formal recognition as 'workers'. They therefore also have very limited protection or rights, including the right to organise unions, and as migrant workers occupy an incredibly precarious position within the domestic labour market, continuously living in fear of being deported.

The lack of recognition of domestic workers as workers is not just a problem within governments but also extends to unions. As Elizabeth Tang, chief executive for IDWN, pointed out in an interview,

> In the unions' world, they never thought about domestic workers when they tried to think about who to organise.' In recent years, however, this has changed, at least at a formal level: 'the unions also feel [domestic workers] are not workers (…) Nowadays

> no union, I think even the most conservative one, will not say something like this. Maybe they think like this but they dare not say it. (Elizabeth Tang, chief executive at IDWN)

Important to this has been the trend towards global unionism in organising domestic workers. Although GUFs have faced a lot of criticisms over the years, acting predominantly on a symbolic level with little ability to enforce changes in practice, for labour activists concerned with domestic workers, they have been crucial. Most importantly, getting a Domestic Workers Convention adopted at the ILO has allowed for a global standard to be put in place in which domestic work is actually recognised as labour, a significant achievement. This has, in turn, acted as a pressure point upon national governments to conform to global standards. In the Convention the sector is defined as (a) the term *domestic work* means work performed in or for a household or households; and (b) the term *domestic worker* means any person engaged in domestic work within an employment relationship. It also states that (c) a person who performs domestic work only occasionally or sporadically and not on an occupational basis is not a domestic worker (ILO, 2011). This definition and the adoption of the convention has grown out of previous failed attempts. An initiative at the United Nations 4th World Conference on Women in 1995 to build an International Network of Workers in Domestic Service never materialised:

> The global labour movement was still focused on "waged" workers and on formal employment relations, and there was no momentum to support the domestic workers' initiative. Actions to organise domestic workers remained largely at the local level. (Mather, 2013, p. 3)

The first global conference for domestic workers' organisations took place in 2006 in Amsterdam under the title 'Protection for Domestic Workers!'. Hosted by the Dutch trade union confederation, it became important to include unions in what has been—and continues to be as will be further outlined below—a heavily NGO-led movement. As Elizabeth Tang from IDWN said, reflecting on her organising efforts,

> I remember when I started to organise campaigns for the adoption of the convention in 2008 (…) I'm in Hong Kong so I started with the unions around me in Asia and at that time there was almost no union which was interested. I worked with NGOs because they were organising domestic workers or at least they were supportive.

Despite the difficulty in getting unions on board, the 2006 conference agreed to a statement called 'Decent Work for Domestic Workers' that pushed for an ILO Convention on the rights of domestic workers. Upon achieving this in June 2011, the chairperson and previous domestic worker herself Myrtle Witbooi stated:

> On 16 June 2011, our dream became a reality, and we are free—slaves no more, but workers. We cannot stop now. We won't stop until this ILO Convention is carried out. So we have work to do and, yes, we will be united as never before. The voices of domestic workers cannot be silenced. (quoted in Mather, 2013)

The momentum surrounding the ILO Convention illustrates the importance of a formal union structure for the movement: 'domestic workers wanted to have a formal structure; it is their choice (...) if teachers, construction workers, engineers can do it, why can't we?' (Elizabeth Tang, IDWN) It is in this regard that GUFs have come to be significant for organising domestic workers and what motivated the founding congress of an International Domestic Workers Federation in Uruguay in October 2013 as an extension of IDWN that was created in 2009. This formalising of the movement has been particularly important as the nature and conditions of domestic work present a number of challenges for traditional union structures. Not only do unions have to engage with members that might lack basic education and literacy, but issues surrounding lack of salary and precarious wages mean that the regular collection of fees and dues is difficult to implement. The individualised nature of the work also means that there is no collective employer to negotiate or bargain with, nor is it clear whether the employer is the household where the domestic worker works or the agency that organises the placement of domestic workers within households. What is more, in regions such as Asia where domestic work is so widespread, union officials as well as rank and file members will often be employers of domestic workers themselves creating a significant conflict of interest by having employers and domestic workers in the same union.

These issues partly explain the lack of interest that unions have shown in organising domestic workers, but also illustrate why the organising of domestic workers has and continues to be largely informal, dominated to a significant extent by NGOs and informal associations. A key part of the establishment of an International Domestic Workers Federation has therefore been to include only unions as members, largely as a symbolic gesture to signify the sector as becoming a formally organised labour movement: 'when we formalised our structures, we wanted our organisation to be only an organisation of workers but not supporters or advocates' (Elizabeth Tang, chief executive at IDWN). This has involved attempts to make unions a much more central part of the movement working with NGOs and informal associations, rather than operating merely on the margins. This speaks to a concerted effort to move towards a model of social movement unionism within a framework of global unionism in which unions operate within a broader ecology of political activism, cooperating closely with NGOs and other forms of groups and associations, but one in which unions occupy a central ground. As we will see in our discussion of Hong Kong and Singapore, this is difficult to put into practice in contexts in which there are such historical and entrenched constraints on union activity. As recognised by Elizabeth Tang,

> I think we are in such a difficult situation and also traditionally, in many places, it is the civil societies which have been more active in supporting domestic workers. So naturally we work with a wide range of civil society organisations and even professional legal people. (...) But now we try to bring the trade unions in who can help [domestic workers] in talking to the government and bring them to the ILO.

In some ways, therefore, the domestic workers movement is in line with aspects of the broader transformations within the labour movement we have discussed in previous chapters, particularly amongst low-wage workers, in which organising is necessarily being pursued in a more complex, flexible and multifaceted way than what we might think of as traditional trade unionism, and which also involves making use of developments in media technologies. However, in the case of domestic workers, this is being pursued by GUFs as part of a 'catch-up' strategy following years of disinterest and hostility from unions towards the integration of domestic workers into the labour movement, leaving organising and campaigning largely to human rights advocates and migrant community groups.

Migration and Limits to Internationalism

This make-up of the movement is evident in different ways in Hong Kong and Singapore. As a place where unionising domestic workers is legal, Hong Kong has been at the forefront of the domestic workers movement within Asia and it is where much activity is located and developed from. However, in comparison to many other places, the domestic workers movement within Hong Kong is deeply fragmented and is dominated by non-union forms of organisations. There are over 200 registered organisations in Hong Kong working with domestic workers in some form or another, often under the broader label of migrant workers (Parker, 2014). Most of these are associations or NGOs that are either based on some common hobby or interest or concerned with a particular issue or aspect of the lives of domestic workers, such as providing legal advice or shelter. What is more, they are often catering to a specific migrant national group, such as Filipino, Indonesian or Thai domestic workers. This division along nationalities is prevalent amongst the unions as well and is an outcome of earlier efforts to organise domestic workers in a more transnational manner with the Asian Domestic Workers Union (ADWU) formed in 1989. This union was dissolved in the early 2000s with migrant domestic workers preferring to organise along their own nationalities. Rex, a labour activist involved in the ADWU in the 1990s, explained this: 'It was difficult to manage because the concerns of the Filipinos in Hong Kong were common with Thais and others but the national problems were unique; like, for example, when they were campaigning to oust Marcos. So the union has to take a stand but then the Thais would say we don't care who your President is.' Another activist who wanted to remain anonymous on this point said in a more frustrated tone: 'they don't talk to each other, and they're all asking for the same thing and there's a repetition of roles as well and they all talk about capacity and this kind of thing but there's very little teaming up.' He went on, 'our small effort to try and unite some of these groups under very simple, uncontroversial ideas was met with a wall of resistance because I guess there's decades of politics and history which have resulted in this situation.' As such, the multitude of factions that make up the domestic workers movement within Hong Kong have developed out of a combination of the different national landscapes that continue to have significance amongst migrant workers. What is more, issues of different history and culture, not least language, were pointed out by several other organisers as significant dividing aspects within the movement. This is not to say that cooperation between the different groups is absent from the movement; a Hong Kong Federation of Asian Domestic Workers Unions (FADWU) was established in 2009, for example, under the organising efforts of the Hong Kong Confederation of Trade Unions that actively seeks to bring forth a collective voice. However, as we have noted earlier, particularly amongst low-wage migrant workers, the fragmented nature of the movement remains one of its defining features.

In Singapore, the divisions along national lines is less obvious but this is largely due to the limited activity in domestic workers organising in comparison to Hong Kong. Unionising domestic workers is illegal in Singapore and any organising or campaigning is therefore necessarily done outside any form of trade union framework and is primarily carried out by two NGOs, Transient Workers Count Too (TWC2) and Humanitarian Organisation for Migrant Employees (HOME). Although both these organisations approach domestic workers campaigning across national migrant groups, the infrastructure and everyday practices of the organisations illustrate the separation of different community groups along national lines even within these organisations. For example, both these NGOs work with the two largest informal groups amongst domestic workers, the Filipino Family Network and the Indonesian Family Network. What is more, different groups and segments within the organisations are oriented towards different specific community interests that often divide along national lines in which hobbies and social activities organised by NGOs as opportunities for domestic workers to meet tend to be dominated by one particular national group.

Building solidarity across different migrant nationalities is not a straightforward task. Apart from the language barriers, there are also issues regarding the demographics and terms and conditions under which different migrant groups enter the country. For example, Filipino domestic workers tend to be older and will frequently have university degrees, whereas Indonesian domestic workers tend to be younger and with less formal education. What is more, Filipino domestic workers have a longer history in both Hong Kong and Singapore and therefore are prone to see the rapid influx of Indonesian domestic workers, which as a workforce has grown dramatically in the last decade, as a threat and as potentially undermining the sector by accepting worse working conditions and pay. This also has implications for organising collectively and it is the Filipinos that tend to be prominent in the organising of migrant domestic workers more broadly: 'they can easily run a programme on their own and also talk about human rights…maybe they have the time when they fight against a dictatorship and they have good education backgrounds' (Fish, regional organiser at IDWN). On the other hand, several organisers pointed out that it tends to be the young Indonesians who are more militant and willing to take to the streets to protest. Key to organising is, therefore, to create mutual understandings between different groups. This can prove a real challenge, but as Fish from IDWN pointed out, these divisions are often overcome by the shared experience of being migrant workers, a theme that also emerges in our chapter on the Justice for Cleaners movement. Where the real difficulties lie are in creating sustained solidarity between local and migrant domestic workers. This is, again, largely to do with perceived threats and insecurity: '[The] Hong Kong government is all the way saying that this foreign labour is taking away your jobs. So this kind of thing is really deep in the very marginalised local workers. It's very difficult to solve' (Fish, regional organiser at IDWN). As we have discussed in previous chapters, the visions of internationalism that have always been prevalent within the labour movement continuously face this dilemma of imposed competition by state and capital between local and migrant labour.

Therefore, although the international dimension of the domestic workers movement has had important implications in terms of the symbolic significance of formalising the sector, there are real limits to internationalism beyond that, regardless of transformations in media and communication technologies. Certainly communication across borders and between local, regional and global union federations has become easier, but prominent divisions and exclusions remain. Partly this is due to limited access to the technology amongst many domestic workers that simply means they are unable to participate in online discussion and activity in certain parts of the world. More broadly, however, the limits to this virtually-inspired internationalism are contingent upon the dynamics of the actual organising, mobilising and campaigning around domestic workers, which remains localised and community oriented. This is despite indications amongst campaigners and labour activists alike that with migrant workers, in particular, the international dimension is especially important to pursue. For example, Jolovan Wham, an organiser with HOME, one of the major NGOs working with domestic workers in Singapore, said:

> We really need to go international and by that I mean blowing things up. Say, for instance, a Filipino domestic worker who's badly abused [in Singapore], she should have a press conference in the Philippines and get a petition signed over there delivered to the Singapore Embassy. We need to do more of this kind of stuff but at the moment we don't.

Rather, the structure of the movement is based around different silos according to specific country contexts.

Indeed, Alex Au, the media coordinator for TWC2, the other major organisation working with domestic workers in Singapore, backed this up when discussing the media strategy of the organisation:

> If our website begins to look as if we are just an arm of an international network, we will actually have less credibility among Singaporeans. We must sound like Singaporeans speaking to Singaporeans. We must not sound like the mouthpiece of Geneva.

Similarly, Fish from IDWN speaking from Hong Kong said: 'the Hong Kong government responds to local residents. So it means unless you can have enough voice from the local residents who are largely employers of the migrant domestic workers, then maybe you can have some change.' This is important because much discussion on the potentials of the labour movement in a digital media age has concerned the heightened role of international solidarity. Although the pressure of 'global public opinion' may have some impact on domestic policy developments, this remains a marginal concern for campaigners and organisers working with advancing the interests of domestic workers. Rather, efforts in this regard are predominantly targeted at local residents and local activity that are seen to be the key engines of change.

Organising Domestic Workers—Place and Community

The national fractions and local contexts that define the domestic workers movement (also at a global scale) are central to understanding the practices of organising and the place of digital and social media within domestic worker activity. This plays a part not only in terms of the organisational architecture of the movement outlined above, but permeates the lives of migrant domestic workers in general upon which the activities of the movement are contingent. For example, Sunday is a very special day for domestic workers in countries like Hong Kong and Singapore where it is for most domestic workers their only day off. In Singapore, this day off only came into fruition in January 2013 after a ten-year NGO-led campaign, and in fact, it still remains limited to a minority of workers despite it being written into law. For those who are able, however, this day is frequently spent out in public spaces with other domestic workers. This, too, is delineated according to nationalities. In Hong Kong, areas like Central are occupied by Filipino domestic workers in great numbers who spend the day chatting to fellow Filipino domestic workers, sharing food, stories and experiences. By contrast Indonesian domestic workers tend to gather in Causeway Bay and Thai domestic workers in Kowloon Walled City Park. Similarly, in Singapore, Filipino domestic workers gather on Sundays at the shopping district Lucky Plaza, whereas the Indonesians go to another shopping area, City Plaza. Surrounding these locations, an entire sub-industry has emerged in which goods and services are traded and sold to domestic workers, including a saturation of community newspapers, flyers and promotions that are widely distributed. Competing in this commercialised public space are unions and other forms of organisations that seek to reach and mobilise domestic workers. Indeed, in many respects, these public spaces become the 'shop-floor' for the domestic workers movement where 'traditional' organising tactics can take place, which still dominate organising practices within the movement, both in Hong Kong and Singapore. By this is meant that emphasis amongst organisers continues to be placed on meeting in physical locations and on face-to-face interaction above other types of activities. This is not limited to vast open public spaces but also includes religious institutions, such as reaching Filipino domestic workers within the context of the Catholic Church. As an organiser with an NGO offering legal advice to domestic workers in Hong Kong explained:

> Filipinos, especially, are very religious and they belong to churches and when they arrive in Hong Kong that's where they find their sense of belonging. So on Sundays we go to church and talk to Filipinos. And I think it's the same for the Indonesians and the mosque. (Holly, Helping Domestic Helpers)

This type of 'outreach' work is complemented by the arrangement of a host of different activities on Sundays by a cross-section of organisations that will allow for domestic workers to meet and engage with each other. Fish, from IDWN, explained that this will often involve a sense of sharing, for example through cooking together, or handicraft, or other types of interests:

> In this gathering, the domestic workers will share something. Sometimes they share the cooking so that they make themselves happy and also they feel they have more confidence because if you cook for your [employer] family, nobody appreciates it but you come to our sisterhood gathering, all people will feel this is so good and then they share and they feel I can become somebody.

In Singapore, HOME has different organised groups in which activities can take place, whether playing sports, taking cooking classes, or writing for the NGO newsletter. These activities allow for relationships to be built, solidarities to emerge and provide a context in which stories can be shared, problems discussed, and organising can take place. As Leo, an organiser from the Hong Kong Confederation of Trade Unions (HKCTU) also outlined: 'On Sunday they will have their activities and then they will connect them and then in their activity or at the end of their activity, they will give some information from the union and then that is their way to organise.' In Singapore, where union activity is not allowed, these activities become part of building and sustaining communities where domestic workers can informally seek help, find out information about their rights, and discuss how to push for changes.

Crucially organising through these types of activities allows for mobilisation and resistance to remain predominantly a social form of practice, rather than political. This depoliticisation of practices is something that permeates the movement partly because of the dominant role of NGOs, associations and informal groups in the way the movement is organised: '[Unions'] appearance and nature seem more political and it makes a boundary because some of [the domestic workers] may think it's a political organisation and they don't want to join them' (Leo, organiser with HKCTU). What is more, in places like Hong Kong where although unionisation is legal, collective bargaining is not, and unionisation remains marginal across the labour force:

> Even for local people, it's very seldom [that they are] a member of a union. So how do you ask even migrant workers to join a union? And unions, we have to collect the membership fee because as a union our mission is [that] the union is supported by workers. So even now maybe we are not strong enough, we still have a principle which is we have to collect the membership fee. So this is kind of a boundary but we keep it. (Leo, organiser with HKCTU)

In particular, it becomes an issue to define the purpose of unions in such a context:

> There are many groups among the migrant domestic workers, which is good, but then how can the workers be able to know what's the difference between just a group or a union? There are also groups who also fight for rights, so how can you persuade the domestic workers to pay for a membership fee to sustain their own union, and then the fighting for rights is quite hard. This is very difficult. (Elizabeth Tang, chief executive at IDWN)

Therefore, organising migrant domestic workers in actual local contexts comes to be embedded in networks of community groups, in which informal and social mobilisations are highlighted forms of activity. Apart from a reluctance to be seen to be too 'political', which is partly due to the fears of migrant workers that they are vulnerable to deportation, the movement is marked by what Fish from IDWN called 'friends, friends, friends' Whether this be through meeting in open public spaces on Sundays, or cooking and eating together in the offices of one of the organisations of which they are a member, or even speaking to other neighbouring domestic workers whilst walking the dog, these informal and social networks have been and continue to be the underlying feature of the movement, despite the move to formal structures at a global level.

Out of these practices emerge moments of visible resistance, such as public events to lobby for a change in policy or protesting outside the embassy of their home country. Often these events will have developed out of organising tactics such as petitions where domestic workers can be approached to sign their name to a certain issue. For example, Jolovan Wham from HOME explained how they went about organising for a change in policy in 2012 that concerned the safety of domestic workers working in high-rise buildings after a series of accidents where domestic workers had fallen, pushing for tighter regulations:

> What we did was we organised a petition among the domestic workers and we got them to sign, which we submitted to the Minister and to the Indonesian Embassy because many of the domestic workers who were falling off the windows were Indonesian.

These forms of actions are also backed up by research, with organising being done by conducting surveys amongst domestic workers about their working conditions, partly as a way to provide evidence for lobbying, but, perhaps more importantly, as a tactic to engage with domestic workers and alert them of their rights and possibilities for resistance. This is especially the case in Singapore where union activities or the organising of protests are not allowed and these research oriented routes to reaching domestic workers gain greater significance for the movement.

However, often these visible forms of resistance are not necessarily connected to these informal and, perhaps, largely invisible networks of solidarity that mark domestic workers as community groups. Rather, these visible forms of resistance come to be enacted by the formal structures in place, such as local union officials and campaigners or Western-led and/or Western-funded NGOs that come to speak on behalf of migrant domestic workers. As Jolovan Wham from HOME said regarding the One Day Off campaign in Singapore:

> Not too many domestic workers were involved in [the One Day Off campaign] actually. I think at the time the decision was that Singaporeans had to do it. We felt that way because domestic workers, politically the government didn't care what they thought. So even if you had like 10,000 signatures from domestic workers, we didn't

> think that was something which the government would take seriously. How we got them involved was to get their feedback and to hear what they had to say about the issue and what it was that they wanted. But the people who fronted it were mostly Singaporeans. The only way in which we could get their voices heard was to mediate it through us, and this is actually what's happening at the moment still. It still tends to be the Singaporeans who are talking and giving the comments and being the voice. We are the ones who meet policymakers as opposed to the migrant workers themselves.

The issue of making the voice of domestic workers their own rather than being represented for them by an external actor is also partly what has driven activists to push for unions to become more involved and occupy a central role in the movement. As labour activist Rex outlined with regards to his role in pushing for this vision within the Asian Migrant Centre in Hong Kong:

> What we have done is we said we are conscious that NGOs are not representative organisations. They are beholden to their board or funders. So we have always advocated in our centre that the main organising force, if you are to empower domestic workers or women, is how to be a trade union movement because they are the most stable that are there.

Similarly, in Singapore, activists from NGOs recognise the limitations of 'own voice' in the current architecture of the movement:

> I would like it to be possible for domestic workers to form their own union but we shouldn't be a substitute union; we're not and that's not our function. I would hope that we'll evolve to a situation where we become irrelevant to things and let workers have their own institutions which are effective, and that that's just accepted as part of the way things are. But we're not there at the moment so that's why we need to carry on. (John Gee, organiser with TWC2)

Social Media and (Dis)Connected Networks of Resistance

It is within this context that we also have to understand the nature of new and social media practices within the movement. Although developments in new media technologies have not been at the forefront of public debate in discussing events surrounding the struggle to improve working conditions for domestic workers in a way that may have been more the case in our other case studies, they have certainly been recognised as significant in some aspects. *The Guardian*, for example, reported on protests taking place in Hong Kong in

February 2014 that 'social media ensures that information spreads fast, particularly since domestic workers are unusually dependent on their mobile phones for communication with the outside world' (Branigan, 2014). In another article, there was a particular reference to apps such as Viber and WhatsApp as significant communication tools for mobilising and organising amongst migrant domestic workers (Young, 2014). The question of how organisers, activists and domestic workers engage with digital and social media reflect broader structures of the movement, as outlined above. That is, it is defined by national enclaves of community groups that are largely informal and invisible and mainly made up of migrant domestic workers on the one hand, and policy-oriented advocacy campaigning that represent more formalised, visible forms of resistance, on the other and are mainly made up of local or Western organisers and activists. Although there may be some integration between these practices, perhaps especially in moments of outreach, the broader architecture of the movement also limits the possibilities for workers themselves to become the visible faction of the movement's media practices. The domestic workers movement as a case study reveals the ways in which digital media practices do not necessarily 'connect' actors as is often implied in debates surrounding social media and activism (see chapter three) but may also extend and entrench disconnected actors within a movement.

Most organisations and groups involved with domestic workers rights and conditions have a particular online media element to their practices both in Hong Kong and Singapore. That is, organisations will have websites and/or Facebook pages that are considered to be important for their everyday practices. A dominant aspect of this online presence is concerned with advocacy and campaigning that operates in conjunction with more 'traditional' media practices. This is clearly outlined in the case of the One Day Off campaign in Singapore for example. As John Gee from TWC2 explained:

> There were reports that would highlight the issue, how important it was for the domestic workers' rights and also for her effectiveness as a worker (…) We did press releases on it, provided information to the media (…) we could put articles in our newsletters so that would get messages out to our members. We did interviews with the press. We also wrote articles which got into the media. So it was just a matter of just over a long period of time trying to find every way possible of highlighting the issue.

This was also supported by advocacy by HOME that would upload digestible videos about the campaign. Both HOME and TWC2 have 'storytelling' (Alex Au, media coordinator for TWC2) online sites that they use to write stories with their own voice. Similarly, in Hong Kong issues concerning domestic workers get outlined and described via the online sites of organisations and associations. Key issues have gone 'viral' worldwide according to Tom Grundy from the Hong Kong Helpers Campaign, 'through professional photography and videography and not long-form articles and these kinds of efforts, but more of a kind of viral accessible means.' The target of these digital media practices are often predominantly what may be thought of as 'traditional' mainstream media. As Jolovan Wham from HOME said:

> Despite how I feel about mainstream media, the government still takes what they say very seriously, which is why it's always good to get them to write stuff the way you want them to write because when it gets published, we know that it has the attention of the politicians.

In addition to domestic mainstream media, a key actor in this media strategy is the foreign media and campaigning for their attention. Indeed, both in Hong Kong and Singapore, campaigners regarded foreign news coverage as crucial for putting pressure on domestic governments: 'We believe that the Chinese spotlight, in Hong Kong especially, if it's coming from abroad it can change and keep the momentum as well in Hong Kong into changing [conditions]' (Tom Grundy, Hong Kong Helpers Campaign). Social media activity will therefore also, in this way, have an international or global dimension.

This interplay between new and old, domestic and foreign media activity can perhaps be seen in the campaign surrounding 'the Erwiana case' more than in any other campaign. Erwiana is an Indonesian domestic worker who worked in Hong Kong for eight months and was seriously abused by her employer. After eight months, in February 2014, she was so ill after being abused that her employer wanted to secretly send her back to Indonesia. The employer took her to the airport for a midnight flight back to Indonesia where, at the gate, she met another Indonesian domestic worker who was going back home for a holiday. This other Indonesian domestic worker took a picture of Erwiana and her physical state and posted it on Facebook. The story was widely picked up and became one of the biggest stories the domestic workers movement has ever seen. The story made both domestic news in Hong Kong and Indonesia, as well as international news in Europe and the US. In April 2014, *TIME* magazine listed Erwiana as one of the 100 most influential people in the world as an 'icon' for migrant workers. There are different understandings as to how and why this story became so significant. There have been previous cases of severe abuse of domestic workers; in fact, only a few months prior to the Erwiana case another domestic worker suffered a similar fate but the story did not garner nearly as much media attention. Partly this was due to the reaction by the Indonesian consulate to previous cases where it has been fast to take over abuse cases and limit attention paid to them. However, some activists interviewed also believe that the Erwiana case grew as a story to some extent due to its social media visibility: 'the thing is for Erwiana you have a photo. It was really a very scary photo which shows a person being seriously abused' (Fish, regional organiser at IDWN). It was therefore also shared widely on the social network and could be picked up by a number of organisations who brought the story forward. One of those organisations was the Hong Kong Helpers Campaign, which made an effort to highlight the story, not as an individual victim story, but as a systemic critique of the working conditions for domestic workers: 'we were able to speak and basically get everyone on the same message and to push the spotlight onto how the government enables this kind of abuse' (Tom Grundy, Hong Kong Helpers Campaign). This allowed for the image of Erwiana to become a symbol for the campaign to change the conditions under which migrant domestic workers are employed within households. In particular, it called for the government to ensure tighter regulation on employment agencies. According to the union organiser in charge of the organising of domestic workers for the HKCTU, the Erwiana case and the media attention it received also acted as a trigger point for mobilising domestic workers:

> After the terrible case of Erwiana, her case showed in the newspapers, especially the Indonesian organisations, including the unions, etc., they actually had two very important rallies; they mobilised more than 3,000 to 5,000 Indonesian workers on the streets. (Leo, organiser with HKCTU)

The Erwiana case, however, is arguably the social media campaigning exception rather than the rule. Social media campaigns are generally not very sophisticated amongst the domestic workers organisations, and it is something most of the organisers and activists interviewed said they wished they could improve on, especially amongst the unions:

> The other groups have a lot of full time people and full time officers, then they really exploit [social media]. That's why they are all over the media and in a way…it's very disempowering because then our unions are saying so why can't you do that? So how do you get people? …[Y]ou also need [media attention] so that you can find a kind of self-affirmation. (Rex, labour activist)

Perhaps more importantly, the connection among informal Facebook groups, formal domestic worker organisations, and the offline mobilisation of domestic workers (as evidenced in the Erwiana case) is not a feature that otherwise defines the role of social media in the domestic worker movement. Indeed, the more prominent feature of the movement is precisely a disconnected relationship among these different activities. That is, the networks that migrant domestic workers operate in have a social media element to them in that they communicate with each other informally using platforms such as Facebook and WhatsApp. These communications are an extension of migrant community dynamics in which social media platforms are used to exchange information both amongst migrant workers, as well as, and perhaps predominantly, with family and friends back in their home countries. The nature and purpose of engagement with social media amongst migrant communities therefore mean that to some extent they are 'always on' (Madianou, 2014) in order to communicate across distant physical locations, which facilitates a level of 'bonding capital' that resides in what Komito (2011) describes as an 'ambient' awareness of others.

In theory, using social media for mobilising amongst migrant domestic workers would, therefore, be an obvious extension of these community practices: 'most of them have to connect with their family by these tools and so that's why most of them are very familiar with Facebook, WhatsApp, Skype. So that's why they can always use it and they have the ability to use it' (Leo, organiser with HKCTU). Indeed, reaching and keeping in contact with workers who may be in difficult situations has been made easier for organisations by many of them engaging with these tools already. As Fish from IDWN said, 'during the daytime when you are working you cannot put the telephone on but the messaging is not so obvious (…) so I can contact some domestic workers through messaging on Facebook or Whatsapp but I cannot call them.' Even within IDWN, there are only four full-time members of staff but another part-time staff member has been brought in who is fully dedicated to doing social media and the website: 'you see how important it is (…) we rely a lot on this technology because it's very, very difficult for us to go to the countries and meet domestic workers' (Elizabeth Tang, chief executive at IDWN). In particular, this means having an online presence for domestic workers organisations that may need resources and assistance. Such a presence may also serve as providing simple practical information about rights and services available to domestic workers.

Certainly, there is also some evidence of social media being used for mobilising workers into collective actions to advance their interests. Labour activist Rex said, 'what democratised our access even for organising was cellphones so we can text them. Now the smartphones also revolutionised it because then they can have Facebook and it makes it more easy.' In particular, this has been seen amongst Indonesian domestic workers in Hong Kong who have been especially active in terms of organising protests: 'the Indonesians use [social media] a lot for organising and also for calls for action. So every time if there is a call for action, they put everything on Facebook and then they forward and share and then they come up with an infographic and share and send to everybody' (Fish, regional organiser at IDWN). These practices that are commonly of the kind that we associate with digital activism, however, do not really stretch across the movement. Rather, social media practices among migrant domestic workers are less about organising and mobilising towards protests and direct action or about organising collectively into formal groups and organisations, and more about informal ways of connecting with other domestic workers from the same communities, exchanging information and stories about their lives as migrant domestic workers, largely without any political motivations. This is often done in rather closed networks of communication, in their own language, that are intended to be a space for workers themselves to connect. As one activist said, 'it's often within the bubble.'

Of course there is an attempt by organisations to 'tap into' these online community groups, either by engaging with domestic workers within these groups, or by providing platforms for them to meet each other according to different interests and hobbies, under the umbrella of the organisation. This, for example, has been the approach of HOME in Singapore, which has been active in using social media to organise migrant domestic workers. The Facebook page *HOME Gabriela* (based on the female Filipino heroine Gabriela Silang who led a revolt against Spain in the eighteenth century), for example, allows for informal connections and exchanges to be made amongst Filipino domestic workers around the world but it also provides a way to inform new workers about the activities of HOME. As domestic worker and organiser Cecilia explained 'we say oh, you want to join Gabriela, you are a domestic worker and you want to join Gabriela, then we will add them. Then they will know there what's been going on with HOME.' However, the non-political tone and content is crucial for making it a space that works for this community:

> We are very careful in posting, like we don't want to hurt the Singapore government and we also don't want to hurt our government or any government of any nationalities. We don't want to complicate ourselves. We are workers yes, we want justice, we want our rights, but not to the extent that we will go against them or whatever rules they have. (Cecilia, Filipino domestic worker and organiser with HOME)

These precautions reach also to the HOME newsletter, an initiative that is, perhaps, the most direct attempt at connecting the informal community with a more formal form of representation where domestic workers themselves have an official platform to voice their issues or concerns. The newsletter 'My Voice' is largely run by domestic workers themselves, with some editorial responsibilities residing with HOME staff, and is intended as a media outlet 'that domestic workers use to express their views on issues' (Jolovan Wham, HOME). However, again, this has a distinctly social and non-political tone in the nature of communication. As Jolovan Wham from HOME explained:

> They can write pretty much whatever they want, as long as it doesn't stray into politics, otherwise we might lose the licence for this because we had to get a permit (…) So we're also very conscious that they shouldn't write anything too critical because they might lose their jobs. (Jolovan Wham, HOME)

Although it is leisure-oriented, creating social media spaces under the umbrella of the organisation has also allowed for the HOME Facebook page to have a wide reach amongst domestic workers that can use it as a platform to ask for help:

> What happens on [the HOME Facebook page] where we have about 17,000 members, every day someone posts something. It's either a question about their employment or a question about what kind of administrative procedures they need to undergo to get a passport or that kind of stuff. So very practical day to day kind of questions that need to be answered and the domestic workers all answer for themselves. It's pretty much like a self-help kind of thing. Only when there's abuse or exploitation, that's when I'll come in. So I will personally say and give my perspective or my opinion on what this particular person should do in such a situation but other than that, it's pretty much self-run. (Jolovan Wham, HOME)

In many ways, these practices illustrate the richness and level of social solidarity that is expressed within these communities connecting online and they speak to the potential of the movement to act collectively as a resistance movement. However, media practices within the domestic workers movement are predominantly not oriented towards organising a form of long-term, sustainable resistance movement, certainly not one that could be visible. Rather, these migrant community networks that are prevalent within the movement remain rather invisible and disconnected from the sometimes rather sophisticated media advocacy campaigns that are specifically targeted at changing government policy and regulation. That is, the strong community networks that underpin the lives of domestic workers have yet to become politicised in a way that allows them to also be the face of their own resistance movement. They themselves are still invisible, on the margins, and in the shadows, continuously suppressed by the precarity of their lives as migrant domestic workers and the fear of retaliation from government and employers. Developments in media technologies have not overcome these much broader structural constraints that limit the possibilities for domestic workers to become empowered and be the voice of their own resistance. As Jolovan Wham from HOME reflected:

> I guess social media is the tool in which you get people to come together to build alliances, to build solidarity (…) really to support one another. Ideally, of course, to push for the kind of change that they want to see. But I think if you are dealing with migrant workers, there are a lot of limitations (…) If you are too aggressive or you're seen to be political, and these things are never defined, the boundaries are never clear, so you just have to police yourself.

Conclusion

What the case of domestic workers, as a labour movement, illustrates, especially in Southeast Asia, is the multitude of opportunities and possibilities that exist for workers to resist corporate exploitation today. Domestic workers have gone from being a labour force that existed largely informally, in the shadows, excluded from national labour and employments laws, and invisible from unions, to being formally recognised as workers by the International Labour Organisation, brought in to a union structure, however nominally, and that is beginning to gain rights through government policy through the adoption of the Convention 189. These developments go against the grain that organising precarious workers is a contemporary impossibility and show rare momentum within the existing structures of organised labour, particularly with regards to GUFs and global unionism. However, the case of domestic workers in Hong Kong and Singapore also illustrates the extreme challenges that surround some of the most marginalised workers in today's corporate dominated global economy that make organising resistance in these circumstances incredibly difficult. Hong Kong and Singapore are two very contrasting political and legislative environments in which migrant domestic workers are a significant part of the workforce and contribute significantly to sustaining and nurturing the growth of global capital in both contexts. In Hong Kong, domestic workers are, formally at least, included in the employment ordinance, recognised as a workforce, and allowed to legally form unions and engage in direct action such as strikes and protests. In Singapore, by contrast, domestic workers are not covered by employment law and by extension are not recognised as workers in any comparative aspect to other sectors of the workforce. They, therefore, also do not have the right to unionise and by Singaporean law do not have the right to stage direct actions such as street protests. Despite these contrasting contexts, however, similarities can be found in the practices of organising migrant domestic workers and the way that media is perceived, used and practiced within what might be thought of as a regional domestic workers movement.

The global dimension of the movement has been important in some aspects. In particular, this has been about providing an international standard to use as a lobbying mechanism to put pressure on the government and, along with that, garnering international media attention to 'shame' domestic governments into changing conditions for migrant domestic workers. However, as a movement of migrants, the transnational character of activities is surprisingly limited. No real coordination exists to build cross-national actions and solidarity, even around the same migrant community that exists in different countries. Rather, international solidarity remains largely symbolic in nature along with the GUF structure that marks the formalisation of the sector within the trade union movement. Instead, organising and campaigning practices are much more concerned with domestic solidarity building across different groups and communities. This is particularly prominent in the media practices of campaigners and advocates of domestic workers' rights who see the main target of their efforts to be advancing a particular public image of the domestic workers movement to local publics and governments. This is especially advanced by NGOs and associations who dominate the representation of the domestic worker voice in public debate. Despite the integration of domestic workers into the trade union movement, the history of a prominent lack of union interest in organising domestic workers means that non-union types of organisations, in particular charities and NGOs, have become the formal face of domestic worker resistance. These groups have engaged with developments in media technologies, not to organise and mobilise domestic workers particularly, but more in ways that may be thought of as a form of media activism in which alternative platforms have been created to provide news and information about the working conditions of domestic workers. These have been created to inform and change perceptions amongst local members of the public, but also, importantly, to communicate directly with and lobby local/national government. In many respects, these media practices and these organisations have become the visible face of the movement. Unions have struggled to develop the same level of sophistication in their media campaigns and have found it challenging to embrace developments in digital media in the same way. Union engagement with media technologies has been primarily in terms of limited outreach using social media. However, organising and mobilising practices continue in what may be considered quite traditional form; going to physical locations such as public spaces where migrant domestic workers gather on their days off, running classes and training in their offices and reaching workers through friendship networks within the community.

Where organising potential using digital media may be much more significant within the movement is largely away from unions, and even other kinds of formal organisations such as NGOs. Rather, solidarity building amongst domestic workers has been built largely through existing community networks that have moved and grown online. Informal networks such as the Filipino Family Network and the Indonesian Family Network in Singapore, or even friendships made in places like Central in Hong Kong, have grown and manifested themselves as online community groups that include different segments of migrant domestic workers. Within these social media networks, connections can be made, information exchanged and stories shared that in many ways are part of building a solid and robust movement that can mobilise around shared interests and form collective actions. However, although these practices are incredibly important for the day-to-day protection and advancement of domestic workers' rights, they remain within 'bubbles' of communication that do not reach institutions of power and do not form into collective, organised networks of resistance. Rather, these practices are largely apolitical, largely individualised and fragmented, and largely invisible from the recognised 'voice' of resistance. This is not to say that these informal exchanges are not significant for our understanding of domestic worker resistance. Indeed, these informal community groups are where domestic workers predominantly engage in activity as domestic workers in solidarity with others. What we do see with these social media practices in the context of the architecture of the movement as a form of resistance, however, is a lack of contact between these informal connections amongst domestic workers and the voice of the movement in confronting exploitation and power. The challenge facing organisers and campaigners as well as domestic workers is how to make these rich networks of solidarity that reside within online communities of migrant domestic workers an expression of collective power in which the resistance against exploitation is led by the voice and actions of domestic workers themselves. The structural constraints and political and economic environments that continue to shape organising and advocacy activities encourage a fragmented and considerably disconnected movement of resistance. Media practices, including the incorporation of social media in movement strategies and activities, are contingent upon this movement infrastructure and rather than necessarily connecting actions and voices, shifting the make-up of resistance, may also come to exacerbate the fragmentation and disconnection that mark the struggle to improve the conditions for domestic workers in such contexts. This, then, becomes part of the challenge facing unions in the twenty-first century.

· 7 ·

ONLINE LABOUR ACTIVISM AND STATE-CORPORATE CONTROL

"It's like holding all your political meetings at McDonald's and ensuring that the police come and film you while you do so." (Yossarian, Indymedia programmer on the use of commercial social media platforms by activists, quoted in Uldam, 2014, p. 10)

As we have argued in this book, the shape and form that worker resistance is taking in the twenty-first century illustrate significant challenges and opportunities for how an organised labour movement can stay relevant and advance workers' interests against increasingly expanding global corporate powers. Our case studies highlight the ways in which developments in media forms, in particular, can become an integral part to new ways of organising, mobilising and campaigning amongst previously unorganised sectors of the labour market. However, they also highlight some of the substantial difficulties that unions and labour organisations are facing in creating democratic, sustainable and strong resistance movements amongst low-wage workers that limit the potentials for changing media practices to challenge global corporate power. When looking at transformations in labour movements and the ways in which digital and social media become integrated into struggles over working conditions it is important not to abstract these technologies from the context in which they are being used. What is more, the nature and development of these technologies have their own histories and processes that need to form part of any analysis. Indeed, social movements and protests have shown over the years that communication and media platforms are not separate from broader power struggles and conflict. Media systems—and the internet—are contingent upon the processes and power relations of the modern world-system, and the ways in which movements are able to engage with these technologies needs to be understood in this context. We have highlighted this by outlining the background to the current crisis of the labour movement and the nature of global corporate power that also informs and shapes engagement with new technologies and digital media practices.

In this chapter we want to continue this contextual approach to understanding the relationship between media forms and worker resistance by also situating the development of digital and social media in the broader context of the modern world-system that becomes significant for understanding the potential of these technologies with regards to struggles over labour and capital. The history of digital media technologies and the struggle over the internet reflects the twin dynamics of Globalisation From Above (GFA) and Globalisation From Below (GFB) that we have outlined throughout this book. From its outset, the development of the internet has reflected the battle over control and ownership of information and content that has combined the military-industrial complex and commercial interests with a counter-culture movement that marked the early philosophy of the internet. The 'new' protest environment that the labour movement now has to navigate in resisting forces of state and capital therefore introduces important questions regarding the autonomy and control of exchanges and communication that takes place within these digitally enabled networks of resistance. As virtual solidarity networks, online communities, and digital advocacy campaigns have become part of contemporary media practices of social movements, so have ever-innovative ways of practicing state-corporate control firmly been incorporated into these mediated processes. In conjunction, corporations and states have sought to find ways to curb, control and direct the activities of activist groups, using a range of technologies and (in)filtration techniques that make up a complex and intensive surveillance regime of both private and government agencies and intermediaries. Simultaneously, the commercialisation of the online space has seen the rise of a digital oligarchy that now in themselves have come to represent the very global corporate power that their platforms and services are being (albeit marginally) used to challenge.

However, at the same time as the internet is increasingly becoming a space in which regulations and policing of online activities overwhelmingly favour the manifestation of state-corporate control, resistance to such control is also proliferating. The battle over the architecture of the internet continues to be fiercely fought over in a multitude of ways, from proactive technological responses to amend the technical infrastructure of the internet to advocacy campaigns and street protests targeted at changing policy and governance structures of the web. In recent years, this type of activism has become ever more pertinent as ownership over digitally produced data is being used as a central currency in contemporary forms of state-corporate control in all aspects of social life. As we will argue in this chapter, if unions are to be a significant force in today's global system as a genuine challenge to state and capital, labour movements will need to be part of this struggle against digital state-corporate control and within a broader political ecology, as in social movement unionism, represent an *independent* source of resistance to contemporary digital developments. This will require an engaged labour movement that is able to make links and connections and build a broad base around workers' interests in a digital economy outside of the corporatist and business union models.

The Struggle Over the Internet: Control and Counter-Control

The history of the internet speaks to the long-standing struggles and relations between state, capital and resistance that mark the modern world-system. Its development is contextualized by a continuous opposition and negotiation between GFA and GFB, incorporating multiple social visions and narratives. It combines forces of control and counter-control and a technology rooted in military expansion as well as conceptual roots in philosophies of counter-culture. Dating back to calculating artillery range tables during World War II, the electronic computer has its origins in the US military as much as its, perhaps more celebrated, origins in the counter-culture revolution of 1960s California that sought to challenge technocratic society and develop technology as a way of giving 'power to the people' (Roszak, 1969). Similarly, the internet developed out of a military and scientific need to share information about research in these fields as well as a vision of the mass popularization of shared information and knowledge as envisioned by such figures as World Wide Web inventor Tim Berners Lee (Barnes, 2010). The development of social media has only furthered these tensions, embedded as it is within a range of features that have long been seen as central to the Web as a communications infrastructure, such as the scope for participation, interactivity, collaborative learning and social networking. As Curran (2010) has pointed out, such developments have served to advance a longer standing narrative and discourse surrounding the transformative potential of technologies for creating a better society. Such 'techno-fantasies' (Curran, 2010) are frequently constructed and circulated. The internet was met early on with widespread enthusiasm because of its impact on the economy, supported by frequent accounts of so-called 'dotcom' entrepreneurs making fortunes in record time. As Curran outlines, for the most part, British newspapers were content to chronicle the accumulation of wealth during the dotcom boom without properly investigating whether it was based on a secure foundation, and neglected to foresee the inevitable dotcom bust before it happened. Similarly, as features of social media have been further and further commercialized, discourses around the potential for entirely new business models based on 'innovative' interactions between producers and consumers in a space free of regulatory constraints have been omnipresent. This free market digital space is said to have introduced a new kind of economy that is markedly different from that of traditional corporate media. As Freedman (2012) outlines, a number of internet commentators, such as *Wired* magazine editor Chris Anderson, coalesce around the notion that web culture is ushering in a far more efficient, creative, smoother, democratic and participatory form of capitalism with a media economy based on niches and not mass markets, on flexibility and not on standardisation, on abundance and not scarcity, and on entrepreneurial start-ups and not on the industrial corporations that dominated the twentieth century. This has allowed for a media market to develop where transaction and distribution costs are so low that 'an entirely new economic model' has emerged, one of 'Free' (Chris Anderson quoted in Freedman, 2012). That is, in the digital economy it is possible to make money by giving things away for 'free' and what matters in this economy is 'linking' rather than 'owning', peer-to-peer exchanges, nodes 'connecting people with information, action, and each other' (Jeff Jarvis quoted in Freedman, 2012). As Freedman puts it, the idea is that in the pre-digital age, innovation largely took place within the walls of the company and inside the laboratory; now, the web allows for collective forms of innovation that originate in garages, bedrooms, studies and living rooms. We have a new 'grassroots' economy, an economy of niches produced by a mass of collaborators; it is highly specialized, but organised on collective principles that profit from the 'wisdom of crowds'.

Accompanying this enthusiasm for the transformative potential of the 'sharing economy' (Benkler, 2006) for business, discourses around the political potentials of these digital technologies, and social media in particular, have also been prevalent. As we have already discussed in chapter three, and evidenced in all our case studies, there has been widespread enthusiasm for a shift in power relations and a new potential for challenging forms of domination and control with the emergence of digital media technologies. The notion has been from the 'cyber-optimist' camp that these technologies provide solutions to significant social problems by facilitating civic engagement, giving voice to the voiceless and allowing for more direct democratic accountability and deliberation between government and citizens (Hacker & Van Dijk, 2000; Fisher & Wright, 2001; Chadwick, 2006). The internet, according to this reading, is seen as a communications medium 'uniquely suited to providing multiple arenas for public debate that are relatively spontaneous, flexible, and above all, self-governed' (Chadwick, 2006, p. 89). What is more, reinvigorated notions of the 'global village' (McLuhan, 1964) and the fostering of new global solidarities and consciousness based on principles of cosmopolitanism have been brought to the fore with the advent of these digital media technologies, particularly social media (Dencik, 2012; Chouliariaki & Blaagaard, 2013). The notion is that in these spaces we form 'natural' collectivities, communicate and mobilise into movements, unrestrained from institutional interests and agendas (Couldry, 2013).

Importantly, Curran (2010) argues that the waves of enthusiasm for the promises of new media for business and society over the last couple of decades have, more often than not, been advanced by the business interests promoting these new media. That is, hyping has come deliberately from interested parties such as companies seeking to expand, politicians seeking to offset the decline of the manufacturing economy with the 'new information economy' and technology experts in industry and universities. These were also promoted by an excited media finding the stress on novelty particularly suited to traditional news values. Moreover, Curran makes the point that these narratives of progress that surround digital media technologies are part of a broader cultural frame at the core of modernity, namely the belief that science and technology is the midwife to social and economic advance.

Such narratives have served to instill digital media with a great deal of power as a discourse of change and progress that, as we have seen in our case studies, can also be effectively and strategically used to advance certain interests and causes. It has also made digital media a key discursive battlefield in geopolitical and diplomatic relations with government leaders scrambling to present their internet infrastructures as the most unregulated as a symbol for broader social and political freedom (Fontaine & Rogers, 2011). However, these narratives become problematic when we start to situate the development of the internet within the broader context of the world-system and start to delineate how internet infrastructures and architectures have come to be increasingly shaped by the interests of state and capital. This presents some significant challenges for the labour movement as they seek to integrate online activism into practices of resistance to corporate power.

The Political Economy of Digital Media: Exploiting Participation

What much of the debate surrounding the transformative potential of digital media and the internet lacks, especially with regards to digital activism and the possibilities for grassroots-driven social change, is a substantial consideration for the important processes that shape the very infrastructure and architecture of the technologies that are supposedly at the heart of these social and political transformations. Curran and others have pointed out that drawing transformative potential from the internet's technology leads to a techno-internet-centrism that obscures a key insight from political economy, namely that the wider external context affects the impact of the internet, and that capitalism has influenced the internet more than the digital economy has fundamentally changed capitalism (Curran, Fenton, & Freedman, 2012; McChesney, 2013; Hardy, 2014). Indeed, for many, the early promise of the internet of a democratic and decentralised alternative to commercial mass media was quickly swept aside as governments deregulated their communications markets in the 1990s to give greater power to dominant corporate interests (Mosco, 2008; McChesney, 2013; Schiller, 2000). The emerging patterns of internet governance have largely come to resemble the corporate-dominated societies where they have operated with these elites shaping government policy for their own interests. That is, the development of the global internet can best be understood as being driven by the demands of transnational corporations and the US government for a globally integrated computing and communications network aimed at promoting the expansion of operations and markets worldwide without much government interference (Schiller, 2000).

This has led, not to a proliferation of new actors onto the playing field through the democratization of access and production, but rather a digital media economy that resembles previous information technology markets that have gone before; what Wu (2011) has described as a cyclical closure of information empires in which technologies disrupt existing industries, allow for a period of innovation and decentralization, only to close and become centralized once more around a few dominant players. The internet is monopolized by a handful of giant corporations that dominate their respective digital media markets, whether in search (Google), file-sharing (Apple) or social networking (Facebook) (Hindman, 2009; Wu, 2011). Moreover, as the internet has become increasingly mobile and infrastructure focus has shifted to apps and platforms, the digital media economy has tended towards acquisition and concentration, and ownership predominantly confined to the global North, if not just Silicon Valley. Indeed, as Jin (2013) has illustrated, we are seeing an extended form of media imperialism with the development of digital media as platforms are not being supported and developed in the periphery, but are, rather, overwhelmingly developed within or bought by corporations in the US, a situation that Jin describes as 'platform imperialism'.

When looking at the nature of the digital media economy, these patterns of media ownership and control have become more relevant as sources of power, not less. Indeed, the notion that a 'sharing economy' based on a model of 'free' exchange would obliterate undemocratic hierarchical business models as outlined above is based on a misguided abstraction of digital media developments from the broader context of the intertwined advancement of state and capital within the modern world-system. In such a context 'free' and 'sharing' come to serve as convenient panaceas for the exploitation of resources for commercial profit. Freedman (2012), for example, argues that in the case of news, 'free' content is simply paid for at a different point in the chain: through advertising, print sales, and in the case of the BBC, a licence fee. Moreover, 'free', while having obvious benefits for consumers in the short term, is not likely, *in the context of the capitalist market*, to generate the revenues needed to pay journalists, writers, directors and casts that are required to produce original and high-quality content (Freedman, 2012).

What is more, whether something is 'free' or not has little to do with commodification, it is simply to do with *what* or *who* is being sold. This is fundamental for understanding the 'social' character of digital media and the implications these platforms have for shifts in activist practices. Although concepts such as social media have often been seen as leading to a more participatory culture in which the networked nature of communications and the emphasis on 'sharing' is said to have allowed for a more horizontal and inclusive politics, more critical accounts of digital media technologies illustrate the ways in which the underlying structures of such communication platforms actually limit citizen empowerment in a way that introduce some significant dilemmas for the labour movement. Fuchs, for example, has been eager to illustrate how these networks of 'mass self-communication' (Castells, 2009b) and the sharing of content by users themselves are embedded in a deeply exploitative business model that limits the ways in which we can see this as 'participatory' activity (Fuchs, 2014). That is, when we look at how social media companies generate revenue, it is, in fact, from the collecting and selling of the data we, as users, 'freely' provide companies with when we voluntarily contribute our time and energy (our labour) in order to produce and share content on their platforms. In fact, these companies would not survive without our labour creating content for them, yet they keep all the profits they make from it, epitomized by campaigns such as *wagesforfacebook.com* or *paymefacebook.com*. Certainly parts of the labour movement are waking up to these developments and have tried to draw attention to the exploitative nature of the digital media economy by drawing connections between 'creativity', 'participation' and 'sharing' and the further entrenchment of neoliberal restructurings in the nature of work and working conditions (Lovink, Olma & Rossiter, 2014; Senalp & Senalp, 2014).

What these struggles highlight in a broader sense is the increasingly familiar dilemma for activists, not least labour activists, of using corporate platforms entrenched in a profit-seeking commercial system over which they have no control or ownership for anti-corporate and anti-systemic activity. This is not a new dilemma per se, and one we have seen the labour movement negotiate for years with regards to how they have sought to work within as well as resist a largely hostile capitalist mainstream media. However, as these social media platforms are seeking to become the new 'mainstream' in how we consume, exchange, and produce information, whilst keeping their corporate agendas and operations relatively hidden, this dilemma takes on further significance. When activism incorporates a digital element, it does so in a contested environment in which these practices also become embedded in processes that are divorced from their intended consequences. Online activity can therefore be said to have what Andrejevic (2012) has referred to as a 'dual' character: the conscious action and the captured information. That is, the online space may be an arena that facilitates for the intentional actions of alerting others to certain information or posting a photo for a campaign or sharing stories of experiences with fellow workers, but all these actions also generate additional *unintentional* information: data about user-behaviour captured by the (commercial) platform. For Andrejevic, this signifies the alienating dimension of online activity: 'To the extent that this information can be used to predict and influence user behaviour it is an activity that returns to the users in an unrecognisable form, turned back upon them as a means of fulfilling the imperatives of others. Estrangement, or alienation, in Marx's account, occurs when our own activity appears as something turned back against us as, "an alien power"' (Andrejevic, 2012, p. 85). Therefore, these online spaces are not autonomous spaces of communication as such and when organisers, campaigners, and workers incorporate digital (commercial) media practices into their repertoire of actions to challenge global corporate power, they do so without any ownership over the data they produce, both intentionally and unintentionally. Rather, this data is predominantly commodified within algorithmic processes that monitor and capture content for the purposes of marketing. Indeed, the algorithmic filtering of user data in order to decide who gets what information and when has become the marker of contemporary forms of commercial practice—and largely done in a way that is entirely obscure to the user (Turow, 2011).

As such, these social media platforms and digital media more broadly are not 'alternative' media in the way that has traditionally been understood in which they serve as alternative channels to mainstream capitalist media. Rather, they are the new mainstream capitalist media, designed to exploit users for the purposes of profit, above all else. They have not been designed with resistance in mind, despite claims of the opposite at opportune moments by their chief executives, such as Mark Zuckerberg's celebration of Facebook as an instigator of the Arab Spring just as the company was about to go public on the stock exchange (Chen, 2012). These new digital corporate giants are certainly not designing technologies with the intent to challenge labour relations and corporations' stronghold over global politics. Rather, they have become central actors in consolidating state-corporate relations in the modern world-system. This has become further evident in accounts of Google's relationship with the US government, for example, in which they are said to have received support and protection in exchange for advancing US foreign policy (Assange, 2014).

Digital Media, State-Corporate Surveillance and Regimes of Governance

The commercialisation of online networks and the corporate exploitation of social media platforms as spaces for user interaction and communication make them problematic as tools for resistance to corporate power. These technologies are designed and developed out of a particular set of power relations that do not necessarily favour citizens, let alone trade unions that are keen to challenge these power relations. In fact, the digital space has proven itself to be an increasingly complex terrain of not only corporate and commercial interests, but a frequently blurred and obscure extension of private-public strategies for control, particularly the control of dissent. In some instances this has been made overt through the complete shutdown of the internet directly by the state in times of social unrest, such as in Iran during the protests of 2009 or in Egypt in January 2011 at the outset of the Arab Spring (Howard, Agarwal & Hussain, 2011). Often, state interference will be more selective than this, such as shutting off particular servers, closing down political websites or portals or by proxy, through controlling Internet Service Providers (ISPs) or by forcing companies to deny access to disagreeable content. As Howard et al. (2011) point out, this form of interference is by no means limited to authoritarian governments. Rather, while authoritarian regimes practice controlling full-networks, subnetworks, and nodes more than democratic governments do, democracies are the most likely to target civil society actors by proxy by manipulating ISPs (Howard et al., 2011, pp. 223–224). Indeed, frequently obstacles to free online communication originate partly in government policy and partly in business practices, and often it is combinations and interactions of the two that result in online censorship (Hintz, 2013). Filtering practices (often initiated with the rationale of restricting content such as child pornography), discussion over temporary blockages of social networking platforms (as in the case of the London Riots), discrimination in frequency allocation (such as towards digital forms of community broadcasting), denial of services by resource applications (such as Paypal or App stores), and data retention and installment of eavesdropping hardware by ISPs (as revealed in the Snowden leaks) all indicate the multitude of strategies being pursued to manage and interfere with communication within the digital space; and this is not to mention the many 'offline' tactics that are exercised to control information (such as imprisoning political activists like whistleblowers) (Hintz, 2013).

The development of digital media technologies therefore needs to be contextualized by the political and economic interests that permeate the modern-world-system, and although significant in some aspects for anti-systemic movements, these technologies have also been integrated into a system of ever-extending social control. As was revealed in June 2013 by the National Security Agency whistleblower Edward Snowden, digital media forms are a central part of the twenty-first century regulatory framework that merges corporate and state actors into an extensive regime of surveillance (Lyon, 2014). The Snowden leaks highlighted the increasingly sophisticated ways in which the monitoring of digital communication by both corporations, private agencies and state actors have become a key part of contemporary forms of governance. Government programmes such as PRISM in the United States and Tempora in the United Kingdom, which are strategies pursued by intelligence agencies that seek to use digital technologies for collecting information on citizens both domestically and abroad, illustrate how social media companies and telecommunications providers have become intermediaries in the regulation of citizen activities by collecting and sharing data on their users (Hintz, 2015). These form part of what Lyon (2001) has described as the rise of 'surveillance society', a social context characterised by an increasing amount of surveillance taking place alongside an explosion in the possible methods and means for observing and monitoring people's behaviours. In such a society, the question is no longer one of determining the means for targeted surveillance but, rather, indicate a significant shift towards *mass* surveillance in which all citizens are now subject to their data being collected and shared. In such a context, citizens have become both consumers and potential suspects.

Activists and anti-systemic movements occupy a particularly precarious position in this regard. Journalist Glenn Greenwald, who was one of the journalists to publish the documents leaked by Snowden, has outlined how the Snowden leaks form part of a longer history of government agencies attempting to intercept citizen communication in order to squash dissent. In his book on the Snowden leaks *No Place to Hide*, he writes:

> The perception that invasive surveillance is confined only to a marginalized and deserving group of those 'doing wrong'—the bad people—ensures that the majority acquiesces to the abuse of power or even cheers it on. But that view radically misunderstands what goals drive all institutions of authority. "Doing something wrong" in the eyes of such institutions encompasses far more than illegal acts, violent behaviour and terrorist plots. It typically extends to meaningful dissent and any genuine

> challenge. It is the nature of authority to equate dissent with wrongdoing, or at least with a threat. The record is suffused with examples of groups and individuals being placed under government surveillance by virtue of their dissenting views and activism—Martin Luther King, the civil rights movement, anti-war activists, environmentalists. In the eyes of the government and J. Edgar Hoover's FBI, they were all "doing something wrong": political activity that threatened the prevailing order. (Greenwald, 2014)

This was evidenced in documents exposed by Snowden showing how monitoring was carried out on online activities of individuals who were considered to have 'radical' ideas and one of the documents leaked detailed how any visitor to the WikiLeaks site was monitored by the British intelligence agency GCHQ's ability to tap into the fibre-optic cables that form the backbone of the internet, allowing it to collect the IP addresses of visitors to the site in real time as well as the search terms visitors had used to reach the site through search engines such as Google (Greenwald & Gallagher, 2014).

The multitude of ways in which state agencies, in conjunction with corporations and private agencies, have incorporated digital technologies into their efforts to monitor and control dissent and activism needs to form part of the debate on transformations within the labour movement and the role that new media forms might play in this. Of course, as we have discussed in previous chapters, there is a long history of state and corporate hostility towards unions and labour activism and, in this regard, labour activists may be rather unsurprised to discover that online activities are part of a regime of state-corporate surveillance. However, it is an important point to remember if unions seek to overcome and circumvent some of the challenges they are faced with in the modern world-system by turning to digital media technologies for building and mobilising worker resistance.

Corporate 'Management' of Online Activism: Eliminating Risks to the Brand

In some regards, as we have seen in our case studies, the advent of 'surveillance society' is not limited to the advantages of GFA, state and capital, but can also provide a context in which it is possible for anti-systemic movements to monitor and subject state and capital to surveillance that can be used as part of activist campaigns as part of GFB. Exposing misconduct, such as systematic under-payment of workers or inhumane treatment of informal labour, has become easier, a system that has been called 'sousveillance' in which citizens 'from below' are able to monitor and surveil the activities of institutions of power (Mann, 2004; Richards, 2013). However, as Uldam (2014) points out, the exposure of such misconduct often relies on civil society actors such as activists to make them visible, and this, in turn, makes such activists visible to political and corporate actors. At the same time there have been developments of extensive forms of corporate management of 'risks' and potential harmful activity to their 'brand' and business coming from civil society. Within the workplace, ubiquitous surveillance has become the norm, particularly for low-wage workers who are becoming accustomed to a working life in which their every activity is monitored and tracked and subsequently used to pressure workers for 'increased productivity'.

Ironically, these very digital media companies that were said to introduce a new, more democratic and participatory form of capitalism based on a 'grassroots economy', as discussed above, have been revealed to implement some of the most oppressive working conditions in this regard. Investigations into tech giants such as Amazon and Apple, for example, have shown how the conditions under which products and services representing the twenty-first century lifestyle and progress are provided based on miserable working conditions, with long shifts and minimum wages, resembling the early days of industrial capitalism combined with a state-of-the-art corporate surveillance infrastructure. Head (2014) describes Amazon's shopfloor processes as an extreme variant of Taylorism in which management experts take the basic workplace tasks at Amazon, such as the movement, shelving, and packaging of goods, and break down these tasks into their subtasks, usually measured in seconds; then rely on time and motion studies to find the fastest way to perform each subtask; and then reassemble the subtasks and make this 'one best way' the process that employees must follow. This is pursued with a regime of workplace pressures, in which targets for the unpacking, movement, and repackaging of goods are relentlessly increased to levels where workers have to struggle to meet their targets. Investigations have shown how Amazon tags its employees with personal sat-nav computers that tell them the route they must travel to shelve goods, set target times for their journeys and then measure whether targets are met, often over ten-hour shifts. All this information is available to management in real time, and if a worker is behind schedule she will receive a text message pointing this out and telling her to reach her targets or suffer the consequences (O'Connor, 2013; Head, 2014). These levels of workplace monitoring and surveillance have become part of a broader corporate culture of extensive management of activities, especially those that may challenge business, both from inside and outside the organisation.

Indeed, a report published in 2013 on corporate espionage on activists argued that the corporate capacity for espionage has skyrocketed in recent years (Ruskin, 2013). Most major companies now have a chief corporate security officer tasked with assessing and mitigating 'threats' of all sorts, including from activist groups in various guises. The report goes on to claim that a few giant corporations, such as Walmart, have essentially replicated in miniature an entire CIA directorate of intelligence—for their own private use. The rise of this form of activity has come from an amalgamation of developments that includes the rising availability of former intelligence officials and the outsourcing of government intelligence operations to private intelligence firms alongside the spread and rising sophistication of digital surveillance. This, of course, is further embedded in a system of entrenched state-corporate ties that has meant that engaging in corporate surveillance and espionage of activists has not been adequately regulated and punished (Ruskin, 2013, p. 7).

The incorporation of digital media technologies into schemes of surveillance that, amongst other practices, targets anti-corporate activity has become an established part of broader understandings of corporate management and 'risk assessment' Lubbers (2012), in one of the few studies exploring this development, argues that this increasingly includes hidden and obscure measures for obtaining information and covert actions to try and prevent resistance from materialising. Business intelligence now goes beyond details about the economy and competition, but must now also include an evaluation of the risks of becoming the target of campaigners, boycotters or digital activists. We saw evidence of this in chapter five and our case study on fast food workers where McDonald's outlined in their 2013 annual report that the Fast Food Forward campaign was a potential 'risk' to the company that needed to be monitored. In fact, McDonald's has a substantial history of corporate spying on activists that ranges back to the infiltration of London Greenpeace in the late 1980s by private detectives hired by McDonald's to monitor activities organised against the company (Lubbers, 2012). That McDonald's monitoring now includes an extensive 'risk assessment' effort dedicated to digital media is exemplary of contemporary corporate surveillance. According to Lubbers, Shell was one of the first companies to develop an online strategy following a successful Greenpeace campaign to stop the sinking of a redundant oil platform. The company hired specialist, external services to trawl the web daily, listing all the places the company was mentioned, and in which context. Services such as eWatch that scan online publications, discussion forums, bulleting boards and electronic mailing lists on behalf of clients are widely used by large corporations (Lubbers, 2012, p. 116). Uldam's study of British Petroleum and Shell illustrate the extent to which corporations are using digital media to engage in surveillance of activities they view as potential 'risks' to their brand and corporate reputation. This 'management of visibility' (Uldam, 2014) includes monitoring activists' activities on social media platforms, often done through contracting risk assessment and PR agencies.

Unsurprisingly, labour activism and union organising is of particular interest in such corporate management of online activism. As we have outlined in previous chapters, union-busting has a long history in liberal democracies and authoritarian states alike. It has become standard practice in many corporations to limit possibilities for workers to organise as part of management strategy and this has become entrenched through extensive levels of workplace surveillance as discussed above. Although not much research has been done in this area, corporate monitoring of social and digital media uses, both inside and outside the workplace, has provided a further avenue to pursue such strategies. Lubbers (2012) recounts the use of a service called CyberSleuth in the early 2000s by Northwest Airlines to track down the alleged organisers of an employee 'sickout' that had nearly halted flights over the Christmas holidays. The airline fired the alleged organisers. This was one of the first times that people discussing labour conditions on a public website had been the target of a far-reaching virtual and real investigation. When hacktivist group Anonymous decided to support the campaign being pursued by OURWalmart to improve working conditions for Walmart workers, their first online action was to hack into the Walmart management system and leak documents that outlined the union-busting techniques being pursued by the company. In 2007 the *Wall Street Journal* reported that Walmart has a roughly 20-person Threat Research and Analysis Group that is dedicated to monitor online media and trolls colleagues' emails looking for 'misbehaviour' (Zimmerman & McWilliams, 2007). Despite this significant history in labour relations at Walmart, one of the leading organisers of the OURWalmart group explained in an interview with us that fears of such practices were necessarily played down within the campaign in order to take advantage of the reach that such platforms afforded:

> We just made a decision from the very beginning that we were just not going to make that choice for people and that we were just going to open it up...over 40,000

> Walmart workers are now on the page and people are very public. It is amazing to me that so many people are willing to step out and be public on Facebook. (Andrea, OURWalmart organiser)

This statement illustrates a pressing dilemma for organisers and labour activists with regards to social media. The use of these 'mainstream' platforms allows them to go where workers are and potentially reach people that they would not otherwise be able to reach with limited resources. However, it also puts the workers they are seeking to protect at risk, often under a cloud of confusion regarding what is and is not public in this context, and often unaware of the social media monitoring practices that many corporations now engage in. In fact, as we have seen in our case studies, the groups that tend to be most conscious of the monitoring of their (online) activities are the ones that have long occupied precarious positions within the labour market, such as migrant domestic workers who are used to balancing on the margins of the law. A long history of 'invisibility' in the global economy has made these communities particularly accustomed to keeping their online discourses apolitical and in the shadows.

Of course, labour organisers seek to limit and manage the risks workers expose themselves to when engaging in online activities if possible. As Andrea from OURWalmart went on to explain, their social media engagement with workers also includes internal groups where privacy settings depend on what the group wants. However, in a social media context in which these public-private distinctions are endlessly being blurred and difficult to maintain, decisions on social media practices often come to rest on a different kind of logic: 'as a community, OURWalmart just decided Walmart's only going to change when people take the risk and stand up and do it' (Andrea, OURWalmart organiser). This is despite being aware of the fact that Walmart management have staff that do go on to these Facebook pages and monitor activities: 'They absolutely do it and I think we just believe that the truth and justice will prevail, and that our members will hold their own and we're just not scared of their stuff because the truth prevails' (Andrea, OURWalmart organiser). Such a stance is admirable in many regards, but it requires a solid base and a mass of numbers that many labour organising initiatives lack. What is more, as is the case in many parts of the labour movement, it does not consider the corporate nature of these platforms themselves that make them unlikely allies in anti-corporate activity. Indeed, the contradictions of using corporate platforms for anti-corporate activity is frequently sidelined in the struggle to find new ways of organising and mobilising workers in the context of the modern world-system. The initiative *Cyberunions*, for example, which is an online resource that looks at the relationship between digital media and trade unionism, was created partly to highlight precisely some of these issues. As founder Walton Pantland noted in an interview with us:

> The whole Cyberunions project has allowed me to keep an eye on the politics of software and technology and who controls it and I suppose where the class line runs through questions of technology which is something I think a lot of political activists are quite blind to. The politics might be quite good in many other ways, but when it comes to communicating online there is not enough thought given to who owns and controls the technology, who it is serving.

As states and corporations have jointly sought to manifest their interests in the development of digital media, these considerations raise caution to the wind regarding the enthusiasm that has generally surrounded social media platforms and their potential to transform power relations. What is more, they highlight the importance for the labour movement, if it is to present itself as a genuine form of anti-systemic resistance in the modern world-system, to position itself in opposition to the state-corporate colonization of our digital communications infrastructure.

(Lack of) Resistance to Surveillance and State-Corporate Control: A Techno-Legal Response

With continuous revelations of corporate and government mass surveillance in recent years, along with an increasing number of cases of police infiltration coming to light, activists have been forced to consider, more than ever, the ways in which their activities might be monitored and tracked. This is not a new phenomenon, but the centralisation of practices around digital media platforms of a host of diverging and conflicting social and political actors has pushed this issue up the agenda. Living in a 'surveillance society' of the kind that has emerged in liberal democracies requires a particular kind of consciousness when engaging in forms of digital activism. However, as we have seen throughout our case studies and in our conversations with labour activists, at a time when the labour movement is seeking to take advantage of the possibilities that these media technologies afford political activism, concerns with the infrastructure, design and political economy of these technologies have taken a back seat. Rather, the concern with going 'where workers are' by using mainstream commercial social media platforms for organising and communicating have taken precedence in how labour activists have sought to engage with this new digital protest environment. Despite the Snowden leaks revealing the extent and nature of state-corporate digital surveillance, there has been limited response amongst civil society and particularly little response from labour unions.

Resistance to state-corporate control of the internet has predominantly resided in groups of tech activists who have sought to disrupt existing control of technologies or build alternative technological infrastructures, as well as digital rights and internet freedom advocates who have framed much of the debate around rights to privacy and freedom of expression. With the advent of the internet, efforts to build media and communications channels with a different political economy to the dominant model have proliferated and the notion that it is possible to 'hack' software as part of a political project has become increasingly integrated into contemporary understandings of activism. Jordan and Taylor (2004) trace the emergence of 'hacktivism' back to the anti-globalisation movement of the late twentieth century. In particular, they argue, the communication systems of advanced capitalism create 'dark spots' where institutional control becomes increasingly difficult, and it is in these corners that hacktivism emerges: "Hacktivism is an attempted solution to the problem of carrying out effective political protest against a system that is expanding its global reach in increasingly immaterial forms" (Jordan & Taylor, 2004, p. 30). As they point out, hacktivism as a form of resistance to institutional control takes different guises and they are keen to distinguish between two, not necessarily compatible, forms of hacktivism, namely 'mass action hacktivists' and 'digitally correct hacktivism'. Here they refer to groups such as the Electronic Disturbance Theatre that engaged in online actions in support of the Zapatistas in the late 1990s and early 2000s as a form of 'mass action hacktivists' that 'look to networks to do things for them, to be a place in which protest can occur just as roads are places in which demonstrations can occur' (Jordan & Taylor, 2004, p. 115). In this respect, practices for advocacy and campaigning using digital media as we have seen in our case studies are not too dissimilar from this kind of practice, although what hacktivists are looking to do is to directly use technologies to disturb and disrupt established orders and in this way challenge control. This is more explicit with 'digitally correct hacktivists' that include groups such as The Cult of the

Dead Cow (or Hacktivismo) that are particularly concerned with changing the actual infrastructure of digital technologies: 'Digitally correct hacktivists create purist technologies for an informational politics' (Jordan & Taylor, 2004, p. 115). These types of practices have particularly proliferated in recent years as a response to revelations of digital surveillance. Events such as 'hackathons' in which computer scientists and technologically skilled users come together to focus on changing or developing software for the purposes of secure communications have become widespread and 'crypto-parties' or information security workshops in which online users of different kinds learn how to circumvent surveillance and use encrypted software have been widely popularized.

Practices of hacktivism have helped highlight the mechanisms of control that prevail within digital media technologies and with groups such as Anonymous these practices have entered mainstream public discourse. However, they are often regarded as marking the line between legality and illegality and present a very different understanding of political activism than more traditional practices such as those associated with organised labour. Indeed, this ambivalent attitude towards hacktivists is evident in the response from one of the key organisers at OURWalmart when asked about the support the campaign had received from Anonymous:

> I believe that…everybody is a stakeholder in what happens at Walmart, and the more that people are out there calling for Walmart to change and the more voices are in that mix, the stronger the movement is. Certainly we believe in taking actions and compliance with the law is essential, but we absolutely believe that everybody is a stakeholder. (Andrea, OURWalmart organiser)

The different protest cultures of hacktivists and labour activists are not to be underestimated. As Coleman (2013) explains with regards to Anonymous, they are difficult to pin down and some work independently while others work in small teams or join demonstrators during large-scale campaigns. They epitomize the rise of 'networked individualism' (Wellman, 2001), in that, as a form of a political collective, they can be seen as composed of individuals acting in their own capacity in the context of a loosely connected network (Milan, 2013). They represent a modality of politics exercised by a class of relatively privileged and visible actors who often lie at the centre of economic life whose activities are rooted in 'concrete experiences of their craft—administering a server or editing videos—skills channeled toward bolstering civil liberties, such as privacy' (Coleman, 2013, p. 14). Moreover, their forte is publicity, one they have been successful in creating partly because of their unpredictability and fragmented political goals. As Coleman (2013, p. 16) points out, members of the network will boast with a commonly stated refrain, 'We are not your personal army', which prevents their assimilation and neutralization by established institutional actors.

These features of resistance associated with hacktivism make for a complicated protest environment for activists within the labour movement and, in some ways, the occupation of resistance to state-corporate surveillance and control online by technologically focused activists may have alienated other forms of protest movements from being a part of this struggle. That is, as Jordan and Taylor (2004) also argue, there is a hacker obsession with equating technological means with social ends, which may be rather limiting. What is more, and this has become further explicit in a post-Snowden political context, much of this kind of activism is motivated by liberal values, such as the power of the individual and, particularly, the advancement of human rights, such as free speech and privacy (Coleman, 2011, p. 513). Liberal notions such as transparency as a way of limiting state power as advanced by the whistleblower platform Wikileaks, for example, or free software developers conceptualizing source code as an example of free speech, indicate that rather than the 'practice of deviant subculture…[hacking] reveals the continuing relevance, if also the contradictions, of the liberal tradition of the digital present' (Coleman, 2011, p. 513). Hacktivism, in this regard, is part of the broader movement for internet freedoms and digital rights, often focused on technological infrastructure, which has dominated the post-Snowden anti-surveillance debate.

As a form of resistance, these practices have received a great deal of attention and are in some regards an apt response to what can be seen as a political struggle being fought out via technological means. However, as we have seen throughout this book, there is a danger that such approaches to state-corporate control abstract too much from the possibilities of technologies to transform society in and of themselves rather than situating the development of the internet in the context of the modern world-system. Centring resistance to mass surveillance on privacy and on developing what is commonly referred to as 'privacy-enhancing technologies' is limited in this regard as it does not capture the element of productive power and control at work (Andrejevic, 2012, p. 86). This is not to say that there is no value in articulating resistance to digital surveillance in terms of individual rights to privacy and in facilitating opportunities for changes in individuals' online behaviour. Certainly, for activists there is a strong interest in pushing for the creation of (online) spaces that are free from corporate and state surveillance on these terms, in particular for the purposes of organising and mobilising resistance. However, the tech-privacy paradigm fails to address the extent to which relations of power in the online economy mirrors and is contingent upon relations of power in the modern world-system. As we have seen, the global labour movement has a role to play in such a critique, by highlighting the connection between the state, capital and the consciousness industries, of which digital surveillance has now become a central part.

A Labour Response to Digital State-Corporate Control: An Opportunity for Independent Social Movement Unionism?

Although resistance to digital surveillance as an extension of mediated state-corporate control has been dominated by a tech-centric privacy-focused framework, the question of what happens to our communication online is of central concern to broader systemic and structural critiques that encompass a key role for the labour movement as well. It does so for a number of reasons. As outlined above, the commercial nature of digital media platforms promotes a business model that is being advanced through the exploitation of 'free' digital labour and alienation of users by collecting, sharing and selling 'unintentional' data trails. As mentioned above, this context potentially offers an entry-point into the resistance efforts to state-corporate control over digital media from a labour perspective. Some of the debates within network initiatives such as *Networked Labour* and *Global Networked Labour Union (GNUnion)* have attempted to make this link between corporate power, the digital media economy, and labour. That is, an attempt to formulate strategies that highlight how the architecture of digital media technologies advances a media landscape where media consumers become media producers who work and create surplus value creating a 'transnational association of consumers/workers' (Karatani, 2005, p. 295) that engages in 'the class struggle against capitalism' of 'workers qua consumers or consumers qua workers' (Karatani,

2005, p. 294). As Andrejevic points out, if consumers are generating value, we can interrogate the conditions of that structure and who is compelled to surrender the economic value generated by their activity and who benefits. Such critiques do more than simply attempt to align consumer (or 'prosumer') exploitation with worker exploitation; they also, and perhaps more importantly, highlight the implications of online commodification for the social and political role played by digital media technologies: 'To speak of consumer exploitation is, in other words, to invoke a strategy for critiquing the emerging online economy against the background of the promise of consumer empowerment and democratisation that have accompanied its development' (Andrejevic, 2012, p. 74).

This exploitation of prosumer data further allows for a regime of state-corporate surveillance to extend possibilities of control, particularly of dissent and anti-corporate or anti-commercial activity. As Fuchs (2012a) points out, Marx saw surveillance, practiced by capital and the nation-state, as a fundamental aspect of the capitalist economy and the nation-state with the aim of controlling the behaviour of individuals and groups. This is now being exercised via electronic, especially social media, means:

> 'In the case of political electronic surveillance, individuals are threatened by the potential exercise of organised violence (of the law) if they behave in certain ways that are undesired, but watched by political actors (such as secret services or the police). In the case of economic electronic surveillance, individuals are threatened by the violence of the market that wants to force them to buy or produce certain commodities and help reproduce capitalist relations by gathering and using information and their economic behaviours with the help of electronic systems. In such forms of surveillance violence and heteronomy are the ultimo ratio.' (Fuchs, 2012a, p. 43)

Thus, surveillance operates as a form of social control and, moreover, it has become the driving force of digital media's political economy. That is, as Cohen (2008) forcefully argues, the business of digital media is underpinned by the 'valorisation of surveillance' in which platforms such as Facebook rely on surveillance as the method by which they aggregate user information for third-party use and specifically target demographics for marketing purposes, and, moreover, surveillance is the main strategy by which the company retains members and keeps them returning to the site (by tracking and revealing the activities of friends and relations through its 'News Feed'). It is the sharing of knowledge, the fostering of relationships, creativity and human agency that have become commodified within this context through the ability to monitor and surveil these activities.

As such, in a digital environment, and with the digitisation of the global economy, distinctions between workplace, workforce, consumer, citizen, economic and political surveillance become blurred as producers and users of digital media platforms merge and the same spaces (platforms) come to consist of a multitude of diverse practices. The struggle over the infrastructure of these spaces, and what happens to both the intentional and unintentional content (data) that circulates within them, therefore cannot be separated from broader social and political structures and relations of power. It necessitates an anti-systemic movement that places digital surveillance in the context of the challenges facing forms of resistance in the modern world-system.

What should be the role and nature of unions in such a movement? Here we want to advance two themes that have been prevalent throughout this book. First of all, the trend towards social movement unionism within the global labour movement is something that speaks to the necessity for unions to build links and networks with a range of different actors and movements in order to build up the support and solidarity that is needed to challenge global corporate power in the twenty-first century. When it comes to the emergence of new media forms and the struggle that continues to mark the development of the internet, situating the labour movement within a broader political ecology of anti-systemic resistance in which unions collaborate and make connections with other movements and activists is particularly pertinent. Digital media is part of a broader development that is changing patterns of working conditions and the ability to challenge GFA. Unions have a significant role here in being part of and creating a broad base of resistance to global corporate power. Of course, this is not limited to making connections with digital rights movements, but rather social movements concerned with issues of social and economic justice more broadly. Initiatives such as *Union Solidarity International Live* (USiLive) speak to such an approach, for example, incorporating a key element for digital media, both as a way to build connections between issues and movements, as well as challenging the dominant political economy of digital media. Similarly, within projects such as *Cyberunions* and *Networked Labour*, where there is a specific interest in digital media technologies, discussions have centred on responses to state-corporate control that draw inspiration from a broader alternative system of economic relations, particularly 'the politics of the commons'. That is, the focus within these communities has emphasized the possibilities for a commons-based internet as an alternative to its dominant structures. This debate incorporates the exploitative dimension of the digital media economy by focusing on the 'expropriation of the common' (Hardt & Negri, 2004) shifting the debate away from questions regarding individual privacy and, instead, argues that knowledge produced collectively and collaboratively has, through the 'valorisation of surveillance', become private property, which obscures the social dimension of wealth production (Cohen, 2008; Lazzarato, 2004). The politics of the commons presents a model of the economy based on the principle of common ownership of the means of (digital) production and one in which production is collectively organised (Sandoval, 2014). In such an understanding of media systems, media are commonly owned, every member of society has the power to participate in decisions regarding the system, and the system would be based on values that support economic and political participation such as solidarity, equality, inclusion, sharing and cooperation. Of course, as Sandoval points out, such a system would require a commons-oriented society in a broader sense. Despite the at times problematic nature of these ideas, what such debate allows for, at least as a starting point, is a space where different forms of activism, spanning across labour activists, hacktivists, internet freedom advocates, and other civil society groups, can meet and possibly converge in their resistance to global corporate power. This requires unions to redefine their purpose more broadly than the workplace as traditionally understood.

Secondly, and related to this, for unions to be relevant within such a resistance movement, labour needs to confront the crisis of its relation to state and capital in the context of the modern world-system. As we have argued in earlier chapters, the corporatist models and versions of business unionism that align with more authoritarian principles have proven to fail the interests of labour in a context of increasing global corporate power and what may be regarded as 'virtual' states coalescing around a broad neoliberal agenda. Although little dialogue exists between labour and digital rights activists and hacktivists, libertarian principles permeate many aspects of these movements and projects such as ROAR, Guerilla Translation and Global Uprising, co-created by hackers, artists, and digital media activists, have sought to open up previously self-enclosed hacker groups to interlock with labour activists and radical worker collectives (Senalp & Senalp, 2014). For unions to present themselves as a genuine challenge to state-corporate control, of which developments in digital media have become increasingly symbolic, they need, in whatever form they take, to define themselves as independent bodies that are able to democratically organise resistance. In this regard, they present an opportunity for other groups that lack institutional memory to engage in broader historical and political understandings of resistance.

Conclusion

The incorporation of digital media technologies as a part of worker resistance strategies is part of an important and transformative shift in how we might understand the nature and role of labour unions in the modern world-system. However, the nature and implications of these online practices cannot be abstracted from the political and economic context in which these digital media forms are being developed. Technology has to be understood within its historical context and transformative potential cannot be explained from technology as its starting point. Rather, both the infrastructures and the uses of these infrastructures are embedded in broader social, cultural, political and economic processes that become crucial to understand and interrogate when examining forms of activism and resistance. As we have seen in this chapter, labour activists are faced with a very difficult dilemma in the 'new' protest environment in which online activism is said to be a central part. Although social media platforms provide unprecedented opportunities to reach and speak with workers in order to organise and mobilise around anti-corporate activity, they do so as thoroughly corporate spaces.

What is more, the data abstracted and aggregated from digital media technologies have become thoroughly integrated into an unprecedented regime of state-corporate surveillance and control that has made it a particularly precarious environment for activists, not least forms of worker resistance. Increasingly, therefore, political activists from across different sections of civil society are forced to confront questions regarding the infrastructure of the technologies they are using to advance their interests. As we have seen in recent years, the issue of who owns and controls this technology and in whose interests is a central concern in the modern world-system. Too much of the debate regarding ways to challenge state-corporate control of online space has been dominated by a tech-centric focus on individual rights to privacy. This is an important part of the resistance to powers of control as it offers opportunities for concrete changes to the technological infrastructure that individuals can use, but it is limited in making the fundamental connection between mechanisms for digital control and the broader functioning of neoliberal states and globalised capital. The struggle against digital mass surveillance is also a struggle against the dominant power relations of the modern world-system. Making such connections provides an opportunity for the labour movement to build solidarity networks and for unions to be part of a broader society-based movement that aims to challenge global corporate power. However, in so doing, as we go on to suggest in our conclusion, unions need to revisit their purpose and function as independent collective worker-led bodies that may have renewed relevance in a digitized world-system.

CONCLUSION: RE-IMAGINING WORKER RESISTANCE IN THE TWENTY-FIRST CENTURY

The interplay between labour movements and media forms that we have outlined and discussed in this book illustrates the extent to which this is linked to broader issues regarding the potential, nature and challenges of resisting dominant power structures in the modern world-system in order to make the idea that *Another World Is Possible* real. If there is a consensus to be reached among the debates surrounding the future of the labour movement in the twenty-first century it is that change, and significant change, is necessary for it to survive and flourish. The disagreement arises, unsurprisingly, over exactly what kinds of changes are needed. In the core of the world-system the major trade unions remain wedded to notions of business unionism or various forms of partnership with the state and corporate sector. The latter have only limited interest in relationships with trade unions, largely where the union is willing to act to police its membership against militant rank and file actions. Commentators such as Gray, a former neoliberal intellectual turned critic, argue that there is no possibility of a return to the golden age of social democracy within which many unions felt secure; that moment in the historical development of the modern world-system (limited as it was to specific parts of the core) has now passed (Gray, 2002).

This conclusion will provide an overview of how the debates around the future of the labour movement have evolved and their relationship to developments amongst the major new social movements that have been influential over the past 20 years, particularly those coalescing, however, tentatively, around the idea of global justice or alternative globalization. In particular, drawing upon the influential work of Benedict Anderson, we argue that what is required is a re-imagining of the global labour movement as a community that works with progressive social movements, promoting solidarity but allowing for diversity and difference (Anderson, 2006).

Although the concept of utopianism has received a largely critical commentary over the past three decades an analysis of social change is inadequate without an account of it. This is not simply because of the problems that are often associated with the idea of utopianism; but because in order to understand what motivates people under the most desperate and dangerous of conditions to form trade unions and aspire to change the world for the better, an understanding of utopianism is crucial. As Mannheim made clear, utopianism is a central part of social theory (Mannheim, 1985). In this respect our conclusion is that what is needed in the labour movement in the twenty-first is a form of *utopian realism*, a conception of a better world that can be built through cooperation and mutual aid in alliance with progressive social movements, in the workplace and in communities. The precise manner of this utopian realism can only emerge from within such a movement and we have shown in the book that a number of principles are emerging that make this utopian realism plausible, if not inevitable.

We have raised the concept of utopianism not only because it is important to the possibility of realizing what the World Social Forum has taken as its motto: that *Another World Is Possible*, but also because the relationship between utopian social thought and technology has been problematic in practice historically for reasons that are also apparent in some of the ways in which the labour movement have begun to incorporate digital media technologies into their practices. In particular there is a danger of placing too much emphasis upon the role that technologies can play in generating progressive social change. As critics of technologically-driven utopian social thought have argued, this can lead to an asocial account of the role that technology plays in transforming society. In some versions it results in a form of technological determinism that says that social change is primarily caused by the impact of technology itself. The influential and important work of Paul Mason is a self-confessed example of this latter argument and it has strong roots in strands of enlightenment thought that have done so much to shape the world politically, socially and economically over the past three centuries (Mason, 2012).

More broadly these tendencies lend themselves towards an overly idealistic view of social change that can encourage the labour movement to embrace, if not mirror, their corporate opponents in prioritizing such things as public relations, professionalized media strategies, and other manifestations of the consciousness industries. In short, in following social theorists such as Castells (who is influential amongst sections of the critical commentariat in the labour movement) there is an exaggeration of the role of communication power at the expense of an emphasis upon organising in the workplace and amongst communities. The fight between the labour movement and corporations in the realm of public relations and social media is a form of asymmetric warfare—whilst the labour movement can win important battles (as our case studies show) it is always a digitized conflict taking place on terrain owned, controlled and developed by the state and subsequently, corporations. As chapter seven has shown, digital technologies are important tools for the labour movement but they are even more important and extensive as forms of power for the state and corporations to monitor, control and survey populations in general and workforces in particular.

This is a balance of social power that cannot be overturned by communication strategies alone, the latter being an idea that is often conveyed in the romanticized role of the 'hacktivist' as the heroic individual fighting against the corporate or political giant. Whist heroic individuals are important in exposing state-corporate malfeasance, crimes and relationships, as WikiLeaks, Ed Snowden and Chelsea Manning have shown, what they also reveal is that without a meaningful social movement behind them they face the danger of becoming isolated forms of protest. Witness the persecution of WikiLeaks staff, the criminalizing and imprisonment of Jeremy Hammond and Chelsea Manning and the hounding of Ed Snowden, all for exposing criminal actions on the part of states and the complicity of corporations in this. Indeed the danger of fetishizing communication is illustrated sharply in the case of Snowden whose leaks have been amongst the most important individual political acts of the past century. The revelations that Snowden has brought into the public realm have sharply exposed the ways in which democracy has been effectively subverted by the state and political and economic elites but it has evoked very little public outrage and protest thus far. The liberal fallacy that in a liberal democracy revealing the truth will somehow correct wrongs is nowhere more starkly revealed than in the aftermath of the Snowden leaks. The rhetorical commitment to supporting whistleblowers that expose criminal actions by the state, political elites and corporations is largely mythical. President Obama, for example, was a strong supporter of whistleblowers whilst a senator but as president has overseen the prosecution of more whistleblowers than any other president (Greene, 2011). As chapter seven made clear, for 'hacktivism' to have lasting and meaningful impact upon existing social relations it can only do so as part of a wider alliance of social movements that should include the labour movement.

The second main argument of the book has been rooted in an analysis of the emergence of the labour movement in the modern world-system. The end of the Cold War has brought about huge geo-political changes in the structure of the world-system that have great significance for the future of the labour movement. The relative decline of US power has seen the rise of trading blocs and groups of states that would have been crushed or subverted much more easily before 1989 by the core states. The rise of many major states in the semi-periphery and the spread of leftist governments in South America are important signs of the fragmentation of geo-political power in the world-system. Whilst this opens up opportunities for a new international to develop this fragmentation has also seen a rise in the break-up of nation-states, often leading to brutal civil wars, as well as more extreme forms of warfare and violence carried out by the US-led core states in many parts of the world-system. The destruction of social life by violence and poverty remains a fundamental feature of many parts of the world-system alongside the establishment of more progressive governments and social movements. Hence in this interregnum the possibilities for a new international labour movement are both difficult and problematic. For example, the struggle of Egyptian trade unions in the overthrow of the Mubarak regime illustrate this clearly in that after the fall of the regime the unions were put firmly back in their place by the newly installed military government, with the support of the US-led core states. The fragmentation of power and ideas in the world-system, its core ideology, has also seen the rise of social movements committed to divisions based on religion, nationalism and ethnocentrism, all of which are fundamentally opposed to the idea of a new international labour movement.

The future of the labour movement in facing these profound obstacles will be derived, in part, from its willingness to revisit its heritage of independent unionism in order to build alliances with social movements that will bring pressure to bear on governments and political parties to pursue policies that support social needs rather than political power and economic privilege.

Such a new international has to take the form of a utopian realism, which builds solidarity in an open manner amongst progressive voices around the world-system. It is a realism that recognizes that whilst power is an ineluctable part of social relations that it is not solely the basis for human actions. The history of the labour movement, for example, cannot be explained simply on the basis of the pursuit of power; it was driven by ideals, hopes and expectations that a better world was possible: in short, utopian realism.

A New International?

The foundations for a new imagined community that might create a humane world-system have been developing for some time and we want to briefly sketch this lineage. The idea and practice of social movement unionism, for example, arose in a number of countries in the periphery and semi-periphery of the world-system in the 1980s and 90s that saw communities organising against the impact of neoliberal restructuring of their economies and societies. Major protests in this period found voice and developed their communities against the IMF and World Bank policies adopted by their governments and against GATT agreements that in their desire to liberalize trade in textiles, agriculture and to extend the realm of intellectual property rights, threatened to destroy vast sections of social life in the periphery and semi-periphery (Wilkin, 2000). These social movements were often faced by violent national police and military forces that were used to suppress rebellious domestic communities. Trade unionists, in particular, have been subject to major human rights abuses throughout the world-system (ITUC, 2012). This fact alone tells us much about how institutions of political power and economic privilege view the threat of an independent labour movement.

From India to South America and Africa communities have had little choice other than to try to organise themselves and their own services in the absence of meaningful support from the state. As Zibechi has shown in detailed and extensive accounts of the rise of social movements in South America over this period, for example, this has led to the emergence of communities trying to build their own services, often against the attempt of the state to destroy them. This includes housing, education, health care and cultural activities such as public libraries (Zibechi, 2010, 2012). The significance of these movements has been immense in South American politics, helping to shift the political culture of the continent and to force governments to adopt policies, however compromised, that espouse a commitment to the marginalized and excluded majority of the population. At the same time in apartheid South Africa the union movement was heavily involved in the defense of the communities from which their members emerged and built alliances and networks of solidarity around the world, culminating in the most powerful global social union movement yet created.

Before Seattle took place the vast protests and social movements developing in the periphery and semi-periphery had gained little public attention in the mainstream media of the core states. It was the appearance of the Zapatista movement in Mexico in 1994 that changed this, becoming the most powerful symbolic resistance to neoliberalism outside of the core. The ideological narrative that the Zapatistas brought into being prefigures many of the themes that have been dominant in the alternative globalization and global justice movements and are heavily influenced by the legacy of libertarian social thought. The Zapatistas, as chronicled by the Marxist scholar Harry Cleaver, were fundamental to new ways of thinking about social movement organisation and espoused a universal commitment to urge the marginalized and oppressed to defend themselves and build new communities of resistance (Cleaver, 1998). This message was delivered through both the communiques of Subcommandante Marcos but also through the long-term practical community building activities of the Zapatistas that sought to help local populations challenge not only the corrupt and violent Mexican state but oppressive social practices within the communities themselves. To promote and build support for their activities the Zapatistas launched their campaign through both the internet, sending emails around the world launching their manifesto for revolutionary change on January 1st, 1994 to media outlets and universities, but also by taking practical action to help communities in Chiapas liberate themselves and take over the organising of their services.

Drawing upon insights from the Situationists, the Zapatistas have emphasized the need for revolutionary movements to build an alternative spectacle to engage audiences and disseminate the truths about the struggles of indigenous and peasant groups in Chiapas. These forms of tactical media interventions both accept the importance of media's role in the modern world-system but also acknowledge the limited resources available to revolutionary and opposition movements. The emphasis is upon strategic and immediate media successes, a form of hit-and-run media spectacle that enables the Zapatistas and indeed the alternative globalization movement to swarm on to the world's media through dramatic events. The Seattle WTO summit was to prove perhaps the greatest example of this tactic and it is a theme that resonates with each of the case studies in this book.

Seattle and Its Aftermath

The importance of the Seattle WTO protests and carnival in 1999 has been rightly viewed as the point at which the alternative globalization movement and resistance to neoliberal capitalism impacted on the world's media. This was, of course, also a reflection of the ethnocentric nature of much of the world's mainstream media who had largely ignored protests throughout the periphery and semi-periphery of the world-system against the very neoliberal policies that were now being embraced by political and economic elites in the core. Seattle was symbolically and politically crucial both because it was taking place in the USA but also because of the way in which it was organised and the diverse array of often antagonistic interests that it brought together. This latter point proved very important to critics of the alternative globalization movement, generally found amongst the mainstream media in the core states, who lambasted the protests on a variety of grounds as being: anti-democratic, unrepresentative, deluded, ill-informed, luddite and reactionary. These criticisms came from across the political spectrum and in part were an understandable reaction to the shock that the protests and carnival had caused. The Seattle protests were unanticipated by the state and political elites and were partly organised through digital media forms. Clearly potential for surprise is largely a thing of the past as the Snowden leaks have revealed conclusively, many states, in conjunction with corporations, have extended their powers of surveillance massively and secret organising is much harder via digital technology. However the Seattle events fit precisely with what the Zapatistas had talked about as an alternative spectacle, a one-off hit and run type media strategy that temporarily disrupts and dominates the mainstream media in the core (effectively the world's dominant media at the time) recognizing that it would be short-lived and that new and different tactics would be required in the years ahead (Wilkin, 2000; Cockburn & St. Clair, 2000).

Seattle should be seen as the beginning of a process of realignment amongst the array of oppressed and exploited groups and communities around the world-system, not the culmination of the search for a new ideology. Indeed the *World Social Forum* (WSF), which emerged from the event and has subsequently led to meetings of activists and groups around the world-system, explicitly embraces plurality of views and open dialogue, recognizing that building an alliance amongst such groups cannot be brought about through the kind of party discipline associated with vanguard revolutionary movements. For all of its problems and faults both Seattle and the WSF represent the possibility of finding ways to build solidarity and alliances amongst social movements and the labour movement that might minimize authoritarian practices. There is nothing inevitable about this process, of course, but it represents the best hope for the labour movement in terms of building a new international that is part of an alliance with other progressive social movements around the world-system. In particular and as we have stressed earlier, the division between unions in the global South and global North have to be overcome if a substantive international is to be built, and this deeply entrenched division, as Arrighi and Silver note, remains the major obstacle to a globally organised labour movement (Silver & Arrighi, 2001).

The development of social media has been an important part of the proliferation of protest groups and social movements around the world-system, providing them with an array of tools through which to organize and coordinate activities in real time, culminating most notably in the arrival of the Occupy Movement and the Arab Spring in 2011. The significance of digital and social media as we have addressed in the book has been in providing platforms that make the web interactive and participatory, allowing groups and individuals to publish, blog, communicate and disseminate ideas in unprecedented volume and speed. As we have seen this has also had important implications for union strategies and coincides with the four main narratives that we have focused on: global unions, community unionism, social movement unionism and syndicalism. All of these strands of the union movement can and have existed without digital and social media but it is also the case that the latter have helped them to evolve and develop with new tactics and strategies. Our case studies have involved each of these four strands of union forms to a greater or lesser degree and the links between the labour movements globally and social movements and the World Social Forum are illustrative of the possibility of a new narrative emerging around the overarching theme of global social justice. Clearly any attempt to overcome the massive global social problems of the twenty-first century is dependent upon the contribution of the labour movement as part of this new alliance. Unsurprisingly the progress thus far has been uneven and marred by significant setbacks including the counter-offensive by the state that began with the Genoa Summit in 2000 and that has accelerated massively after 2001 and the expansion of the global surveillance regime under the auspices of the Bush and Obama Administrations and their 'five-eyes' allies.

Building a Global Alliance?

As we have argued in this book, there are some possibilities emerging for (re)visiting questions around the future of unions that foreground the emerging alliance between the global labour movement and the global justice movement. Peter Waterman (2001a, 2005, 2012) has been part of ongoing debates within the labour movement that delineate a number of principles reflecting this alliance as well as a revived interest in the neglected libertarian tradition that we have highlighted in this book. These include the importance of struggling not simply for better wages and conditions but for increased worker and union control over the labour process, such as investments, new technologies, relocation, subcontracting, training and education policies. Such strategies and struggles should be carried out in dialogue and common action with affected communities and interests so as to avoid conflicts (e.g. with environmentalists, with women) and to positively increase the appeal of the demands. These principles also include struggling against hierarchical, authoritarian and technocratic working methods and relations, for socially-useful and environmentally-friendly products, for a reduction in the hours of waged work, for the distribution of that which is available and necessary, for the sharing of domestic work, for an increase in free time for cultural self-development and self-realisation, and to be active on the terrain of education, culture and communication, stimulating worker and popular culture, supporting initiatives for democracy and pluralism both inside and outside the dominant institutions or media, locally, nationally, globally. What is more, they emphasise dialogue with the movements of other non-unionised or non-unionisable working classes or categories (petty-commodity sector, homeworkers, peasants, housewives, technicians and professionals) as well as other non- or multi-class democratic and pluralistic movements (base movements of churches, women's, residents', ecological, human-rights and peace movements, etc.) in the effort to create a powerful and diverse civil society.

With its emphasis upon self-help, mutual aid, cooperation and an end to hierarchically imposed discipline and ideologies, this agenda is to be welcomed. What is crucial is that the labour movement becomes a meaningful part of these networks of global solidarity and our case studies have each shown ways in which this is developing but also the problems and limitations that such aspirations face. What is crucial is that the labour movement begins to rebuild its activities as an independent movement that is not subordinate to political parties or the state. We have seen that global unionism, a long-standing part of the labour movement, has developed in the twenty-first century through the reinvention and more visible status of the Global Union Federations (GUFs) and as coordinators of action, information and communication they have potentially a significant role to play in the twenty-first century. The International Domestic Workers Network, for example has drawn heavily upon the contribution of the GUFs. However, more progress will depend upon the extent to which they can overcome the weaknesses that have held them back in the past: being too far removed from the union movement, the intrusion of nationalist interests into the GUFs and the general lack of visibility amongst trade unionists. Nonetheless at present it is the twin themes of community unionism and social movement unionism that are perhaps the most important strands in the possible revival of the labour movement. The strengths of these approaches, as we have seen, arise from their willingness to go beyond the workplace to build powerful alliances with communities, NGOs and the international labour movement in pursuit of their goals, building new networks of solidarity. However there are important limitations to these themes in that nearly all unions espouse the rhetoric of building alliances with the community and social movements but as we have also shown mainstream unions are often wedded to practices and ways of thinking and organising that undermine the possibility of a new form of labour movement emerging in genuine alliance with communities and other social movements. The syndicalist current that we have focused upon remains small but important precisely because it is the strongest and most radical of the labour movement traditions and has more natural affinities with community and social movement unionism. It is also the most far-removed from the mainstream unions and there is a tendency in some contemporary literature to overstate the extent of the revival of this particular form. Whatever contribution syndicalism has to make to the labour movement in the twenty-first century it will most likely be as part of the broader alliances with social movements. Nonetheless, its libertarian heritage is central to the re-imagining of the global labour movement.

REFERENCES

Aalto-Matturi, S. (2005). The internet: The new workers' hall and new opportunities for the Finnish trade union movement. *Working USA: The Journal of Labor and Society*, 8(4), 469–481.

Ackers P., & Payne, J. (1998). British trade unions and social partnership: Rhetoric, reality and strategy. *The International Journal of Human Resource Management*, 9(3), 529–550.

Aguiar, L. (2004). Resisting neoliberalism in Vancouver: An uphill struggle for cleaners. *Social Justice*, *31*(3), 105–129.

Aguiar, L., & Ryan, S. (2009). The geographies of Justice for Janitors. *Geoforum*, 40(6), 949–958.

Ahmad, E. (2007). *The selected writings of Eqbal Ahmad*. New York: Columbia University Press.

Alberti, G., Holgate, J., & Tapia, M. (2013). Organising migrants as workers or as migrant workers? Intersectionality, trade unions and precarious work. *The International Journal of Human Resource Management*, *24*(22), 4132–4148.

Albright, J. (2008). Contending rationality, leadership and collective struggle: The 2006 JFJ campaign at the University of Miami. *Labor Studies Journal*, *33*(1), 63–80.

Alinsky, S. (1989). *Rules for radicals*. New York: Vintage.

Allan, S. (2013). *Citizen witnessing: Revisioning journalism in times of crisis*. Cambridge, UK: Polity Press.

Allegretto, S., Doussard, M., Graham-Squire, D., Jacobs, K., Thompson, D., & Thompson, J. (2013). *Fast food, poverty wages: The public cost of low-wage jobs in the fast-food industry*. Berkeley, CA: UC Berkeley Center for Labor Research and Education.

Alperowitz, G. (2011). *America beyond capitalism: Reclaiming our wealth, our liberty and our democracy*. Washington, DC: Democracy Collaborative.

Alzaga, V. (2011, February 7). Justice for Janitors campaign: Open-sourcing labour conflicts against global neo-liberalism. *Open Democracy*. Retrieved from https://www.opendemocracy.net/valery-alzaga/justice-for-janitors-campaign-open-sourcing-labour-conflicts-against-global-neo-libera

Amdur, K. (1986). *Syndicalist legacy*. Urbana: University of Illinois Press.

Amin, A. (1995). *Postfordism: A reader*. Oxford, UK: Wiley-Blackwell.

Amin, S. (1989). *Eurocentrism*. New York: Monthly Review Press.

Anderson, B. (2006). *Imagined communities: Reflections on the origins and spread of nationalism* (Rev. ed.). London: Verso.

Anderson, B. (2007). *Under three flags: Anarchism and the anti-colonial imagination*. London: Verso.

Andrejevic, M. (2012). Exploitation in the data mine. In C. Fuchs, K. Boersma, A. Albrechtslund, & M. Sandoval (Eds.), *Internet and surveillance: The challenges of Web 2.0 and social media* (pp. 71–88). New York and Abingdon, UK: Routledge.

Andrejevic, M. (2014). Alienation's returns. In C. Fuchs & M. Sandoval (Eds.), *Critique, social media and the information society* (pp. 179–190). New York and Abingdon, UK: Routledge.

Antcliff, V., Saundry, R., & Stuart, M. (2007). Networks and social capital in the UK television industry: The weakness of weak ties. *Human Relations*, *22*(2), 178–191.

Armbruster, R. (1998). Cross-border Labour organising in the garment and automobile industries. *Journal of World-Systems Research*. Retrieved from http://www.jwsr.org/wp-content/uploads/2013/05/Armbruster-v4n1.pdf

Arrighi, G., Hopkins, T., & Wallerstein, I. (1989). *Anti-systemic movements*. London: Verso.

Assange, J. (2014, October 23). Assange: Google is not what it seems. *Newsweek*. Retrieved from http://www.newsweek.com/assange-google-not-what-it-seems-279447

Avrich, P. (1973). *Anarchists in the Russian revolution*. New York: Thames & Hudson.

Avrich, P. (2006a). *Russian anarchists*. Edinburgh, Scotland: AK Press.

Avrich, P. (2006b). *Kronstadt, 1921*. Princeton, NJ: Princeton University Press.

Baccaro, L., Hamann, K. & Turner, L. (2003). The politics of labour movement revitalisation: The need for a revitalised perspective. *European Journal of Industrial Relations*, 9(1), 119–133.

Bakan, J. (2005). *The corporation: The pathological pursuit of profit and power*. New York: Robinson Publishing.

Baker, D. (2010a). *Plunder and blunder: The rise and fall of the bubble economy*. San Francisco: Berrett-Koehler.

Baker, D. (2010b). *False Profits: Recovering from the bubble economy*. San Francisco: Berrett-Koehler.

Bakunin, M. (1980). Federalism, socialism anti-theologism. In S. Dolgoff (Ed.), *Bakunin on anarchism* (pp. 102–147). Montreal, Canada: Black Rose Books.

Bakunin, M. (1992). *The basic Bakunin: Writings 1869–71*. New York: Prometheus Books.

Baldwin, R., & Martin, P. (1999). Two waves of globalisation: Superficial similarities, fundamental differences. In H. Siebert (Ed.), *Globalization and labour*. Tübingen, Germany: Mohr Siebeck. Retrieved from http://www.nber.org/papers/w6904.pdf

Banks, A. (1991). The power and promise of community unionism. *Labour Research Review, 1*(18), 17–31.

Barassi, V. (2015, forthcoming). Social media, immediacy and the time for democracy: Critical reflections on social media as 'temporalising practices'. In L. Dencik & O. Leistert (Eds.), *Critical perspectives on social media and protest: Between control and emancipation*. London: Rowman & Littlefield International.

Barassi, V., & Fenton, N. (2011). Alternative media and social networking sites: The politics of individuation and political participation. *The Communication Review, 14*(3), 179–196.

Barnes, R. (2010). *The virtual revolution* [Television series]. London: British Broadcasting Corporation.

Baskerville, S. (2014, July 2). Interview conducted with London Citizens West London organiser.

Baskerville, S., & Stears, M. (2010). London citizens and the labour tradition. *Renewal, 18*(3–4), 65–70.

Bauman, Z. (2006). *Liquid times: Living in an age of uncertainty*. Cambridge, UK: Polity Press.

Beck, P. (1999). Projecting an image of a great nation on the world screen through football: British cultural propaganda between the wars. In B. Taithe & T. Thornton (Eds.) *Propaganda* (pp. 252–278). Gloucestershire, UK: Sutton Publishing Ltd.

Beck, U. (2000). *The Brave new world of work*. Cambridge, UK: Polity Press.

Beck, U., & Beck, E. (2001). *Individualisation: Institutionalised individualism and its social and political consequences*. London: Sage.

Beder, S. (2002). *Global spin: The corporate assault on environmentalism*. Devon, UK: Green Books.

Beder, S. (2006). *Free market missionaries*. London: Earthscan.

Bekken, J. (2009). Peter Kropotkin's anarchist economics for a new society. In F. S. Lee & J. Bekken (Eds.), *Radical economics and labour* (pp. 27–45). New York and Abingdon, UK: Routledge.

Bekken, J., & Thompson, F. W. (2006). *The I.W.W.: Its first 100 years*. Boston: Red Sun Press.

Bello, W. (1994). Dark Victory: The United States, Structural Adjustment and Global Poverty. London, UK: Pluto Press.

Benkler, Y. (2006). *The wealth of networks: How social production transforms markets and freedom*. New Haven, CT and London: Yale University Press.

Bennett, L., & Segerberg, A. (2012). The logic of connective action: Digital media and the personalization of contentious politics. *Information, Communication & Society, 15*(5), 739–768.

Berkman, A. (2009). *The Bolshevik myth*. London: Dodo Press.

Bernays, E. (2005). *Propaganda*. Brooklyn, NY: Ig. (Original work published 1928)

Bernstein, S. (2011, May 18). Fast-food industry is quietly defeating Happy Meal bans. *Los Angeles Times*. Retrieved from http://articles.latimes.com/2011/may/18/business/la-fi-happy-meal-backlash-20110518

Berry, D. (2009). *A history of the French anarchist movement*. Edinburgh, Scotland: AK Press.

Berry, D., & Bantman, C. (Eds.). (2010). *New perspectives on anarchism, labor and syndicalism*. Newcastle-upon-Tyne, UK: Cambridge Scholars Publishing.

Bershad, J. (2012, January 26). Warren Buffett on class warfare: 'If this is war my side has the nuclear bomb'. *Mediate*. Retrieved from http://www.mediaite.com/tv/warren-buffett-on-class-warfare-if-this-is-a-war-my-side-has-the-nuclear-bomb/

Bieler, A. (2012). Neoliberal globalisation, the manufacturing of insecurity and the power of labour. *Labor History*, 53(2), 274–279.

Bieler, A., Lindberg, L., & Pillay, D. (Eds.). (2008a). *Labor and the challenge of globalisation: What prospects for transnational solidarity?* London: Pluto Press.

Bieler, A., Lindberg, L., & Pillay, D. (2008b). The future of the global working class. In A. Bieler, L. Lindberg, & D. Pillay (Eds.), *Labor and the challenge of globalisation: What prospects for transnational solidarity?* (pp. 1–22). London: Pluto Press.

Billig, M. (1995). *Banal nationalism*. London: Sage.

Bittman, M. (2013, July 25). Fast food, low pay. *The New York Times*. Retrieved from http://opinionator.blogs.nytimes.com/2013/07/25/fast-food-low-pay/?_r=0

Bizyukov, P., & Olimpieva, I. (2014). Collective labor protest in contemporary Russia. In I. Ness (Ed.), *New forms of worker organisation: The syndicalist and autonomist restoration of class struggle unionism* (pp. 62–83). Oakland, CA: PM Press.

Bliss, R. (2014, April 20). Social justice unionism seeks to build labor and student movements. *Green Shadow Cabinet*. Retrieved from http://greenshadowcabinet.us/statements/social-justice-unionism-seeks-build-labor-and-student-movements

Blum, W. (2014a). *Killing hope: US military and CIA interventions since World War II*. London: Zed Books.

Blum, W. (2014b). *America's deadliest export – democracy*. London: Zed Books.

Boehm, M. (2014, February 8). Job polarization and middle-class workers' wages. *VoxEU*. Retrieved from http://www.voxeu.org/article/job-polarisation-and-decline-middle-class-workers-wages

Bond, P. (2008, November 12). Against Volcker. *Counterpunch*. Retrieved from http://www.counterpunch.org/2008/11/12/against-volcker/

Bookchin, M. (1994). *To remember Spain: The anarchist and syndicalist revolution of 1936*. Edinburgh, Scotland: AK Press.

Bostock, M., & Fessenden, F. (2014, September 19). 'Stop and frisk' is all but gone from New York. *The New York Times*. Retrieved from http://www.nytimes.com/interactive/2014/09/19/nyregion/stop-and-frisk-is-all-but-gone-from-new-york.html

Bracken, H. (1983). *Mind and language*. Dordrecht, Netherlands: Foris.

Bracken, H. (1994). *Freedom of speech: Words are not deeds*. Westport, CT: Praeger.

Brady, R. (2012). *Business as a system of power*. New York: Forgotten Books. (Original work published 1942)

Branford, S., & Kucinski, B. (1988). *The debt squads*. London: Zed Books.

Branigan, T. (2014, February 28). Foreign domestic workers across Asia rise up over exploitation. *The Guardian*. Retrieved from http://www.theguardian.com/world/2014/feb/28/foreign-domestic-workers-asia-exploitation

Bratton, J., & Gold, J. (2007). *Human resource management: Theory and practice*. Basingstoke, UK: Palgrave.

Braunthal, J. (1967). *History of the International Volume 1: 1864–1914*. New York: Praeger.

Braverman, H. (1998). *Labor and monopoly capital: The degradation of work in the twentieth century*. New York: Monthly Review Press.

Brecher, J., Costello, T., & Smith, B. (2000). *Globalisation from below: The power of solidarity*. Cambridge, MA: South End Press.

Bremmer, I. (2009, May–June). State capitalism comes of age. *Foreign Affairs*. Retrieved from http://www.foreignaffairs.com/articles/64948/ian-bremmer/state-capitalism-comes-of-age

Brenner, R. (2006). *The economics of global turbulence*. London: Verso.

Brenner, R., Brenner, A., & Winslow, C. (2010). *Rebel rank and file: Labor militancy and revolt from below during the long 1970s*. London: Verso.

Brinton, M. (1970). *The Bolsheviks and workers control*. London: Solidarity.

Briskin, L., & McDermott, P. (Eds.). (1993). *Women challenging unions: Feminism, democracy and militancy*. Toronto: University of Canada Press.

Broder, D. (2010). Migrant cleaners and organising solidarity. *The Commune*. Retrieved from http://thecommune.wordpress.com/2010/05/30/migrant-cleaners-and-organising-solidarity/

Bronfenbrenner, K. (Ed.) (2007). *Global unions: Challenging transnational capital through cross-border campaigns*. Ithaca, NY: Cornell University Press.

Buketov, K. (1999). The Russian trade unions: From chaos to a new paradigm. In R. Munck & P. Waterman (Eds.), *Labour worldwide in the era of globalisation: Alternative union models in the new world order* (pp. 124–148). Basingstoke, UK: Macmillan.

Buketov, K. (2014, January 29), Interview with the campaign organiser of the International Union of Food workers (IUF).

Burgmann, V. (1995). *Revolutionary industrial unionism: The Industrial Workers of the World in Australasia*. Cambridge, UK: Cambridge University Press.

Butler, T., & Robson, G. (2003). *London Calling: The middle classes and the remaking of inner London*. London: Berg.

Byrne, D. (2002). *Interpreting quantitative data*. London: Sage.

Byrne, D., & Callaghan, G. (2013). *Complexity theory and the social sciences: The state of the art*. New York and Abingdon, UK: Routledge.

Byrne, S., McGregor, W., & van der Walt, L. (2011). Why May Day matters. *Anarkismo.net*. Retrieved from http://www.anarkismo.net/article/19393?author_name=Lucien+van+der+Walt&

Callinicos, A. (2013, February). Is Leninism finished? *Socialist Review, 376*. Retrieved from http://socialistreview.org.uk/376/leninism-finished

Cammaerts, B., Mattoni, A., & McCurdy, P. (Eds.). (2012). *Mediation and protest movements*. Chicago, IL: Intellect Books.

Cannon, J. P. (1955). Against the IWW. LibCom. Available at https://libcom.org/blog/against-iww-series-part-2-iww-1955-james-p-cannon-23102013, last viewed March 20th, 2015.

Caraway, T. (2007). *Assembling women: The feminisation of global manufacturing*. New York: ILR Press.

Carr, B. (2103). *The Carr Report: The Report of the Independent Review of the Law Governing Industrial Disputes*, available at https://carr-review.independent.gov.uk/wp-content/uploads/2014/10/Carr-Review-Final-Report.pdf, last viewed March 20th, 2015.

Carson, K. (2002). *Liberalism and social control.* Retrieved from http://www.mutualist.org/id7.html

Castells, M. (1997). *The power of identity, the information age: Economy, society and culture* (Vol. II). Oxford, UK: Blackwell.

Castells, M. (2004). Informationalism, networks, and the network society: A theoretical blueprint. In M. Castells (Ed.), *The network society: A cross-cultural perspective*. London: Edward Elgar. Retrieved from http://annenberg.usc.edu/Faculty/Communication/~/media/Faculty/Facpdfs/Informationalism%20pdf.ashx

Castells, M. (2009a). *The rise of the network society* (2nd ed.). London: Wiley-Blackwell.

Castells, M. (2009b). *Communication power.* New York: Oxford University Press.

Castells, M. (2012). *Networks of outrage and hope: Social movements in the internet age.* Cambridge, UK: Polity Press.

Cavanagh, J., Wysham, D., & Arruda, M. (1994). *Beyond Bretton Woods*. London: Pluto Press.

Chadwick, A. (2006). *Internet politics: States, citizens, and new communication technologies.* Oxford, UK: Oxford University Press.

Chang, H. J. (2002). *Kicking away the ladder: Developmental policy in historical perspective.* London: Anthem Press.

Chen, A. (2012, February 2). Mark Zuckerberg takes credit for populist revolutions now that facebook's gone public. *Gawker*. Retrieved from http://gawker.com/5881657/facebook-takes-credit-for-populist-revolutions-now-that-its-gone-public

Chen, M. (2014, June 6). Temp nation: How corporations are evading accountability, at workers expense. *The Nation.* Retrieved from http://www.thenation.com/blog/180151/temp-nation-how-corporations-are-evading-accountability-workers-expense

Chin, J. (2005). Public dramas and the politics of justice: Comparison of janitors union struggles in South Korea and the United States. *Work and Occupation*, *32*(4), 486–503.

Chin, J. (2008). The contested politics of gender and irregular employment: Revitalising the South Korean democratic labour movement. In A. Bieler, I. Lindberg, & D. Pillay (Eds.), *Labour and the challenges of globalisation* (pp. 23–44). London: Pluto Press.

Chomsky, N. (1988). Psychology and ideology. *The Chomsky reader*. New York: Serpents Tail Press.

Chomsky, N. (1999, Summer). Reform and revolution: Noam Chomsky on anarcho-syndicalism. *Anarcho-Syndicalist Review*, *25*, 14–19.

Chomsky, N. (2002). *What Uncle Sam really wants*. New York: Odanian Press.

Chomsky, N. (2003). Interview. In Anton Pannekoek, *Workers' councils* (vii–xvi). Edinburgh, UK: AK Press.

Chomsky, N. (2011). *The state-corporate complex: A threat to freedom and survival.* Retrieved from http://www.chomsky.info/talks/20110407.htm

Chomsky, N., & Herman, E. (1979). *The Washington connection and third world fascism: The political economy of human rights*. Montreal, Canada: Black Rose Books.

Chossudovsky, M. (2003). *The globalisation of poverty and the new world order*. Montreal, Canada: Global Research Institute.

Chouliaraki, L., & Blaagaard, B. (2013). Cosmopolitanism and the new news media. *Journalism Studies*, *14*(2), 150–155.

Christiansen, J. (2009). We are all leaders: Anarchism and the narrative of the IWW. *Working USA: The Journal of Labor and Society, 12*(3), 387–401.

Christie, S., & Meltzer, A. (2010). *The floodgates of anarchy*. Oakland, CA: PM Press.

Citigroup. (2006). The global investigator: The plutonomy symposium – rising tides, lifting yachts. *Citigroup Global Markets*. Retrieved from http://www.correntewire.com/sites/default/files/Citibank_Plutonomy_2.pdf

Clark, I. (2000). *Governance, the state, regulation, and industrial relations*. London and New York: Routledge.

Clawson, D. (2003). *The next upsurge: Labor and the new social movements*. Ithaca, NY: Cornell University Press.

Clawson, D. (2009, June 5). A battle for labor's future. *Z Magazine*. Retrieved from http://zcomm.org/zmagazine/a-battle-for-labors-future-by-dan-clawson/

Cleaver, H. (1998). The Zapatista effect: The internet and the rise of alternative political fabric. *Journal of International Affairs, 51*(2), 621–640.

Cleaver, H. (2000). *Reading capital politically*. Edinburgh, Scotland: AK Press.

Cliff, T. (1960). Trotsky on substitutionism. *International Socialism, 1*(2), 14–17, 22–26.

Cockburn, A., & St. Clair, J. (2000). *Five days that shook the world*. London: Verso.

Cockfield, S. (2003). *Union recruitment and organising on the WW*. Working Paper series. Monash University. Retrieved from http://www.buseco.monash.edu.au/mgt/research/working-papers/2003/wp23-03.pdf

Cohen, N. (2014, June 21). Why we prefer our immigrants to be invisible. *The Guardian*. Retrieved from http://www.theguardian.com/commentisfree/2014/jun/21/immigrants-taken-to-cleaners-living-london-wage

Cohen, N. (2008). The valorization of surveillance: Towards a political economy of facebook. *Democratic Communiqué, 22*(1), 5–22.

Cohn-Bendit, D., & Cohn-Bendit, G. (2001). *Obsolete communism*. Edinburgh, Scotland: AK Press.

Cole, G. D. H. (1965). Proudhon. In G. D. H. Cole, *A History of Socialist Thought Volume 1: The Forerunners* (pp. 201–218). London: St. Martin's Press.

Cole, G. D. H. (1970). *Socialist thought: Marxism and anarchism 1850–1890*. London: Macmillan.

Coleman, G. (2011). Hacker politics and publics. *Public Culture, 23*(3–65), 511–516.

Coleman, G. (2013). Anonymous in context: The politics and power behind the mask. *Internet Governance Papers, 3*, 1–21.

Colling, T. (2009). Court in a trap? Legal mobilisation by trade unionists in the UK. *Warwick papers in Industrial Relations, 91*, 1–30.

Commune, (2009). Latin American workers in Unite: From heroes to pariahs. *The Commune*. Retrieved from http://thecommune.wordpress.com/2009/11/20/latin-american-workers-in-unite-from-heroes-to-pariahs/

Connolly, H., Marino, S., & Lucio, M. (2012). Justice for Janitors goes Dutch. *Buria Working Paper*. Retrieved from http://www2.gre.ac.uk/__data/assets/pdf_file/0010/665740/Lisa-Berntsen-and-Nathan-Lillie.pdf

Conquest, R. (2008). *The great terror*. London: Pimlico Press. (Original work published 1968)

Couldry, N. (2010). *Why voice matters*. London and Thousand Oaks: Sage.

Couldry, N. (2013, November 21). A necessary disenchantment: Myth, agency and injustice in a digital world [Inaugural lecture]. London School of Economics and Political Science. Retrieved from http://www.lse.ac.uk/media@lse/documents/MPP/Nick-Couldrys-LSE-INAUGURAL-SCRIPT.pdf

Cowie, H. (1986). *Imperialism and race relations*. New York: Nelson.

Cranford, C. (2007). Constructing union motherhood: Gender and social reproduction in the LA 'Justice for Janitors' movement. *Qualitative Sociology*, 30(4), 361–381.

Cronin, J. (1989). Strikes and power in Britain: 1870–1920. In L. Haimson & C. Tilly (Eds.), *Strikes, wars and revolution in an international perspective: Strike waves in the late nineteenth and early twentieth centuries* (pp. 79–100). Cambridge, UK: Cambridge University Press.

Crosby, M., & Easson, M. (Eds.). (1992). *What should unions do?* London: Pluto Press.

Crouch, C. (2004). *Post-democracy*. Cambridge, UK: Polity Press.

Croucher, R., & Cotton, E. (2009). *Global unions, global business: Global union federations and international business*. London: Middlesex University Press.

Crozier, M., Huntington, S., & Watanuki, J. (1975). *The crisis of democracy*. New York: New York University Press.

Curran, J. (2010). Technology foretold. In N. Fenton (Ed.), *New media, old news: Journalism and democracy in the digital age* (pp. 19–34). London and Thousand Oaks: Sage.

Curran, J., Fenton, N., & Freedman, D. (2012). *Misunderstanding the internet*. New York and Abingdon, UK: Routledge.

Damier, V. (2009). *Anarcho-syndicalism in the twentieth century*. Edmonton, Canada: Black Cat Press.

Danford, A. Richardson, M., & Upchurch, M. (2003). *New unions, new workplace: A study of union resilience in the restructured workplace*. London: Routledge.

Dani, M. (2000). Social movement networks: virtual and real. *Information, Communication and Society*, 3(3), 386–401.

Darlington, R. (2013). *Radical unionism: The rise and fall of revolutionary syndicalism*. Chicago, IL: Haymarket Books.

Datta, K., McIlwain, C., Evans, Y., Herbert, J., May, J., & Wills, J. (2007). From coping strategies to tactics: London's low-pay economy and migrant labour. *British Journal of Industrial Relations*, 45(2), 404–432.

Davis, M. (2009). *Comrade or brother?* London: Pluto Press.

Dean, A. B. (2014, June 28). 'People make up our city': Why Seattle's $15 minimum wage is a sign of things to come. *Truthout*. Retrieved from http://www.truth-out.org/news/item/24608-people-make-up-our-city-why-seattles-$15-minimum-wage-is-a-sign-of-things-to-come

Dean, J. (2009). *Democracy and other neoliberal fantasies: Communicative capitalism and left politics*. Durham, NC: Duke University Press.

Deborah, Y., & Smith, I. (Eds.) (2002). *Globalisation, employment and the workplace*. London: Routledge.

Deibert, R. (2000). International plug'n play? Citizen activism, the internet and global public policy. *International Studies Perspectives*, *1*, 255–272.

Della Porta, D. (2007). *The global justice movement: Cross-national and transnational perspectives*. Boulder, CO: Paradigm.

Della Porta, D., & Mosca, L. (2005). Global-net for global movements? A network of networks for a movement of movements. *Journal of Public Policy*, *25*(1), 165–190.

Dencik, L. (2012). *Media and global civil society*. Basingstoke and New York: Palgrave.

Dencik, L. (2015, forthcoming). Social media and the 'new authenticity' of protest. In L. Dencik & O. Leistert (Eds.), *Critical perspectives on social media and protest: Between control and emancipation*. London: Rowman & Littlefield International.

Diamond, W., & Freeman, R. (2001). Will unionism prosper in cyberspace? *National Bureau of Economic Research*. Working Paper 8483. Retrieved from http://www.nber.org/papers/w8483

Dicken, P. (2010). *Global shift*. London: Sage.

Dionne Jr., E. J. (2013, September 1). New life for labor. *The Washington Post*. Retrieved from http://www.washingtonpost.com/opinions/ej-dionne-jr-new-life-for-labor/2013/09/01/02401384-1199-11e3-bdf6-e4fc677d94a1_story.html

Dirlik, A. (1993). *Anarchism in the Chinese revolution*. Los Angeles: University of California Press.

Dolgoff, S. (1970). *The relevance of anarchism to modern society*. Available at http://flag.blackened.net/liberty/spunk/Spunk191.txt

Dolgoff, S. (1988). The role of Marxism in the international labour movement. *Libertarian Labor Review*, *5*, 27–35.

Dolgoff, S. (2013). A *critique of Marxism*. Retrieved from http://zabalazabooks.files.wordpress.com/2013/03/a_critique_of_marxism_sam_dolgoff.pdf

Dølvic, J., & Waddington, J. (2004). Organising marketised services: Are trade unions up to the job? *Economic and Industrial Democracy*, *25*(1), 9–40.

Dosemi, M. (2014, January 13). Superman, Clark Kent and the limits of the Gezi uprising. *Roar Mag*. Retrieved from http://roarmag.org/2014/01/superman-limits-turkish-resistance/

Drew, J. (2013). *A social history of contemporary democratic media*. New York and Abingdon, UK: Routledge.

Dubofsky, M. (1987). *Big Bill Haywood*. Manchester, UK: Manchester University Press.

Dunleavy, P., & O'Leary, P. (1987). *Theories of the state*. Basingstoke, UK: Palgrave.

Dunn, B. (2004). *Global restructuring and the power of labour*. Basingstoke, UK: Palgrave.

Ealham, C. (2010). *Anarchism and the city: Revolution and counter-revolution in Barcelona, 1898–1937*. Edinburgh, Scotland: AK Press.

Ebbinghaus, B. (2002). Trade unions changing role: Membership erosion, organisational reform and social partnership in Europe. *Industrial Relations Journal*, *33*(5), 465–483.

Economist, (2013, December 24). Appreciating the BRICS. *The Economist*. Retrieved from http://www.economist.com/blogs/freeexchange/2013/12/emerging-economies

Eder, M. (2002). The constraints on labour internationalism. In J. Harrod & R. O'Brien (Eds.), *Global unions? Theory and strategies of organised labour in the global economy* (pp. 167–184). London: Routledge.

Elger, T., & Smith, C. (Eds.) (1994). *Global Japanization?* Abingdon, UK: Routledge.

Elliott, L., & Atkinson, D. (2009). *The gods that failed*. London: Vintage.

Ellis, C. (2009). *The partnership: The making of Goldman Sachs*. London: Penguin.

El-Ojeili, C. (2012). *Politics, social theory, utopia and the world-system*. Basingstoke, UK: Palgrave.

El-Ojeili, C. (2014). Reflections on Wallerstein: The modern world-system, four decades on. *Critical Sociology*, 1–22.

Erickson, C., Fisk, C., Milkman, R., Mitchell, D., & Wong, K. (2002). Justice for Janitors in Los Angeles: Lessons from three rounds of negotiations. *British Journal of Industrial Relations*, 40(3), 543–567.

Erickson, E. (2010, December 7). New NLRB Decision Legitimizes Unions' Race to the Bottom. *Labour Union Report*. Available at http://www.redstate.com/diary/laborunionreport/2010/12/07/new-nlrb-decision-legitimizes-unions-race-to-the-bottom/

Evren, S. (2012). There ain't no black in the Anarchist flag! Race, ethnicity and anarchism. In R. Kinna (Ed.), *The Continuum companion to anarchism* (pp. 383–406). London: Continuum.

Ewen, S. (1996). *PR! A social history of spin*. New York: Basic Books.

Ewen, S. (2001). *Captain of consciousness: Advertising and the social roots of consumer culture*. New York: Basic Books.

Ewing, K. D. (2005). The function of trade unions. *Industrial Law Journal*, *34*(1), 1–22.

Fairbrother, P. (2000). British trade unions facing the future. *Capital and Class*, *71*, 11–42.

Fairbrother, P., & Hammer, N. (2005). Global unions: Past efforts and future prospects. *Industrial Relations*, 60(3), 405–431.

Fairbrother, P., Williams, G., Barton, R., Gibellieri, E., & Tropeoli, A. (2007). Unions facing the future: Questions and possibilities. *Labor Studies Journal*, *31*(4), 31–53.

Fanon, F. (2006). *The Fanon reader*. London: Pluto Press.

Felix, D. (2003). The past as future? The contribution of financial globalisation to the current crisis of neo-liberalism as a development strategy. University of Massachusetts Working Papers series, 68. Retrieved from http://www.peri.umass.edu/fileadmin/pdf/working_papers/working_papers_51-100/WP69.pdf

Fenton, N. (Ed.) (2010a). *New media and old news: Journalism and democracy in the digital age*. London and Thousand Oaks: Sage.

Fenton, N. (2010b). *Social networking, political citizenship and democracy*. Paper presented at ECREA 3rd Communication Conference, Hamburg.

Ferguson, T., & Johnson, R. (2010). Too big to bail? The "Paulson put," US Presidential Politics, and the global financial meltdown. In M. Konings (Ed.), *The great credit crash*. London: Verso.

Feuer, A. (2013, November 28). Life on $7.25 an hour. *The New York Times*. Retrieved from http://www.nytimes.com/2013/12/01/nyregion/older-workers-are-increasingly-entering-fast-food-industry.html

Fine, J. (2006). *Worker center: Organizing communities at the edge of the dream*. Ithaca, NY: Cornell University Press.

Fink, E. (2014). Sewer syndicalism: Worker self-management in public services. *Nevada Law Journal*, *14*(1), 444–464.

Fisher, D., & Wright, L. (2001). On utopias and dystopias: Toward an understanding of the discourse surrounding the internet. *Journal of Computer-Mediated Communication*, 6(2).

Fitch, R. (2006). *Solidarity for sale*. New York: Public Affairs.

Fitzgerald, I., & J. Hardy. (2010). Thinking outside the box? *British Journal of Industrial Relations*, 48(1), 131–150.

Fitzgerald, I., Hardy, J., & Lucio, M. (2012). The internet, employment and Polish migrant workers: Communication, activism and competition in the new organisational spaces. *New Technology, Work and Employment, 27*(2), 93–105.

Flew, T. (2007). *Understanding global media.* Basingstoke, UK: Palgrave.

Fones-Wolf, E. (1995). *Selling free enterprise: The business assault on labor and liberalism 1945–60.* Champaign: University of Illinois Press.

Fontaine, R., & Rogers, W. (2011). Internet freedom: A foreign policy imperative in the digital age. *Center for a New American Security.* Retrieved from http://akgul.bilkent.edu.tr/Sansur/CNAS_InternetFreedom_FontaineRogers_0.pdf

Forman, E. (2013a, April 15). The 'organising model' goes global. *Labour Notes.* Retrieved from http://www.labornotes.org/2013/04/organizing-model-goes-global

Forman, E. (2013b). Fast food unionism: The unionization of McDonald's and the McDonaldization of unions. *LibCom.* Retrieved from https://libcom.org/library/fast-food-unionism-unionization-mcdonald%E2%80%99s-mcdonaldization-unions

Forman, E. (2014). Revolt in fast-food nation: The Wobblies take on Jimmy John's. In I. Ness (Ed.), *New forms of worker organisation: The syndicalist and autonomist restoration of class struggle unionism* (pp. 205–232). Oakland, CA: PM Press.

Forman, M. (1998). *Nationalism and the international labor movement: The idea of the nation in socialist and anarchist theory.* Philadelphia: University of Pennsylvania Press.

Forstater, M. (2009). Some notes on anarchist economic thought. In F. S. Lee & J. Bekken (Eds.), *Radical economics and labour* (pp. 46–54). New York and Abingdon, UK: Routledge.

Fortune. (2014). Fortune 500 2014. *Fortune.* Retrieved from http://fortune.com/fortune500/

Fox, M. (2012). *The pope's war.* New York: Sterling Ethos.

Fox, M. (2012, December 7). Jon Kest, advocate for low-wage workers in New York, dies at 57. *The New York Times.* Retrieved from http://www.nytimes.com/2012/12/08/nyregion/jon-kest-community-advocate-in-new-york-dies-at-57.html

Fox, M. (2013, March 15). Pope Ratzinger's war on social justice. *Counterpunch.* Retrieved from http://www.counterpunch.org/2013/03/15/pope-ratzingers-war-on-social-justice/

Freedman, D. (2012). Web 2.0 and the death of the blockbuster economy. In J. Curran, N. Fenton, & D. Freedman, *Misunderstanding the internet* (pp. 69–94). Abingdon, UK and New York: Routledge.

Freeman, R. (2002). The labour market in the new information economy. *Oxford Review of Economic Policy, 18*(3), 288–305.

Freeman, R. B. (2013). What, if anything, can labor do to rejuvenate itself and improve worker well-being in an era of inequality and crisis-driven austerity? *Perspektiven der Wirtschaftspolitik, 14*(1–2), 41–56.

Freeman, R., & Rehavi, M. (2008). Helping workers online and offline: Innovation in union and worker involvement using the internet. *National Bureau of Economic Research.* Working Paper 13850. Retrieved from http://www.nber.org/papers/w13850

French, J. D., & James, D. (Eds.). (1997). *The gendered worlds of Latin American women workers.* Durham, NC: Duke University Press.

Friedman, M. (1970, September 13). The social responsibility of business is to increase profits. *The New York Times Magazine.* Retrieved from http://www.umich.edu/~thecore/doc/Friedman.pdf

Friedman, M. (2009). *Capitalism and freedom*. Chicago, IL: University of Chicago Press.

Fuchs, C. (2012a). "Critique of the Political Economy of Web 2.0 Surveillance" In C. Fuchs, K. Boersma, A. Albrechtslund, & M. Sandoval (Eds.), *Internet and surveillance: The challenges of Web 2.0 and social media* (pp. 31–70). New York and Abingdon, UK: Routledge.

Fuchs, C. (2012b). Some reflections on Manuel Castells' book "Networks of outrage and hope: Social movements in the internet age." *Communication, Capitalism and Critique*, *10*(2), 775–797.

Fuchs, C. (2014). *Social Media: A critical introduction*. London and Thousand Oaks: Sage.

Fukuyama, F. (1992a). Capitalism and democracy: The missing link. *Journal of Democracy*, *3*(3), 100–110.

Fukuyama, F. (1992b). *The end of history and the last man*. New York: The Free Press.

Gallin, D. (2002). Labour as a global social force. In J. Harrod & R. O'Brien (Eds.), *Global unions? Theories and strategies of organised labour in the global political economy* (pp. 235–250). London: Routledge.

Gallin, D. (2014). *Solidarity*. London: Labour Start.

Garvey, P., Buketov, K., Chong, H., & Martinez, B. (2007). Global labor organising in theory and practice. *Labor Studies*, *32*(3), 237–256.

George, S. (1991). *The debt boomerang*. London: Pluto Press.

Gerbaudo, P. (2012). *Tweets and the streets: Social media and contemporary activism*. London: Pluto Press.

Gerbaudo, P. (2014, March 27). Occupying the digital mainstream. *The Occupied Times*. Retrieved from http://theoccupiedtimes.org/?p=12853

Ghonim, W. (2012). *Revolution 2.0: The power of the people is greater than the people in power*. New York: Houghton Mifflin Harcourt.

Gibson, J. J. (1986). *The ecological approach to visual perception*. Mahwah, NJ: Lawrence Erlbaum. (Original work published 1979)

Giddens, A. (1987). *The nation-state and violence*. Cambridge, UK: Polity.

Gill, S. (1992). *American hegemony and the trilateral commission*. Cambridge, UK: Cambridge University Press.

Giri, S. (2009, November 21). The dangers are great, the possibilities immense: The ongoing political struggle in India. *Monthly Review*. Retrieved from http://monthlyreview.org/commentary/the-dangers-are-great-the-possibilities-immense/

Girls Intelligence Agency. (2004). Retrieved from http://www.girlsintelligenceagency.com/

Global Wealth Report. (2014, June 9). *Riding a wave of growth*. Retrieved from https://www.bcgperspectives.com/content/articles/financial_institutions_business_unit_strategy_global_wealth_2014_riding_wave_growth/

Glockstein, D. (2011). Workers' councils in Europe: A century of experience. In I. Ness & D. Azzellini (Eds.), *Ours to master and to own: Workers' control from the commune to the present* (pp. 32–47). Chicago, IL: Haymarket Books.

Goldman, E. (2003). My *disillusionment in Russia*. London: Dover.

Golin, S. (1992). *The fragile bridge: Paterson silk strike 1913*. Philadelphia, PA: Temple University Press.

Gorman, A. (2014). Diverse in race, religion and nationality…but united in aspirations of civil progress: The anarchist movement in Egypt 1860–1940. In S. Hirsch & L. van der Walt (Eds.), *Anarchism and syndicalism in the colonial and postcolonial world, 1870–1940* (pp. 3–32). Boston: Brill.

Gorz, A. (Ed.). (1978). *The division of labour: The labour process and class struggle in modern capitalism*. Brighton, UK: Harvester Wheatsheaf.

Gorz, A. (1999). A new task for the union: The liberation of time from work. In R. Munck & P. Waterman (Eds.), *Labour worldwide in the era of globalisation: Alternative union models in the new world order* (pp. 41–63). Basingstoke, UK: Palgrave.

Graeber, D., & Schmid, B. (2012). *Inside Occupy*. Frankfurt, Germany: Campus Verlag Gmbh.

Graham, R. (2015). From the bottom up: The First International and the emergence of European anarchist movements. *Anarcho-Syndicalist Review*, 63, 23–27.

Gray, J. (2002). *False dawn: The delusions of global capitalism*. London: Granta Press.

Gray, J. (2013, February 5). Unions and the internet: 65% of new members in my branch now join on-line. *Union Home*. Retrieved from http://www.unionhome.org.uk/?p=2222

Greene, A., & Kirton, G. (2003). Possibilities for remote participation in trade unions: Mobilising women activists. *Industrial Relations Journal*, 34(4), 319–333.

Greene, A., Hogan, J., & Grieco, M. (2003). E-collectivism and distributed discourse: New opportunities for trade union democracy. *Industrial Relations Journal*, 34(4), 282–289.

Greene, L. (2011, June 30). Obama's war on whistleblowers. *Counterpunch*. Retrieved from http://www.counterpunch.org/2011/06/30/obama-s-war-on-whistleblowers/

Greenwald, G. (2014). *No place to hide: Edward Snowden, the NSA and the surveillance state*. London: Hamish Hamilton.

Greenwald, G., & Gallagher, R. (2014, February 18). Snowden documents reveal covert surveillance and pressure tactics aimed at WikiLeaks and its supporters. *The Intercept*. Retrieved from https://firstlook.org/theintercept/2014/02/18/snowden-docs-reveal-covert-surveillance-and-pressure-tactics-aimed-at-wikileaks-and-its-supporters/

Guerin, D. (1970). *Anarchism: From theory to practise*. New York: Monthly Review Press.

Guerin, D. (2005). *Fascism and big business*. New York: Pathfinder Books.

Guerin, D. (2006). *No gods, no masters: An anthology of anarchism*. Edinburgh, Scotland: AK Press.

Guerin, D. (2012). *Anarchism and Marxism*. New York: Christie Books.

Guest, D. (1987). Human resource management and industrial relations. *Journal of Management Studies*, 24(5), 503–521.

Guest, D. (1999). Human resources management: The workers' verdict. *Human Resource Management Journal*, 9(3), 5–25.

Gumbrell-McCormick, R., & Hyman, R. (2013). *Trade unions in Western Europe: Hard times, hard choices*. Oxford, UK: Oxford University Press.

Gupta, A. (2013, November 11). Fight for 15 confidential. *In These Times*. Retrieved from http://inthesetimes.com/article/15826/fight_for_15_confidential

Habermas, J. (1992). *The structural transformation of the public sphere*. Cambridge, UK: Polity Press. (Original work published 1962)

Hacker, L. H., & Van Dijk, J. (Eds.). (2000). *Digital democracy*. London: Sage.

Hahnel, R. (2007). The case against markets. *Journal of Economic Issues*, *XLI*(4), 1139–1159.

Haimson, L. (1989a). The historical setting in Russia and the West. In L. Haimson & C. Tilly (Eds.), *Strikes, wars and revolution in an international perspective: Strike waves in the late nineteenth and early twentieth centuries* (pp. 18–32). Cambridge, UK: Cambridge University Press.

Haimson, L. (1989b). Conclusion. In L. Haimson & C. Tilly (Eds.), *Strikes, wars and revolution in an international perspective: Strike waves in the late nineteenth and early twentieth centuries* (pp. 525–535). Cambridge, UK: Cambridge University Press.

Haimson, L., & Tilly, C. (1989). *Strikes, wars and revolution in an international perspective: Strike waves in the late nineteenth and early twentieth centuries*. Cambridge, UK: Cambridge University Press.

Hamnett, C. (2003). *Unequal city: London in the global arena*. London: Routledge.

Hardt, M., & Negri, A. (2004). *Multitude: War and democracy in the age of empire*. New York: Penguin Press.

Hardy, J. (2014). *Critical political economy of the media: An introduction*. Abingdon, UK and New York: Routledge.

Harrod, J., & O'Brien, R. (Eds.). (2002a). *Global unions? Theories and strategies of organised labour in the global political economy*. London: Routledge.

Harrod, J., & O'Brien, R. (2002b). Organised labour and the global political economy. In J. Harrod & R. O'Brien (Eds.), *Global unions? Theories and strategies of organised labour in the global political economy* (pp. 3–28). London: Routledge.

Harvey, D. (2007). *A brief history of neoliberalism*. Oxford, UK: Oxford University Press.

Hattingh, S. (2013). The Marikana massacre. *Anarcho-Syndicalist Review*, *60*, 11–18.

Hattingh, S. (2014). Exploding anger: Workers' struggles and self-organisation in South Africa's mining industry. In I. Ness (Ed.), *New forms of worker organisation* (pp. 97–114). Oakland, CA: PM Press.

Head, S. (2014, February 23). Worse than Wal-Mart: Amazon's sick brutality and secret history of ruthlessly intimidating workers. *Salon*. Retrieved from http://www.salon.com/2014/02/23/worse_than_wal_mart_amazons_sick_brutality_and_secret_history_of_ruthlessly_intimidating_workers/

Healy, G., Heery, E., Taylor, P., & Brown, W. (Eds.). (2004). *The future of worker representation*. Basingstoke, UK: Palgrave.

Hearn, J., & Bergos, M. (2011). Latin American cleaners fight for survival: Lessons for migrant activists. *Race and Class*, *53*(1), 65–82.

Heery, E. (2005). Sources of change in trade unions. *Work, Employment and Society*, *19*(1), 91–100.

Heery, E., Delbridge, R., Salmon, J., Simms, M., & Simpson, D. (2002). Global labour? The transferring of the organising model to the UK. In Y. Deborah & I. Smith (Eds.), *Globalisation, employment and the workplace* (pp. 41–68). London: Routledge.

Heery, E., & Kelly, J. (1994). Professional, participative and managerial unionism: An interpretation of change in trade unions. *Work, Employment and Society*, *8*(1), 1–22.

Heimeshoss, L-M., & Schwenken, H. (Eds.). (2011). *Domestic workers count: Global data on an often invisible sector*. Kassel, Germany: Kassel University Press.

Helmore, E. (2013, August 10). US fast-food workers in vanguard of growing protests at 'starvation' wages. *The Guardian*. Retrieved from http://www.theguardian.com/world/2013/aug/10/us-fast-food-protests-wages

Henwood, D. (2012, January 29). Reflections on the current disorder. *Left Business Observer News*. Retrieved from http://lbo-news.com/2012/01/29/reflections-on-the-current-disorder/

Herman, E., & McChesney, R. (1997). *Global media: The new missionaries of global capitalism*. New York: Continuum.

Herman, E., & McChesney, R. (1998). *The global media: Missionaries of global capitalism*. London: Cassell.

Herman E., & Chomsky, N. (2002). *Manufacturing consent: The political economy of the mass media*. New York: Pantheon. (Original work published 1988)

Herod, A. (2002). Organising globally, organising locally: Union spatial strategy in a global economy. In J. Harrod & R. O'Brien (Eds.), *Global unions? Theory and strategies of organised labour in the global economy* (pp. 83–99). London: Routledge.

Herod, A., & Aguiar, L. (2006). Cleaners and the dirty work of neoliberalism. *Antipode, 38*(3), 425–434.

Heyes, J. (2009). Recruiting and organising migrant workers through education and training: A comparison of Community and the GMB. *Industrial Relations Journal, 40*(3), 182–197.

Higgins, C. (2014, August 18). BBC's long struggle to present the facts without fear or favour. *The Guardian*. Retrieved from http://www.theguardian.com/media/2014/aug/18/-sp-bbc-report-facts-impartial

Hind, D. (2008). *The threat to reason*. London: Verso.

Hind, D. (2012). *The return of the public: Democracy, power and the case for media reform*. London: Verso.

Hindman, M. (2009). *The myth of digital democracy*. Princeton, NJ: Princeton University Press.

Hintz, A. (2013). Dimensions of modern freedom of expression: WikiLeaks, policyhacking, and digital freedoms. In B. Brevini, A. Hintz, & P. McCurdy (Eds.), *Beyond WikiLeaks: Implications for the future of communications, journalism and society* (pp. 146–165). Basingstoke, UK: Palgrave.

Hintz, A. (2015, forthcoming). Social media censorship, privatised regulation, and new restrictions to protest and dissent. In L. Dencik & O. Leistert (Eds.), *Critical perspectives on social media and protest: Between control and emancipation*. London: Rowman & Littlefield International.

Hirsch, S., & van der Walt, L. (2014). *Anarchism and syndicalism in the colonial and postcolonial world, 1870–1940*. Boston: Brill.

Hirst, P., Thompson, G., & Bromley, S. (2009). *Globalisation in question* (3rd ed.). Cambridge, UK: Polity Press.

Hobart, A. (1977). *Organised labour in Latin America*. New York: Harper and Row.

Hobsbawn, E. (1999). *Industry and empire: From 1750 to the present day*. London: Penguin.

Hobsbawn, E. (2007). *Revolutionaries*. London: Abacus.

Hodkinson, S. (2001). *Reviving trade unions: Globalisation, internationalism and the internet*. Retrieved from http://citeseerx.ist.psu.edu/viewdoc/download?doi=10.1.1.201.2351&rep=rep1&type=pdf

Hogan, J., Nolan, P., & Grieco, M. (2010). Unions, technologies of coordination, and the changing contours of globally distributed power. *Labor History*, *51*(1), 29–40.

Holgate, J. (2009). Contested terrain: London's living wage campaign and the tension between community and union organising. In J. McBride & I. Greenwood (Eds.), *Community unionism: A comparative analysis of concepts and contexts* (pp. 49–74). Basingstoke, UK: Palgrave.

Holgate, J. (2013a). Faith in unions: From safe spaces to organised labour? *Capital and Class*, *37*(2), 239–259.

Holgate, J. (2013b). Community organising in the UK: A new approach for trade unions? *Economic and Industrial Democracy*. Available at http://lubswww.leeds.ac.uk/fileadmin/webfiles/ceric/Documents/EDI_paper_Holgate.pdf

Holton, B. (1976). *British syndicalism 1900–1914*. London: Pluto Press.

Hopkins, E. (1995). *Working class self-help in nineteenth-century England*. London: UCL Press.

Horwitt, S. (1989). *Let them call me rebel: Saul Alinsky – His life and legacy*. London: Vintage.

Hossein-Zadeh, I. (2014, August 26). Keynes is dead; long live Marx! *Counterpunch*. Retrieved from http://www.counterpunch.org/2014/08/26/keynes-is-dead-long-live-marx/

House of Commons. (2011). Regeneration: Sixth report of session 2010–12, Vol. 1: Report, together with formal minutes, oral and written evidence (House of Commons Papers). *House of Commons Papers*. London: TSO Publishers.

Howard, P., Agarwal, S., & Hussain, M. (2011). When do states disconnect their digital networks? Regime responses to the political uses of social media. *Communication Review*, *14*(3), 216–232.

Hudson, M. (2005). *Global fracture: The new international economic order*. London: Pluto Press. (Original work published 1977)

Hudson, M. (2012a). *Finance capitalism and its discontents*. Dresden, Germany: Islet.

Hudson, M. (2012b). *The bubble and beyond*. Dresden, Germany: Islet.

Hugill, P. J. (1999). *Global communications since 1844: Geopolitics and technology*. Baltimore, MD: Johns Hopkins University Press.

Human Rights Watch. (2013). *World report 2013: Russia*. Retrieved from http://www.hrw.org/world-report/2013/country-chapters/russia

Humboldt, L. (1993). *The limits of state action*. New York: Liberty Fund Inc.

Hunya, G., & Stöllinger, R. (2009). *Foreign direct investment flows between the EU and the BRICs*. The Vienna Institute for Economic Studies Research Report 359.

Hwang, D. (2014). Korean anarchism before 1945. In S. Hirsch & L. van der Walt (Eds.), *Anarchism and syndicalism in the colonial and postcolonial world, 1870–1940* (pp. 95–130). Boston: Brill.

Hyams, E. (1979). *Pierre-Joseph Proudhon*. London: John Murray.

Hyman, R. (1999). Imagined solidarities? Can trade unions resist globalisation? *Globalisation and Labour Relations*. Available at http://www.antenna.nl/~waterman/hyman2.html

Hyman, R. (2001). European integration and industrial relations: A case of variable geometry? In P. Waterman & J. Wills (Eds.), *Place, space and the new labour Internationalism* (pp. 164–179). Oxford, UK: Blackwell.

Hyman, R., & Gumbrell-McCormick, R. (2010). Trade unions, politics and parties: Is a new configuration possible? *Transfer: European Journal of Labour and Research, 16*(3), 315–331.

International Labour Organization (ILO). (2011). *C189 – Domestic workers convention, 2011*. Retrieved from http://www.ilo.org/dyn/normlex/en/f?p=NORMLEXPUB:12100:0::NO::p12100_instrument_id:2551460

International Labour Organization (ILO). (2014). *Domestic workers: Making decent work a reality for domestic workers worldwide*. Retrieved from http://www.ilo.org/global/topics/domestic-workers/lang--en/index.htm

International Trade Union Confederation (ITUC). (2012, June 6). *Annual survey of violation of trade union rights*. Retrieved from http://www.ituc-csi.org/annual-survey-of-violations-of,11418

International Workers of the World (IWW). (2011). IWW cleaners rally in Parliament raises call to unite our struggles. *Solidarity Forever*, p. 3. Retrieved from http://www.autrefutur.net/IMG/pdf/Solidarity_Forever1_11.pdf

Jaffe, S. (2014, January 16). How Walmart organisers turned the internet into a shop floor. *In These Times*. Retrieved from http://inthesetimes.com/article/16116/how_walmart_organizers_turned_the_internet_into_a_shop_floor

Jakobsen, K. (2001). Rethinking the international confederation of free trade unions and its inter-American regional organisation. In P. Waterman & J. Wills (Eds.), *Place, space and the new labour internationalism* (pp. 59–79). Oxford, UK: Blackwell.

Jakobsen, K., & Barbosa, A. (2008). Neoliberal policies, labor market restructuring and social exclusion: Brazil's working class response. In A. Bieler, I. Lindberg, I., & D. Pillay (Eds.), *Labour and the challenges of globalisation* (pp. 115–138). London: Pluto Press.

Jennings, J. (1990). *Syndicalism in France*. Basingstoke, UK: Macmillan.

Jessop, B. (2002). *The future of the capitalist state*. Cambridge, UK: Polity Press.

Jewkes, Y., & Yar, M. (Eds.). (2009). *The handbook of internet crime*. London: Routledge.

Jin, D. Y. (2013). The construction of platform imperialism in the globalization era. *Triple-C: Communication, Capitalism & Critique, 11*(1). Retrieved from http://www.triple-c.at/index.php/tripleC/article/view/458

Johnson, P. (2000). The resurgence of labour as citizenship movement in the new labour relations environment. *Critical Sociology*, 26(1–2), 139–160.

Johnson, S. (2009, May). The quiet coup. *The Atlantic Online*. Retrieved from http://www.uvm.edu/~wgibson/Classes/11f09/Of_interest/Simon%20Johnson.pdf

Jones, D. (2012). *Who cares wins: Why good business is better business*. Harlow, UK: Pearson.

Jones, N. (2009, March 6). Miner's strike anniversary: Journalists owe a collective apology over vindictive pit closures [Web log]. Retrieved from http://www.nicholasjones.org.uk/40-articles/trade-union-reporting/92-miners-strike-anniversary-journalists-owe-a-collective-apology-over-vindictive-pit-closures

Jordan, T., & Taylor, P. A. (2004). *Hacktivism and cyberwars: Rebels with a cause?* London and New York: Routledge.

Jun, N. (2009). Anarchist philosophy and working class history: A brief history and commentary. *Working USA: The Journal of Labour and Society, 12*(3), 505–519.

Juris, J. (2005). The new digital media and activist networking within anti-corporate globalisation movements. *Annals of the American Academy of Political and Social Sciences*, *597*, 189–208.

Juris, J. (2008). *Networking futures: The movements against corporate globalisation*. Durham, NC: Duke University Press.

Juris, J. (2012). Reflections on #occupy everywhere: Social media, public space, and emerging logics of aggregation. *American Ethnologist*, 39(2), 259–79.

Justice for cleaners. (2013). Sticky scrubbing, wretched wages. *Justice for Cleaners*. Retrieved from http://justiceforcleaners.webs.com/

Kahmann, M. (2003). Trade unions and the growth of the information economy. *Department of Work and Pensions*. Retrieved from http://library.fes.de/pdf-files/gurn/00314.pdf

Kapstein, E. (1996). Workers and the world economy. *Foreign Affairs*, *75*(3), 16–37.

Kapstein, E. (2000). Winners and losers in the global economy. *International Organisation*, *54*(2), 359–384.

Karatani, K. (2005). *Transcritique*. Cambridge, MA: MIT Press.

Kaun, A. (2015, forthcoming). 'This Space Belongs to Us!': Protest spaces in times of accelerating capitalism. In L. Dencik & O. Leistert (Eds.), *Critical perspectives on social media and protest: Between control and emancipation*. London: Rowman & Littlefield International.

Keane, J. (1991). *The Media and democracy*. Cambridge, UK: Polity Press.

Keane, J. (2013). *Democracy and media decadence*. Cambridge, UK: Cambridge University Press.

Kellner, D. (1999). Globalisation from below? Towards a radical democratic technopolitics. *Angelaki*, 4(2),101–113.

Kemp, D. (2011). *How facebook changed the world* [Television series]. London: British Broadcasting Corporation.

Kerr, A., & Waddington, J. (2013). E-Communications: An aspect of union renewal or merely doing things electronically? *British Journal of Industrial Relations*, 2(3), 1–24.

Khatib, K., Killijoy, M., & McGuire, M. (Eds.). (2012). *We are many: Reflections on movement strategy from occupation to liberation*. Edinburgh, Scotland: AK Press.

Khuri-Makdisi, I. (2010). *The Eastern Mediterranean and the making of global radicalism, 1860–1914*. Los Angeles: University of California Press.

Kirkpatrick, J. (2011). The IWW cleaners branch union in the UK. In Ness, I. (Ed.). (2014b). *New forms of worker organisation: The syndicalist and autonomist restoration of class struggle unionism*. Oakland, CA: PM Press, 233–257.

Klein, N. (2000). *No logo*. London: Fourth Estate.

Klein, N. (2008). *Shock doctrine: The rise of disaster capitalism*. London: Penguin.

Kollock, P., & Smith, M. (1999). Communities in cyberspace. In P. Kollock & M. Smith (Eds.), *Communities in cyberspace* (pp. 3–28). London: Routledge.

Komito, L. (2011). Social media and migration: Virtual community 2.0. *Journal of the American Society for Information Science and Technology*, 62(6), 1075–1086.

Koonings, K., Kruijt, D., & Wils, F. (1995). The very long march of history. In H. Thomas (Ed.), *Globalisation and third world trade unions*. London: Zed Books. Retrieved from http://www.daga.org.hk/press/gtwtu/gtwtupart2section5.html

Kornbluth, J. (2011). *Rebel voices: An IWW anthology*. Edinburgh, Scotland: AK Press.

Kropotkin, P. (2010). *Kropotkin's revolutionary pamphlets*. New York: Kessenger.

Laforcade, G. (2014). Straddling the nation and the working world: Anarchism and syndicalism on the docks and rivers of Argentina, 1900–1930. In S. Hirsch & L. van der Walt, *Anarchism and syndicalism in the colonial and postcolonial world, 1870–1940* (pp. 321–362) Boston: Brill.

Lambert, R. (2002). Labour movement renewal in the era of Globalisation: Unions' responses in the South. In J. Harrod & R. O'Brien (Eds.), *Global unions? Theories and strategies of organised labour in the global political economy* (pp. 185–203). London: Routledge.

Lash, S., & Urry, J. (1991). *The end of organised capitalism*. Cambridge, UK: Polity Press.

Lazonick, W. (1993). *Business organisation and the myth of the market economy*. Cambridge, UK: Cambridge University Press.

Lazzarato, M. (2004). From capital-labour to capital-life. *Ephemera*, 4(3), 187–208.

Lee, E. (1997). *The labour movement and the internet: The new internationalism*. London: Pluto Press.

Lee, E. (2000). How the internet is changing unions. *Working USA*, 4(2), 56–72.

Lee, E. (2005a). *How internet radio can change the world: An activist's handbook*. Lincoln, NE: iUniverse.

Lee, E. (2005b). Menshevism in Iraq [Web log]. Retrieved from http://www.ericlee.info/2005/02/menshevism_in_iraq.html

Lee, E. (2013, December 16). Interview with founder of *Labour Start*.

Lee, E., & Mustill, E. (2013). *Campaigning online and winning*. Marston Gate: LabourStart.

Lee, F. S., & Bekken, J. (2009). *Radical economics and labour*. New York and Abingdon, UK: Routledge.

Lehman, C. (2012, March 21). Winging it: The battle between Reagan and PATCO. *The Nation*. Retrieved from http://www.thenation.com/article/166938/winging-it-battle-between-reagan-and-patco

Leimgruber, M. (2007, September). *Bringing private insurance back in: An international insurance think tank for the post Keynesian decades: the "Geneva Association" (1971–2000s)*. Paper presented at the 11th conference of the European Business History Association, Geneva. Retrieved from http://www.ebha.org/ebha2007/pdf/Leimgruber.pdf

Leistert, O. (2015, forthcoming). The revolution will not be liked: On the systemic constraints of corporate social media platforms for protests. In L. Dencik & O. Leistert (Eds.), *Critical perspectives on social media and protest: Between control and emancipation*. London: Rowman & Littlefield International.

Lenin, V. (1987). *Essential works of Lenin: What is to be done?* H. M. Christman (Ed.). New York: Dover.

Lerner, S. (2007). Global corporations, global unions. *Contexts*, 6(3), 16–22.

Levy, C. (2010). The rooted cosmopolitan: Errico Malatesta, syndicalism, transnationalism and the international labour movement. In D. Berry & C. Bantman (Eds.), *New perspectives on anarchism, labor and syndicalism* (pp. 61–79). Newcastle-upon-Tyne, UK: Cambridge Scholars Publishing.

Lewis, J. (2013). *Beyond consumer capitalism: Media and the limits to imagination*. Cambridge, UK: Polity Press.

Lewis, J. (2014). Mission statement. *John Lewis Partnership*. Retrieved from http://www.johnlewispartnership.co.uk/content/cws/resources/faqs/general.html

LibCom. (2011). IWW meeting at Parliament. *LibCom*. Retrieved from http://libcom.org/forums/general/real-27092011?page=1

Lippmann, W. (1922). *Public opinion*. New York: Retrieved from http://xroads.virginia.edu/~Hyper2/CDFinal/Lippmann/cover.html.

Lippmann, W. (2013). *Public opinion*. New York: Merchant Books. (Original work published 1922)

Logan, J. (2002). Consultants, lawyers and the 'union free' movement in the USA since the 1970s. *Industrial Relations Journal*, *33*(3), 197–214.

Logan, J. (2006). The union avoidance industry in the United States. *British Journal of Industrial Relations*, *44*(4), 651–675.

London's Poverty Profile. (2013). *Key facts*. Retrieved from http://www.londonspovertyprofile.org.uk/key-facts/

Long, R. T. (1998). Toward a libertarian theory of class. *Social Philosophy and Policy*, *15*(2), 303–349.

Lovell, J. (1984). *From Marx to Lenin*. Cambridge, UK: Cambridge University Press.

Lovink, G., Olma, S., & Rossiter, N. (2014). On the creative question – Nine Theses. *MyCreativity, Institute of Network Cultures*. Retrieved from http://networkcultures.org/mycreativity/2014/11/19/on-the-creative-question-manifest-by-geert-lovink-sebastian-olma-ned-rossiter/

Lowery, B. R. (2013). The Authority of Anyone. Tedx Talks, Houses of Parliament, June.

Lowy, M. (2014). A common banner: Marxists and anarchists in the first international. *Socialism and Democracy*, *28*(2), 107–114.

Lubbers, E. (2012). *Secret manoeuvres in the dark: Corporate and police spying on activists*. London: Pluto Press.

Lubin, G. (2011, March 2). Hillary Clinton says Al Jazeera is putting American media to shame. *Business Insider*. Retrieved from http://www.businessinsider.com/hillary-clinton-al-jazeera-2011-3

Lucio, M., Walker, S., & Trevorrou, O. (2009). Making networks and (re)making trade union bureaucracy. *New Technology, Work and Employment*, *24*(2), 115–130.

Lutz, H. (2008). *Migration and domestic work: A European perspective on a global theme*. Farnham, UK: Ashgate.

Lynd, S., & Gross, D. (2011). *Solidarity unionism at Starbucks*. Oakland, CA: PM Press.

Lynd, S., & Thompson, F. (1992). *Solidarity unionism: Rebuilding the labour movement from below*. New York: Charles H. Kerr.

Lyon, D. (2001). *Surveillance society: Monitoring everyday life*. Buckingham and Philadelphia: Open University Press.

Lyon, D. (2014). Surveillance, Snowden, and big data: Capacities, consequences and critique. *Big Data and Society*, *1*(2). Retrieved from http://bds.sagepub.com/content/1/2/2053951714541861

Madianou, M. (2014). Smartphones as polymedia. *Journal of Computer-Mediated Communication*, *19*, 667–680.

Mair, P. (2013). *Ruling the void: The hollowing of Western democracy*. London: Verso.

Malatesta, E. (2014). *The method of freedom: An Errico Malatesta reader*. Edinburgh, Scotland: AK Press.

Mann, M. (2005). *The dark side of democracy*. Cambridge, UK: Cambridge University Press.

Mann, M. (2011). *Power in the twenty-first century*. Cambridge, UK: Polity Press.

Mann, M. (2012). *The sources of social power: Volume 2, the rise of classes and nation-states, 1760–1914*. Cambridge, UK: Cambridge University Press.

Mann, S. (2004). 'Sousveillance': Inverse surveillance in multimedia imaging. *Multimedia '04: Proceedings of the 12th annual ACM international conference on Multimedia* (pp. 620–627). New York: ACM.

Mannheim, K. (1971). *Man and society in an age of reconstruction*. London: Routledge.

Mannheim, K. (1985). *Ideology and utopia*. New York: Mariner.

Marx, K., & Engels, F. (2003). *The communist manifesto*. London: Bookmarks. (Original work published 1848).

Mason, P. (2008). *Live working or die fighting: How the working class went global*. London: Vintage.

Mason, P. (2010). *Meltdown: The end of the age of greed*. London: Verso.

Mason, P. (2012). *Why it's kicking off everywhere: The new global revolutions*. London and Brooklyn: Verso.

Mason, P. (2013). *Why it's STILL kicking off everywhere*. London: Verso.

Mather, C. (2013). *'Yes, we did it!' How the world's domestic workers won their international rights and recognition*. Cambridge, MA and Manchester: WIEGO.

Mattick, P. (1978). *Anti-Bolshevik communism*. London: Merlin Press.

Maximoff, G. P. (1940). *The guillotine at work*. Chicago, IL: Cienfuegos Press.

May, J., Wills, J., Datta, K., Evans, Y., Herbert, J., & McIlwaine, C. (2007). Keeping London working: Global cities, the British state and London's new migrant division of labour. *Transactions of the Institute of British Geographers*, *32*(2), 151–167.

Mazzucato, M. (2015). The innovative state. *Foreign Affairs*, *94*(1), 61–68.

Mbah, S., & Igariwey, I. G. (1997). *African anarchism: The history of a movement*. Tucson, AZ: Sharp Press.

McBride, J., & Greenwood, I. (Eds.). (2009). *Community unionism: A comparative analysis of concepts and contexts*. Basingstoke, UK: Palgrave.

McCallum, J. (2013). *Global unions, local power*. Ithaca, NY: Cornell University Press.

McCaughey, M., & Ayers, M. (Eds). (2003). *Cyberactivism: Online activism in theory and practice*. London: Routledge.

McChesney, R. (2013). *Digital disconnect: How capitalism is turning the internet against democracy*. New York: The New Press.

McDonald's Corporation. (2014). *Annual report*. Retrieved from http://www.sec.gov/Archives/edgar/data/63908/000006390814000019/mcd-12312013x10k.htm

McKay, I. (2012). Laying the foundations: Proudhon's contribution to anarchist economics. In D. Shannon, A. J. Nocella, & J. Asimakoulos (Eds.), *The accumulation of freedom: Writings on anarchist economics* (pp. 64–79). Edinburgh, Scotland: AK Press.

McKay, I. (2015). The London dock strike of 1889. *Anarcho-Syndicalist Review*, *63*, 30–33.

McLuhan, M. (1964). *Understanding media: Extensions of man*. New York: Manor.

McNair, B. (2010), *Political Communication in Britain: The leader debates, the campaign and the media in the 2010 general election*. Basingstoke, UK: Palgrave.

McNally, D. (2011). *Global slump*. Oakland, CA: PM Press.

McNeill, W. (1979). *A world history*. Oxford, UK: Oxford University Press.

McVeigh, K. (2013, August 29). Fast-food workers continue fight against low wages: 'This is our right'. *The Guardian*. Retrieved from http://www.theguardian.com/world/2013/aug/29/fast-food-workers-low-pay-nationwide-walkout

Meikle, G. (2014). Social media, visibility, and activism: The *Kony 2012* campaign. In M. Ratto & M. Boler (Eds.), *DIY citizenship: Critical making and social media* (pp. 373–384). Cambridge, MA: MIT Press.

Mertes, T. (Ed.) (2004). *A movement of movements: Is another world really possible?*, London and New York: Verso.

Mestrovic, S. (1994). *The Balkanisation of the West*. London: Routledge.

Meyerson, H. (2013, August 27). The link between civil and economic rights. *The Washington Post*. Retrieved from http://www.washingtonpost.com/opinions/harold-meyerson-the-link-between-civil-and-economic-rights/2013/08/27/18390a18-0f48-11e3-bdf6-e4fc677d94a1_story.html

Michels, R. (1968). *Political parties*. London: Simon & Schuster.

Mies, M. (1998). *Patriarchy and accumulation of a world-scale: Women in the international division of labour*. London: Zed Books.

Mignolo, W. (2000). *Local histories/global designs: Coloniality, subalterns knowledges and border thinking*. Princeton, NJ: Princeton University Press.

Migrant Voice. (2014). Justice for cleaners - Consuelo's story. *Migrant Voice*. Retrieved from http://www.migrantvoice.org/voices/headlines/justice-for-cleaners-consuelo%E2%80%99s-story.html

Mihyo, P., & Schiphorst, F. (1995). A context of sharp economic decline. In H. Thomas (Ed.), *Globalisation and third world trade unions* (pp. 169–200). London: Zed Books.

Milan, S. (2013). WikiLeaks, Anonymous, and the exercise of individuality: Protesting in the Cloud. In B. Brevini, A. Hintz, & P. McCurdy (Eds.), *Beyond WikiLeaks: Implications for the future of communications, journalism and society* (pp. 191–208). Basingstoke, UK: Palgrave.

Miller, D., & Dinan, W. (2008). *A century of spin: How public relations became the cutting edge of corporate power*. London: Pluto Press.

Mills, C. W. (2001). *The new men of power: America's labour leaders*. Champaign: University of Illinois Press. (Original work published 1948)

Mintz, F. (2013). *Anarchism and workers' self-management in revolutionary Spain*. Edinburgh, Scotland: AK Press.

Mishel, L., & Shierholz, H. (2013). A decade of flat wages. Briefing Paper #365. *Economic Policy Institute*. Retrieved from http://www.epi.org/publication/a-decade-of-flat-wages-the-key-barrier-to-shared-prosperity-and-a-rising-middle-class/

Mitchell, M. (1937). *Storm over Spain*. London: Martin Secker and Warburg.

Moloney, K. (2000). *Rethinking public relations: The spin and the substance*. London: Routledge.

Monks, J. (1992). A British view. In M. Crosby & M. Easson (Eds.), *What should unions do?* (pp. 78–95). London: Pluto Press.

Montgomery, D. (1979). *Workers' control in America*. Cambridge, UK: Cambridge University Press.

Moody, K. (2007). *US Labor in troubled times: The failure of reform from above, the promise of revival from below*. London: Verso.

Moore, B. (1967). *The social origins of dictatorship and democracy*. London: Penguin.

Moore, S. (2011). *New trade union activism: Class consciousness or social identity?* Basingstoke, UK: Palgrave.

Moore, S., & Watson, M. (2009). *Unison: Migrant workers participation project*. Retrieved from http://www.workinglives.org/fms/MRSite/Research/wlri/News/UNISON%20migrant%20workers%20evaluation%20report.pdf

Moore Jr., B. (1987). *Authority and inequality under capitalism and socialism*. Oxford, UK: Clarendon Press.

Morris, B. (1994). Flores Magon and the Mexican Liberal Party. *The Anarchist Library*. Retrieved from http://theanarchistlibrary.org/library/brian-morris-flores-magon-and-the-mexican-liberal-party

Mosco, V. (2008). *The political economy of communication* (2nd ed). London and Thousand Oaks: Sage.

Moses, J. A. (1990). *Trade union theory from Marx to Walesa*. Oxford, UK: Berg.

Mullins, D., & Pawson, H. (2011). *After council housing: Britain's new social landlords*. Basingstoke, UK: Palgrave.

Munck, R. (2002). *Globalisation and labour: The new 'Great Transformation'*. London: Zed Books.

Munck, R., & Waterman, P. (Eds.). (1999). *Labour worldwide in the era of globalisation: Alternative union models in the new world order*. Basingstoke, UK: Macmillan Press.

Munro, A. (2001). A feminist trade union agenda? The continued significance of class, gender and race. *Gender, Work and Organisation*, 8(4), 454–471.

Munusamy, R. (2012, October 25). Cyril Ramaphosa: Betrayal does not get more painful than this. *The Guardian*. Retrieved from http://www.theguardian.com/world/2012/oct/25/cyril-ramaphosa-marikana-email

Musthill, E. (2013). *The global labour movement: An introduction*. CreateSpace.

Ness, I. (2011). *Guest workers and resistance to US corporate despotism*. Chicago: University of Illinois Press.

Ness, I. (2014a). New forms of worker organisation. In I. Ness (Ed.), *New forms of worker organisation: The syndicalist and autonomist restoration of class struggle unionism* (pp. 1–19). Oakland, CA: PM Press.

Ness, I. (Ed.). (2014b). *New forms of worker organisation: The syndicalist and autonomist restoration of class struggle unionism*. Oakland, CA: PM Press.

Ness, I., & Azzellini, D. (2011). *Ours to master and to own: Workers' control from the commune to the present*. Chicago, IL: Haymarket Books.

Nettlau, M. (2000). *A short history of anarchism*. London: Freedom Press.

North American Congress on Latin America (NACLA). (2014). *Mexico: The state against the working class*. Available at https://nacla.org/edition/10161

Notes from nowhere. (2003). *We are everywhere: The irresistible rise of global anticapitalism*. London: Verso.

O'Connor, C. (2014, January 28). With minimum wage on state of the union agenda, fast food workers are guests of honor. *Forbes*. Retrieved from http://www.forbes.com/sites/clareoconnor/2014/01/28/with-minimum-wage-on-state-of-the-union-agenda-fast-food-workers-are-guests-of-honor/

O'Connor, M. (2013, March 6). 10 Top social media monitoring & analytics tools. *Tweak Your Biz*. Retrieved from http://tweakyourbiz.com/marketing/2013/03/06/10-top-social-media-monitoring-analytics-tools/

O'Connor, S. (2013, February 8). Amazon unpacked. *Financial Times*. Retrieved from http://www.ft.com/cms/s/0/ed6a985c-70bd-11e2-85d0-00144feab49a.html#slide0

Olasky, M. (2011). *Corporate public relations: A new historical perspective*. Abingdon, UK: Routledge.

Organisation for Economic Co-operation and Development (OECD). (2002). *Intra-industry and intra-firm trade and the internationalisation of production*. Retrieved from http://www.oecd.org/economy/outlook/2752923.pdf

Organisation for Economic Co-operation and Development (OECD). (2010). Competition, state aids and subsidies. *Policy Roundtables*. Retrieved from http://www.oecd.org/competition/sectors/48070736.pdf

Organisation for Economic Co-operation and Development (OECD). (2014). *Introduction to regional trade agreements*. Retrieved from http://www.oecd.org/trade/benefitlib/regionaltradeagreements.htm

Orwell, G. (2005). Politics and the English language. In *Orwell: In front of your nose – 1945–50* (pp. 127–139). Boston: Nonpareil Books.

Oxenbridge, S., & Brown, W. (2004). A poisoned chalice? Trade union representation in partnership and cooperative employer-union relationships. In G. Healey, E. Heery, P. Taylor, & W. Brown (Eds.), *The future of worker representation* (pp. 187–206). Basingstoke, UK: Palgrave.

Palumbo-Liu, D., Robbins, B., & Tanoukhi, N. (Eds.). (2011). *Immanuel Wallerstein and the problem of the world*. Durham, NC: Duke University Press.

Pannekoek, A. (2003). *Worker's councils*. Edinburgh, UK: AK Press.

Parker, J. (2006). Trade union women's groups and their effect on women's goals and strategies. *Human Resources Management Journal, 16*(4), 411–443.

Parker, T. (2014, July 5). Interview with researcher on domestic workers.

Pearson, R., & Syfang, G. (2001). New hope or false dawn? Voluntary codes of conduct, labour regulation and social policy in a globalising world. *Global Social Policy, 1*(1), 48–77.

Peck, J., & Tickell, A. (2002). Neoliberalising space. *Antipode, 34*, 38–404.

Pelling, H. (1988). *A history of British trade unionism*. London: Penguin.

Pelloutier, F. (1896). *Art and revolt*. Retrieved from http://libcom.org/library/art-revolt-fernand-pelloutier

Però, D., & Solomos, J. (2010). Migrant politics and mobilization: exclusion, engagement, incorporation. *Ethnic and Racial Studies, 35*(1), 1–18.

Peschek, J. (1989). Free the Fortune 500! The American Enterprise Institute and the politics of the capitalism class in the 1970s. *Critical Sociology, 16*(2–3), 165–180.

Petley, J. (2004). Fourth rate estate. *Index on Censorship*, *33*(2), 68–75.

Petley, J. (2013). The state journalism is in: Edward Snowden and the British press. *Communication Ethics*. Retrieved from http://journals.communicationethics.net/free_article.php?id=00057

Pinta, S. (2009). Anarchism, Marxism and the ideological composition of the Chicago idea. *Working USA: The Journal of Labor and Society*, *12*(3), 421–450.

Polanyi, K. (1944). *The great transformation: The political and economic origins of our times*. New York: Beacon Press.

Poole, M. (1981). *Theories of trade unions: A sociology of industrial relations*. London: Routledge and Kegan Paul.

Pouget, E. (1905). What is the union? *Le Syndical*. Retrieved from https://libcom.org/library/what-union-emile-pouget

Proudhon, P-J. (2003). *What is property? An inquiry into the principle of right and of government*. New York: Indypublish. (Original work published 1840)

Proudhon, P-J. (2011). *Property is theft: A Pierre-Joseph Proudhon anthology*. Edinburgh, Scotland: AK Press.

Rasmus, J. (2014). Economists discover inequality (but have yet to explain it) [Web log]. Retrieved from http://jackrasmus.com/2014/05/13/economists-discover-income-inequality-but-have-yet-to-explain-it/

Raw, L. (2014, July 2). Trouble at the Met. *Morning Star Online*. Retrieved from http://www.morningstaronline.co.uk/a-50d0-Trouble-at-the-Met/#.VBGfARZGQQY

Reid, A. J. (2004). *United we stand: A history of Britain's trade unions*. London: Penguin Press.

Renshaw, P. (1999). *The Wobblies: The story of the IWW and syndicalism in the United States*. Chicago, IL: Ivan R. Dee.

Richards, N. M. (2013, November 4). Watching the watchers. *Wired*. Retrieved from http://papers.ssrn.com/sol3/papers.cfm?abstract_id=2350002

Ridley, F. (2008). *Revolutionary syndicalism in France*. Cambridge, UK: Cambridge University Press.

Robinson, W. (2006). 'Aqui estamos y no nos vamos!' Global capital and immigrant rights. *Race and Class*, 48(1), 77–91.

Rocker, R. (1937). *Nationalism and culture*. Los Angeles, CA: Rocker Publications Committee.

Rocker, R. (2004). *Anarcho-syndicalism: Theory and practise*. Edinburgh, Scotland: AK Press.

Rodriguez, E., Ramos, R., & Samis, A. (2003). *Against all tyranny! Essays on anarchism in Brazil*. London: Kate Sharpley Library.

Rosenberg, H. (1946). Political and social consequences of the Great Depression 1873–1896 in Central Europe. *The Economic History Review*, *13*(1), 58–73.

Rosencrance, R. (1996, July/August). The rise of the virtual state. *Foreign Affairs*. Retrieved from http://www.foreignaffairs.com/articles/52241/richard-rosecrance/the-rise-of-the-virtual-state-territory-becomes-pass%C3%83%C2%A9

Roszak, T. (1969). *The making of counter culture*. New York: Anchor Books/Doubleday.

Rudy, P. (2004). 'Justice for Janitors' not 'compensation for custodians'. In R. Milkman & K. Voss (Eds.), *Rebuilding labour: Organising and organisers in the new union movement* (pp. 133–149). Ithaca, NY: Cornell University Press.

Ruskin, G. (2013). Spooky business: Corporate espionage against nonprofit organizations. *Corporate Policy*. Retrieved from http://www.corporatepolicy.org/spookybusiness.pdf

Salerno, S. (1989). *Red November black November: Culture and community in the Industrial Workers of the World*. Albany: State University of New York Press.

Sanburn, J. (2013, July 30). Fast food strikes: Unable to unionise, workers borrow tactics from 'Occupy.' *Time*. Retrieved from http://business.time.com/2013/07/30/fast-food-strikes-unable-to-unionize-workers-borrow-tactics-from-occupy/

Sandoval, M. (2014). Social media?: The unsocial character of capitalist media. In C. Fuchs & M. Sandoval (Eds.), *Critique, social media and the information society* (pp. 144–165). New York and Abingdon, UK: Routledge.

Sassen, S. (1991). *The global city: New York, London, Tokyo*. Princeton, NJ: Princeton University Press.

Savage, L. (2006). Justice for Janitors: Scale of organising and representing workers. *Antipode, 38*(3), 645–666.

Sayer, A. (1992). *Method in social science*. London: Routledge and Kegan Paul.

Schiller, D. (2000). *Digital capitalism*. Cambridge, MA: MIT Press.

Schmidt, M. (2013). *Cartography of revolutionary anarchism*. Edinburgh, Scotland: AK Press.

Schmidt, M., & van der Walt, L. (2009). *Black flame: The revolutionary class politics of anarchism and syndicalism*. Edinburgh, Scotland: AK Press.

Scholte, J. (2008). Defining globalisation. *World Economy, 31*(11), 1471–1502.

Scott, A., & Street, J. (2000). From media politics to E-Protest. *Information, Communication and Society, 3*(2), 215–240.

Scott, J. (1998). *Seeing like a state*. New Haven, CT: Yale University Press.

Sen, A. (2014). The struggle for independent unions in India's industrial belt. In I. Ness (Ed.), *New forms of worker organisation: The syndicalist and autonomist restoration of class struggle unionism* (pp. 84–96). Oakland, CA: PM Press.

Senalp, Ö., & Senalp, G. (2014). Transnational networks of radical labour research. *Networked Labour*. Retrieved from http://www.networkedlabour.net/wp-content/uploads/2014/03/Transnational-Networks-of-Radical-Labour-Research-and-Hactivism.doc

Shaffer, K. (2005). *Anarchism and counter-cultural politics in early twentieth-century Cuba*. Gainesville: University Press of Florida.

Shaffer, K. (2013). *Black flag boricuas: Anarchism, antiauthoritarianism and the left in Puerto Rico, 1897–1921*. Champaign: University of Illinois Press.

Shaikh, A. (Ed.). (2013). *Globalization and the myths of free trade*. Abingdon, UK: Routledge.

Shaikh, A. (2014). *Explaining the global crisis*. Retrieved from http://www.scribd.com/doc/226053804/Anwar-Shaikh-Explaining-the-Global-Crisis

Shannon, D., Nocella, A. J., & Asimakoulos, J. (2012). *The accumulation of freedom: Writings on anarchist economics*. Edinburgh, Scotland: AK Press.

Shantz, J. (2013). *Commonist tendencies: Mutual aid beyond communism*. New York: Punctum Books.

Shea, G. (2001). *Spoiled silk: The red mayor and the great Paterson silk strike*. Bronx, NY: Fordham University Press.

Shirky, C. (2008). *Here comes everybody: The power of organising without organisations*. London: Allen Lane.

Shub, D. (1953). Kropotkin and Lenin. *Russian Review, 12*(4), 227–234.

Siebert, H. (Ed.). (1999). *Globalisation and labour*. Tübingen, Germany: Mohr Siebeck.

Silver, B. (2003). *Forces of labor: Workers' movements and globalisation since 1870*. Cambridge, UK: Cambridge University Press.

Silver, B., & Arrighi, G. (2001). Workers north and south. In L. Panitch & C. Leys (Eds.), *Socialist register 2001: Working classes, global realities* (pp. 53–76). London: Merlin Press.

Simms, M., & Holgate, J. (2010). Organising for what? Where is the debate on the politics of organising? *Work, Employment and Society*, 24(1), 157–168.

Simms, M., Holgate, J., & Heery, E. (2013). *Union voices: Tactics and tensions in UK organising*. Ithaca, NY: Cornell University Press.

Simon, S. F. (1946). Anarchism and anarcho-syndicalism in South America. *The Hispanic American Historical Review*, 26(1), 38–59.

Sklair, L. (2002). *Globalisation: Capitalism and its alternatives* (3rd ed.). Oxford, UK: Oxford University Press.

Smith, J. W. (2003). *Economic democracy: The political struggle of the twenty-first century*. New York: Institute for Economic Democracy.

Snell, D. (2007). Beyond workers' rights: TNCs, human rights abuse and violent conflict in the global south. In K. Bronfenbrenner (Ed.), *Global unions: Challenging transitional capital through cross-border campaigns* (pp. 195–212). Ithaca, NY: Cornell University Press.

Snell, S. (1992). Control theory in strategic HRM. *Academy of Management Journal, 35*(2), 292–327.

Snowden, E. (2013). *Everything you know about the constitution is wrong*. CreateSpace.

Sobel, D. (1990, August 20). B. F. Skinner, the champion of behaviourism, is dead at 86. *The New York Times*. Retrieved from http://www.nytimes.com/1990/08/20/obituaries/b-f-skinner-the-champion-of-behaviorism-is-dead-at-86.html

Solimano, A. (2001). International migration and the global economic order: An overview. *The World Bank*. Retrieved from http://demografi.bps.go.id/phpfiletree/bahan/kumpulan_tugas_mobilitas_pak_chotib/Kelompok_7/Andres_Solimano_International_Migration_and_The_Global_Economic_Order.pdf

Solimano, A., & Watts, N. (2005). International migration, capital flows and the global economy: The long run view. *CEPAL*. Retrieved from http://www.cepal.org/publicaciones/xml/7/22007/lcl2259i.pdf

Solis, B., & Breakenridge, D. (2009). *Putting the public back in public relations*. Upper Saddle River, NJ: Pearson.

Staffing Industry Analysts. (2013). Adecco, Randstad, ManpowerGroup top list of largest global staffing firms. *Staffing Industry*. Retrieved from http://www.staffingindustry.com/Research-Publications/Daily-News/Adecco-Randstad-ManpowerGroup-top-list-of-largest-global-staffing-firms-27641

Standing, G. (1989). Global feminisation through flexible labour. *World Development, 17*(7), 1077–1095.

Stern, A. (2006). *A country that works: Getting America back on track*. New York: The Free Press.

Stevis, D. (2002). Union, capital and states. In J. Harrod & R. O'Brien (Eds.), *Global unions? Theory and strategies of organised labour in the global economy* (pp. 130–150). London: Routledge.

Stevis, D., & Boswell, T. (2007). International framework agreements: Opportunities and challenges for global unions. In K. Bronfenbrenner (Ed.), *Global unions: Challenging transnational capital through cross-border campaigns* (pp. 174–194). Ithaca, NY: Cornell University Press.

Suriano, J. (2010). *Paradoxes of utopia: Anarchist culture and politics in Buenos Aires 1890–1910.* Edinburgh, Scotland: AK Press.

Swank, D., & Betz, H-G. (2003). Globalisation, the welfare state and right-wing populism in Europe. *Socio-Economic Review, 1*(2), 215–245.

Tabor, R. (1987). *A look at Leninism.* New York: Aspect Foundation.

Taibbi, M. (2009, July). The great American bubble machine. *Rolling Stone.* Retrieved from http://www.rollingstone.com/politics/news/the-great-american-bubble-machine-20100405

Tattersall, A. (2007). Labor-community coalitions, global union alliances and the potential of the SEIU's global partnerships. In K. Bronfenbrenner (Ed.), *Global unions: Challenging transnational capital through cross-border campaigns* (pp. 155–173). Ithaca, NY: Cornell University Press.

Taylor, P. (2003). *Munitions of the mind: A history of propaganda.* Manchester, UK: Manchester University Press.

Taylor, R. (1994). *The future of trade unions.* London: Andre Deutsch.

Tedlow, R. (1996.) *New and improved: The story of mass marketing in America.* Boston: Harvard Business Press Review.

Terry, M. (2003). Partnership and the future of trade unions. *Economic and Industrial Democracy, 24*(4), 485–507.

Thomas, H. (Ed.). (1995a). *Globalisation and third world trade unions.* London: Zed Books.

Thomas, H. (1995b). The erosion of trade unions. In H. Thomas (Ed.), *Globalisation and third world trade unions* (pp. 3–27). London: Zed Books.

Thompson, E. P. (1963). *The making of the English working-class.* London: Penguin.

Thompson, F. W., & Bekken, J. (2006). *The I.W.W.: Its first 100 years.* Boston: Red Sun Press.

Thompson, J. B. (1991). *Ideology and modern culture.* Stanford, CA: Stanford University Press.

Thompson, J. B. (1995). *The media and modernity: A social theory of the media.* Cambridge, UK: Polity Press.

Thompson, P. (1983). *The nature of work.* Basingstoke, UK: Macmillan Press.

Thompson, P., & Ackroyd, S. (1995). All quiet on the workplace front? A critique of recent trends in British industrial sociology. *Sociology,* 29(4), 615–633.

Thorpe, V. (1999). Global unionism: The challenge. In R. Munck & P. Waterman (Eds.), *Labour worldwide in the era of globalisation: Alternative union models in the new world order* (pp. 218–228). Basingstoke, UK: Macmillan Press.

Thorpe, W. (1991). Afterword: The Hungarian minority socialists in European perspective. In J. Bak (Ed.), *Liberty and socialism: Writings of libertarian socialists in Hungary 1884–1919* (pp. 233–272). Lanham, MD: Rowman and Littlefield.

Thussu, D. (2007). *International Communication: Continuity and Change.* London: Bloomsbury.

Tilly, C. (1985). War making and state making as organised crime. In P. Evans, D. Rueschemeyer, & T. Skocpol (Eds.). *Bringing the state back in* (pp. 169–191). Cambridge, UK: Cambridge University Press.

Tilly, C. (1989). Theories and realities. In L. Haimson & C. Tilly (Eds.), *Strikes, wars and revolution in an international perspective: Strike waves in the late nineteenth and early twentieth centuries* (pp. 3–17). Cambridge, UK: Cambridge University Press.

Tilly, C. (1992). *Coercion, capital and European states; 990–1992 A.D.* London: Wiley-Blackwell.

Tilly, C. (1995). Globalization threatens Labor's Rights. *International Labor and Working-Class History*. 47(2) 1–23.

Tilly, C., & Blockmans, W. (1994). *Cities and the rise of states in Europe A.D. 1000 to 1800*. Boulder, CO: Westview Press.

Tilly, C., & Wood, L. J. (Eds.). (2013). *Social movements: 1768–2012*. Boulder, CO: Paradigm.

Todd, R., & Coates, K. (Eds.). (2008). *One big union: Reviewing the history of a big idea*. Nottingham, UK: Spokesman Press.

Tracey, M. (1998). *Decline and fall of Public Service Broadcasting*. Oxford, UK: Oxford University Press.

Turcato, D. (2009). European anarchism in the 1890s: Why labor matters in categorising anarchism. *Working USA: The Journal of Labour and Society*, *12*(3), 451–466.

Turow, J. (2011). *The daily you*. New Haven, CT and London: Yale University Press.

Uldam, J. (2014, July 1). Corporate management of visibility and the fantasy of the post-political: Social media and surveillance. *New Media & Society*. DOI: 1461444814541526

UNCTAD. (2014). *World investment report*. Geneva, Switzerland: UN Publications.

Urbina, I. (2010, March 19). Acorn on brink of bankruptcy, officials say. *The New York Times*. Retrieved from http://www.nytimes.com/2010/03/20/us/politics/20acorn.html?pagewanted=all&_r=0

Van Aelst, P. & Walgrave, S. (2004). New media, new movements? The role of the internet in shaping the "anti-globalization" movement. In van de Donk, W. et al. (Eds.), *Cyberprotest: New Media, Citizens, and Social Movements* (pp. 97–122). New York: Routledge.

van der Linden, M. (1998). Second thoughts on revolutionary syndicalism. *Labor History*, 63(2), 182–196.

van der Linden, M. (2004). Proletarian internationalism. In I. Wallerstein (Ed.), *The modern world-system in the long durée* (pp. 107–132). Boulder, CO: Paradigm.

Van Laer, J., & Van Aelst, P. (2009). Cyberprotest and civil society: The internet and action repertoires of social movements. In Y. Jewkes & M. Yar (Eds.), *The handbook of internet crime* (pp. 230–255). London: Routledge.

Veblen, T. (2005). *Conspicuous consumption*. London: Penguin Books.

Vltchek, A. (2014). *Fighting against Western imperialism*. Jakarta, Indonesia: Badak Merah Semesta.

Voline, (1982). *The unknown revolution*. Montreal, Canada: Black Rose Books.

Walker, S. (2002). Internet training in trade unions: A comparison of 4 European confederations. *Internet Research*, *12*(4), 294–304.

Waldinger, R., Erickson, C., Milkman, R., Mitchell, D., Valenzuela, A., Wong, K., & Zeitlin, M. (1996). *Helots no more: A case study of the justice for janitors campaign in Los Angeles*. Working Paper 15. Retrieved from https://escholarship.org/uc/item/15z8f64h

Wallerstein, I. (1989). 1968, revolution in the world-system. *Theory and Society, 18*, 431–449.

Wallerstein, I. (1998). *The so-called Asian crisis: Geopolitics in the long durée*. Retrieved from http://www.binghamton.edu/fbc/archive/iwasncrs.htm

Wallerstein, I. (2001). *Unthinking social science: The limits of nineteenth-century paradigms*. Philadelphia, PA: Temple University Press.

Wallerstein, I. (2003). *The decline of American power*. New York: The New Press.

Wallerstein, I. (2004). *World-systems-analysis: An introduction*. Durham, NC: Duke University Press.

Wallerstein, I. (2006). *European universalism: The rhetoric of power*. New York: The New Press.

Wallerstein, I. (Ed.) (2007). *The modern world-system in the long durée*. Colorado, CO: Paradigm.

Wallerstein, I. (2011a). *The modern world-system I: Capitalist agriculture and the origins of the European world economy in the sixteenth century*. Los Angeles: University of California Press.

Wallerstein, I. (2011b). *The modern world-system IV: Centrist liberalism triumphant*, 1789–1914. Los Angeles: University of California Press.

Wallis, V. (2011). Workers' control and revolution. In I. Ness & D. Azzellini (Eds.), *Ours to master and to own: Workers' control from the commune to the present* (pp. 10–31). Chicago, IL: Haymarket Books.

Walsh, G. (1988). Trade unions and the media. *International Labour Review, 127*(2), 205–220.

van der Walt, L. (2014). Reclaiming syndicalism: From Spain to South Africa to global labour today [Web log]. Retrieved from http://lucienvanderwalt.wordpress.com/2014/07/04/van-der-walt-2014-reclaiming-syndicalism-from-spain-to-south-africa/

Wang, Z., & Winters, A. (2000). After Seattle: Regaining the WTO's momentum. *New Economy, 7*(4), 205–209.

van Wanrooy, B., Bewley, H., Bryson, A., Forth, J., Freeth, S., Stokes, L., & Wood, S. (2011). *The 2011 workplace employment relations study*. Retrieved from https://www.gov.uk/government/uploads/system/uploads/attachment_data/file/336651/bis-14-1008-WERS-first-findings-report-fourth-edition-july-2014.pdf

Ward, C. (1973). *Anarchy in action*. London: Allen and Unwin.

Ward, S., & Lessoli, W. (2003). Dinosaurs in cyberspace? Trade unions and the internet. *European Journal of Communication, 18*(2), 147–179.

Waring, M. (1990). *If women counted: A new feminist economics*. San Francisco: HarperCollins.

Warnecke, W. (2007). Transnational Collective action – already a reality? *European Review of Labor and Research, 13*(1), 149–156.

Waterman, P. (1984). Needed: a new communications model for a new working class internationalism. In Waterman, P. (ed.), *For a New Labour Internationalism: A Set of Reprints and Working Papers*, The Hague, Netherlands: International Labour, Education, Research and Information Foundation, pp. 233–55.

Waterman, P. (1992) International Labour Communication by Computer: The Fifth International?, *Working Paper*, No. 129, Institute of Social Studies, The Hague, Netherlands.

Waterman, P. (2001a). Trade union internationalism in the age of Seattle. In P. Waterman & J. Wills (Eds.), *Place, space and the new labour internationalism* (pp. 8–32). Oxford, UK: Blackwell.

Waterman, P. (2001b). *Globalisation, social movements and the new internationalism*. London: Continuum.

Waterman, P. (2002). Labour internationalism in the transition from a national/industrial/colonial capitalism to an informational/globalised one...and beyond. Available at http://www.researchgate.net/publication/228542216_Labour_Internationalism_in_the_Transition_from_a_National Industrial Colonial_Capitalism_to_an_Informatised Globalised_One_and_Beyond

Waterman, P. (2004 edition). *Globalisation, social movements and the new internationalism*. London: Continuum.

Waterman, P. (2005). Labor and new social movements in a globalising world-system: The future of the past. *Labor History*, 46(2), 195–207.

Waterman, P. (2012). The global justice and solidarity movement and the world social forum: A backgrounder. *Antecedents*. Retrieved from http://www.choike.org/documentos/wsf_s110_waterman.pdf.

Waterman, P., & Timms, J. (2005). Trade union internationalism and a global civil society in the making. In K. Anheier, M. Kaldor, & M. Glasius (Eds.), *Global civil society 2004–5* (pp. 175 – 205). London: Sage.

Waterman, P., & Wills, J. (Eds.). (2001). *Place, space and the new labour internationalism*. Oxford, UK: Blackwell.

Watson, M. (2013, July 30). IWGB: Two small unions? [Web log] Retrieved from http://maxwatsonunison.blogspot.fr/2013/07/iwgb-two-small-unions.html

Watson, M. (2014, May 13). Interview with Unison organiser at London Metropolitan University.

Wearing, D. (2014, May 22). Where's the worst place to be a worker? Most of the world. *The Guardian*. Retrieved from http://www.theguardian.com/commentisfree/2014/may/22/worker-world-index-employment-rights-inequality

Weber, M. (1977a). *For Max Weber*. C. Wright Mills & H. Gerth (Eds.). London: Routledge and Kegan Paul.

Weber, M. (1977b). Politics as a vocation. In C. Wright Mills & H. Gerth (Eds.), *For Max Weber*. (77–128) London: Routledge and Kegan Paul.

Weissman, J. (2014, September 7). The fast-food strikes have been a stunning success for organized labor. *Slate*. Retrieved from http://www.slate.com/blogs/moneybox/2014/09/07/the_fast_food_strikes_a_stunning_success_for_organized_labor.html

Wellman, B. (2001). Physical place and cyberplace: The rise of personalised networking. *International Journal of Urban and Regional Research*, 25(2), 227–252.

Wilkin, P. (1996). New myths for the South. *Third World Quarterly*, 17(2), 227–238.

Wilkin, P. (1999). Chomsky and Foucault on human nature and politics: An essential difference? *Social Theory and Practice*, 25(2), 177–205.

Wilkin, P. (2000). Solidarity in a global age – Seattle and beyond. *Journal of World-Systems Research*, 6(1), 19–64.

Wilkin, P. (2001). *The political economy of global communication*. London: Pluto Press.

Wilkin, P., & Boudeau, C. (2015). Public participation and public services in British liberal democracy: Colin Ward's anarchist critique. *Environment and Planning* C. DOI:10.1068/c1367

Wilkinson, R. (2002). Peripheralising labour: The ILO, WTO and the completion of the Bretton Woods Agreement. In J. Harrod & R. O'Brien (Eds.), *Global unions? Theories and strategies of organised labour in the global political economy* (pp. 204–220). London: Routledge.

Williams, A., Wahl-Jorgensen, K., & Wardle, C. (2011). 'More real and less packaged': Audience discourse on amateur news content and its effects on journalism practice. In K. Anden-Papadopoulous & M. Pantti (Eds.), *Amateur images and global news* (pp. 193–210). Bristol: Intellect.

Wills, J. (1998). Taking on the Cosmocorps? Experiments in transnational labour organisation. *Economic Geography*, *74*(2), 111–130.

Wills, J. (2001). Community unionism and trade union renewal in the UK: Moving beyond the fragments at last. *Transactions of the Institute of British Geography*, *26*, 465–483.

Wills, J. (2001a). Uneven geographies of capital and labour. In P. Waterman & J. Wills (Eds.), *Place, space and the new labour internationalism* (pp. 180–205). Oxford, UK: Blackwell.

Wills, J. (2001b). *Mapping low pay in East London*. Retrieved from http://www.york.ac.uk/res/fbu/documents/mlpinel_sep2001.pdf

Wills, J. (2008). Making class politics possible: Organising contract cleaners in London. *International Journal of Urban and Regional Research*, *32*(3), 305–323.

Wills, J., Datta, K., Evans, Y., Herbert, J., May, J., & McIlwaine, C. (2009). Religion at work: The role of faith-based organisation in the LLWE. *Cambridge Journal of Regions, Economy and Society*, *2*(3), 443–461.

Wills, J., & Simms, M. (2004). Building reciprocal community unionism in the UK. *Capital and Class*, *28*(1), 59–84.

Wimmer, A., & Schiller, N. (2002). Methodological nationalism and beyond: Nation-state building, migration and the social sciences. *Global Networks*, *2*(4), 301–334.

Winslow, C. (2009, February 2). Stern's Gang seize UHW Union hall. *Counterpunch*. Retrieved from http://www.counterpunch.org/2009/02/02/stern-s-gang-seizes-uhw-union-hall/

Winslow, C. (2010). *Labor's civil war in America*. Oakland, CA: PM Press.

Wolf, M. (2001). Will the nation-state survive globalisation? *Foreign Affairs*, 80(1), 178–190.

Wrench, J. (1986). *Unequal comrades: Trade unions, equal opportunity and racism*. Retrieved from http://web.warwick.ac.uk/fac/soc/CRER_RC/publications/pdfs/Policy%20Papers%20in%20Ethnic%20Relations/PolicyP%20No.5.pdf

Wu, T. (2011). *The master switch: The rise and fall of information empires*. London: Atlantic Books.

Yerrill, P., & Rosser, L. (1987). *Revolutionary unionism in Latin America: The FORA in Argentina*. New York: ASP.

Young, M. (2008). Between Christianity and the libertarian left: How wide the gap? *Anarcho-Syndicalist Review*, 48/49, 20–23.

Young, H. (2014, February 27). Connected women: Using mobile phones to protect migrants. *The Guardian*. Retrieved from http://www.theguardian.com/global-development-professionals-network/2014/feb/27/international-labour-organisation-freedom-women-migration

Zaharna, R. S. (2004). From propaganda to public diplomacy in the Information Age. In Y. Kamalipour & N. Snow (Eds.), *War, Media and Propaganda*. Lanham, MD: Rowman and Littlefield. Retrieved from http://www.american.edu/soc/faculty/upload/zaharna_Propaganda.pdf

Zibechi, R. (2010). *Dispersing power: Social movements as anti-state forces*. Edinburgh, Scotland: AK Press.

Zibechi, R. (2012). *Territories in resistance: A cartography of Latin American social movements*. Edinburgh, Scotland: AK Press.

Zibechi, R. (2014). *The new Brazil: Regional imperialism and the new democracy*. Edinburgh, Scotland: AK Press.

Zimmerman, A., & McWilliams, G. (2007, April 4). Inside Wal-Mart's 'threat research' operation. *The Wall Street Journal*. Retrieved from http://www.wsj.com/articles/SB117565486864559297

INDEX

D

E

F

G

H

I

J

K

L

M

N

O

P

R

S

T

U

W

Z

Simon Cottle, *General Editor*

From climate change to the war on terror, financial meltdowns to forced migrations, pandemics to world poverty, and humanitarian disasters to the denial of human rights, these and other crises represent the dark side of our globalized planet. They are endemic to the contemporary global world and so too are they highly dependent on the world's media.

Each of the specially commissioned books in the *Global Crises and the Media* series examines the media's role, representation, and responsibility in covering major global crises. They show how the media can enter into their constitution, enacting them on the public stage and thereby helping to shape their future trajectory around the world. Each book provides a sophisticated and empirically engaged understanding of the topic in order to invigorate the wider academic study and public debate about the most pressing and historically unprecedented global crises of our time.

For further information about the series and submitting manuscripts, please contact:

Dr. Simon Cottle
Cardiff School of Journalism
Cardiff University, Room 1.28
The Bute Building, King Edward VII Ave.
Cardiff CF10 3NB
United Kingdom
CottleS@cardiff.ac.uk

To order other books in this series, please contact our Customer Service Department at:

(800) 770-LANG (within the U.S.)
(212) 647-7706 (outside the U.S.)
(212) 647-7707 FAX

Or browse online by series at:

www.peterlang.com

www.ingramcontent.com/pod-product-compliance
Lightning Source LLC
Chambersburg PA
CBHW070939050326
40689CB00014B/3263

* 9 7 8 1 4 3 3 1 2 4 9 8 3 *